ACCLAIM FOR *BEYOND STOICISM*

"A must-read for anyone interested in practical philosophy."
—**Donald J. Robertson**, author of *How to Think Like a Roman Emperor*

"This is a great introduction to the rich variety of philosophical schools in the ancient world, bringing them to life by inviting readers to test them out and compare them for themselves. Everyone should find something to inspire them in this wealth of ancient wisdom."
—**John Sellars**, author of *The Pocket Stoic* and *The Pocket Epicurean*

"Written by self-professed practitioners of Stoicism, this book (hence its title) explores the entire range of Greek and Roman philosophies of life. These philosophies include the Epicurean doctrines of pleasure and avoidance of pain, the Stoic and Aristotelian focus on virtuous character, and the radical doubt and search of Pyrrhonism. The authors invite their readers to try out one or more of these philosophies for themselves by exercises that apply the teaching to their lives. As a comprehensive and practical guide to ancient wisdom, this book is in a class of its own. I recommend it with enthusiasm."
—**A. A. Long**, author of *Epictetus: A Stoic and Socratic Guide to Life*

"*Beyond Stoicism* introduces readers to the vast variety of philosophies practiced as ways of living in ancient Greek and Roman cultures. After competently and imaginatively explaining what was distinctive to each of the philosophical schools or traditions, Pigliucci, Lopez, and Kunz provide five days' worth of well-designed exercises intended to help people apply and experiment with those key concepts and practices. This book is a veritable smorgasbord of substantive philosophical treats that can be sampled at each reader's preferred pace."
—**Greg Sadler**, editor of *Stoicism Today*

"Refreshing, engaging, and thought-provoking, *Beyond Stoicism* is a welcome addition to any Stoic library. Pigliucci, Lopez, and Kunz invite readers to expand their horizons by placing Stoicism (which focuses on character) within a broader framework that also embraces the importance of pleasure and the value of doubt. Far more than just an educational guide on different philosophies of well-being, *Beyond Stoicism* opens readers' eyes to the vast richness of thought that exists beyond Stoic principles. The authors inspire and challenge: Stoicism is powerful—but so are other philosophies. Why not enrich our lives by embracing a wider vision?"
—**Dr. Chuck Chakrapani**, editor of *The Stoic Gym Journal* and Distinguished Visiting Professor, Toronto Metropolitan University

"An engaging and illuminating journey through ancient philosophical thought that encourages the reader to incorporate those philosophies into their own lives. I'm excited for the impact *Beyond Stoicism* will have on its audience."
—**Matthew Van Natta**, author of *The Beginner's Guide to Stoicism*

"*Beyond Stoicism* offers an inspiring guide for those eager to articulate and practice a personal philosophy of life. Becoming acquainted with the wisdom traditions of key Greek and Roman philosophers on whose shoulders we stand, we can thereby wisely elevate our moral and practical efforts toward lives of dignity and meaning."
—**Sharon Lebell**, author of *The Art of Living: The Classical Manual on Virtue, Happiness, and Effectiveness* and coauthor with Brother David Steindl-Rast of *The Music of Silence: Entering the Sacred Space of Monastic Experience*

"A valuable addition to the practical philosophy literature, ideal for modern Stoics who are curious about other sources of ancient wisdom. Especially valuable are the practical exercises for each philosophy, which the reader can try out as experiments in living. I'll be recommending *Beyond Stoicism* to all therapy clients and colleagues who are interested in reading an accessible and engaging introduction to ancient practical philosophy."
—**Tim LeBon**, director of research for Modern Stoicism and author of *365 Ways to Be More Stoic*

"This ambitious book is full of everything you need to know about 13 ancient Greek and Roman philosophies of life. The authors expertly weave together relatable stories, well-grounded theoretical explanations, surprising biographical facts, and practical suggestions for applying these philosophies on your own. Brimming with useful tips and information, *Beyond Stoicism* is perfect for all the curious seekers out there who want to learn about, question, and test philosophical ideas for themselves!"
—**Brittany Polat**, cofounder and president of Stoicare, author of *Journal Like a Stoic*, and coauthor of *Stoic Ethics: The Basics*

"A remarkable combination of a very wide-ranging survey of ancient philosophical approaches with guidance on applying them in practice today. The inclusion of skepticism (very clearly explained) is a particularly striking feature."
—**Christopher Gill**, Emeritus Professor of Ancient Thought, University of Exeter, and coauthor of *Stoic Ethics: The Basics*

"An important contribution to both philosophy and psychology, *Beyond Stoicism* creates a much-needed bridge between ancient wisdom and modern research. This book can help you better understand complex philosophical ideas, so that you can apply them in your life. A practical guide toward a happier, healthier, and calmer life."
—**Tal Ben-Shahar**, author of *Happier, No Matter What* and *Choose the Life You Want*

"This book is an excellent resource for anyone who wants not only to learn about the ancient Greek and Roman philosophies of life but wants to 'test drive' these philosophies by living in accordance with them for a time. As a result of these experiments, you might decide to adopt one of these philosophies, or you might combine ideas from several to create a philosophy that is tailor-made for your life and circumstances. Either way, you will be taking an important step toward optimizing the one life you have to live."
—**William B. Irvine**, Professor Emeritus, Wright State University

"It takes more than intelligence to write intelligently on the subject of philosophical wisdom. The confident and inspiring voices of this trio of seasoned writers illuminate multiple schools of thought with clarity and engaging exercises. Excavating practical ideas on how we can live more fulfilling lives, *Beyond Stoicism* shines a light on how selected philosophies can teach us about the art of living. I'm buying two copies, one for each eye."
—**Karen Duffy**, *New York Times*–bestselling author of *Model Patient, Backbone*, and *Wise Up*

"This impressive book elucidates essential distinctions between various schools of ancient philosophy. It is both comprehensive in its coverage and accessible. The exercises at the end of each chapter help the reader sharpen their understanding of these distinctions. One can learn and then work at putting into practice many of the philosophical ideas and strategies outlined in this book. Readers will be grateful for the collective efforts of Pigliucci, Lopez, and Kunz, whose collaboration has resulted in a fine book that offers a rich and diverse perspective on ancient philosophy."
—**Walter J. Matweychuck**, PhD, REBT psychologist

BEYOND
STOICISM

BEYOND STOICISM

A Guide to the Good Life with Stoics, Skeptics, Epicureans, and Other Ancient Philosophers

MASSIMO PIGLIUCCI
GREGORY LOPEZ
MEREDITH ALEXANDER KUNZ

THE EXPERIMENT

NEW YORK

The Experiment, LLC
220 East 23rd Street, Suite 600
New York, NY 10010-4658
theexperimentpublishing.com

This book contains the opinions and ideas of its authors. It is intended to provide helpful and informative material on the subjects addressed in the book. It is sold with the understanding that the authors and publisher are not engaged in rendering medical, health, or any other kind of personal professional services in the book. The authors and publisher specifically disclaim all responsibility for any liability, loss, or risk—personal or otherwise—that is incurred as a consequence, directly or indirectly, of the use and application of any of the contents of this book.

THE EXPERIMENT and its colophon are registered trademarks of The Experiment, LLC. Many of the designations used by manufacturers and sellers to distinguish their products are claimed as trademarks. Where those designations appear in this book and The Experiment was aware of a trademark claim, the designations have been capitalized.

The Experiment's books are available at special discounts when purchased in bulk for premiums and sales promotions as well as for fund-raising or educational use. For details, contact us at info@theexperimentpublishing.com.

Library of Congress Cataloging-in-Publication Data

Names: Pigliucci, Massimo, 1964- author. | Lopez, Gregory, author. | Kunz,
   Meredith Alexander, author.
Title: Beyond stoicism : a guide to the good life with stoics, skeptics,
   epicureans, and other ancient philosophers / Massimo Pigliucci, Gregory
   Lopez, Meredith Alexander Kunz.
Description: New York : The Experiment, [2025] | Includes bibliographical
   references.
Identifiers: LCCN 2024047892 (print) | LCCN 2024047893 (ebook) | ISBN
   9798893030334 (paperback) | ISBN 9798893030341 (ebook)
Subjects: LCSH: Stoics. | Ethics, Ancient. | Philosophy.
Classification: LCC B528 .P528 2025 (print) | LCC B528 (ebook) | DDC
   188--dc23/eng/20241029
LC record available at https://lccn.loc.gov/2024047892
LC ebook record available at https://lccn.loc.gov/

ISBN 979-8-89303-033-4
Ebook ISBN 979-8-89303-034-1

Cover and text design by Beth Bugler
Cover and interior Stoic illustrations public domain and by Adobe Stock (Aristippus, Epictetus, Hipparchia, Hypatia, Stilpo)
Additional illustrations courtesy of the authors

Manufactured in the United States of America

First printing January 2025
10 9 8 7 6 5 4 3 2 1

To Caley and Jennifer. Hopefully all my philosophizing is making me more bearable.—**MASSIMO PIGLIUCCI**

To Taya, my family, and my friends: harbors and guiding stars on this journey.—**GREGORY LOPEZ**

To Elizabeth and Shannon—you inspired me. To Bob and Susan— you believed in me.—**MEREDITH ALEXANDER KUNZ**

CONTENTS

The philosopher . . . alone lives by looking at nature and the divine. Like a good helmsman, he moors his life to what is eternal and unchanging, drops his anchor there, and lives his own master.

—Aristotle, *Protrepticus*
(in *Aristotle and Other Platonists* by Lloyd P. Gerson)

TIMELINE OF PHILOSOPHERS AND EVENTS

The philosophers covered in the book are highlighted in boldface.

776 BCE	First Olympic games
753 BCE	Founding of Rome
590 BCE	The poet Sappho flourishes on the island of Lesbos
585 BCE	Thales of Miletus, the first philosopher, predicts an eclipse of the Sun
570 BCE	**Pythagoras** is born
509 BCE	The Romans overthrow the monarchy, the Republican period begins
508 BCE	The tyrant Hippias is forced to leave Athens, the Democratic period begins
499 BCE	Beginning of the Greco-Persian wars
495 BCE	**Pythagoras** dies
492 BCE	First Persian invasion of Greece
490 BCE	**Protagoras** (Sophists) is born; the Greeks defeat the Persians at the battle of Marathon
484 BCE	Aeschylus wins at the Dionysia festival
480 BCE	The Greeks, led by the Spartan king Leonidas I, defeat the Persians at Thermopylae; the Persians are also defeated in a pivotal naval battle at Salamis
469 BCE	**Socrates** is born
468 BCE	Sophocles defeats Aeschylus for the Athenian Prize for drama
460 BCE	The First Peloponnesian War begins
449 BCE	The Peace of Callias puts an end to the Greco-Persian wars; Herodotus writes History of the Greco-Persian War from 490 to 479
445 BCE	The First Peloponnesian War ends
441 BCE	Euripides wins the Athenian Prize
435 BCE	**Aristippus** (Cyrenaics) is born; **Euclid** of Megara (Megarians) is born
431 BCE	The Second Peloponnesian War begins
429 BCE	Pericles dies during the Athenian plague

428 BCE (or 424 BCE)	**Plato** is born
425 BCE	Aristophanes wins the Athenian Prize
421 BCE	The Peace of Nicias brings a temporary ending to the Second Peloponnesian War, but is actively undermined by Alcibiades
420 BCE	**Protagoras** (Sophists) dies
415 BCE	Athens lays siege to Syracuse
413 BCE	Athenians defeated by the Syracusans
411 BCE	The Four Hundred overthrow the democratic government in Athens; they will be expelled the following year
404 BCE	Athens capitulates, end of the Second Peloponnesian War; reign of the Thirty Tyrants, which will last one year
399 BCE	**Socrates** dies
383 BCE	**Plato** founds the Academy (as late as 387 BCE)
384 BCE	**Aristotle** is born
365 BCE	**Pyrrho** is born (as late as 360 BCE); **Euclid** of Megara (Megarians) dies
360 BCE	**Stilpo** (Megarians) is born
356 BCE	**Aristippus** (Cyrenaics) dies
350 BCE	**Hipparchia** (Cynics) is born
347 BCE	**Plato** dies
342 BCE	**Aristotle** begins mentoring Alexander the Great
341 BCE	**Epicurus** is born
338 BCE	Philip II of Macedon defeats Athens and Thebes
336 BCE	Alexander the Great succeeds Philip II (who was assassinated)
334 BCE	**Zeno** of Citium (Stoics) is born
332 BCE	Alexander the Great founds Alexandria in Egypt
323 BCE	Alexander the Great dies, the Hellenistic period begins
322 BCE	**Aristotle** dies
300 BCE	Euclid publishes Elements
284 BCE	**Diodorus Cronus** (Megarians) dies, we do not know when he was born
280 BCE	**Hipparchia** (Cynics) dies; **Stilpo** (Megarians) dies

275 BCE (as late as 270 BCE)	**Pyrrho** dies
270 BCE	**Epicurus** dies
265 BCE	Archimedes discovers specific gravity and anticipates the discovery of integral calculus
262 BCE	**Zeno** of Citium (Stoics) dies
241 BCE	First Punic War between Rome and Carthage ends
218 BCE	Second Punic War begins between Rome and Carthage
214 BCE	**Carneades** (Academic Skeptics) is born
149 BCE	Third Punic War begins between Rome and Carthage
146 BCE	Final defeat of Carthage by Rome
129 BCE	**Carneades** (Academic Skeptics) dies
106 BCE	Marcus Tullius **Cicero** (Academic Skeptics) is born
100 BCE	Julius Caesar is born
86 BCE	Sack of Athens by the Roman general Lucius Cornelius Sulla Felix; diaspora of the philosophers throughout the Mediterranean
60 BCE	The First Triumvirate (Caesar, Pompey, and Crassus) informally controls Rome
49 BCE	Julius Caesar crosses the Rubicon thus declaring war against the Roman Senate
44 BCE	Assassination of Julius Caesar
43 BCE	Second Triumvirate (Octavian, Mark Antony, Lepidus); Marcus Tullius **Cicero** is assassinated
31 BCE	Octavian defeats Mark Antony and Cleopatra at the Battle of Actium; the Hellenistic period ends, the Roman Empire begins
27 BCE	The Roman Senate grants Octavian the title of Augustus
4 BCE	**Seneca** the Younger (Stoics) is born
14 CE	Octavian Augustus dies
50 CE	**Epictetus** (Stoics) is born
65 CE	**Seneca** the Younger (Stoics) dies
68 CE	Nero orders his secretary, Epaphroditus, to kill him; end of the Julio-Claudian dynasty

69 CE	Vespasian becomes emperor; beginning of the Flavian dynasty
96 CE	Domitian is assassinated; end of the Flavian dynasty
97 CE	Nerva becomes emperor; the period of the Five Good Emperors begins
121 CE	**Marcus Aurelius** (Stoics) is born
135 CE	**Epictetus** (Stoics) dies
165 CE	The Antonine plague kills five million people throughout the Roman Empire
180 CE	**Marcus Aurelius** (Stoics) dies; the period of the Five Good Emperors ends
204 CE	**Plotinus** (Neoplatonists) is born
212 CE	The emperor Caracalla extends the rights of Roman citizenship to all who live within the confines of the Empire
234 CE	**Porphyry** (Neoplatonists) is born
245 CE	**Iamblichus** (Neoplatonists) is born
270 CE	**Plotinus** (Neoplatonists) dies
305 CE	**Porphyry** (Neoplatonists) dies
313 CE	Constantine the Great declares Christianity to be the official religion of the Roman Empire
325 CE	**Iamblichus** (Neoplatonists) dies
350– 370 CE	**Hypatia** (Neoplatonists) is born
363 CE	Julian the Apostate, the last pagan Roman emperor, dies
412 CE	**Proclus** (Neoplatonists) is born
415 CE	**Hypatia** (Neoplatonists) dies
476 CE	End of the Western Roman empire
485 CE	**Proclus** (Neoplatonists) dies
529 CE	Emperor Justinian I closes the Academy
1453 CE	End of the Eastern Roman empire
1462 CE	Cosimo de' Medici reestablishes the Academy in Florence

PROLOGUE

What is a good life? And how can we build that life for ourselves?

This book is designed to help you think through these big questions by drawing inspiration from the biographies, ideas, and practices of thirteen of the most prominent philosophies of ancient Greece and Rome.

Please don't let the word "philosophies" scare you off. There will be no final exam, no multiple-choice questions asking you to name that philosopher or when he or she was born and died. Instead, we'll use the best of ancient ideas as a compass to find a new path forward today, one with a sense of purpose and intentionality. By doing so, we intend for this book to help you create your own meaningful life philosophy to navigate a world filled with uncertainty.

Together, we'll traverse the foremost ancient Greek and Roman schools of thought. Along the way, each chapter will combine a glimpse into a philosopher's life with an exploration of that thinker's practical philosophy, closing with exercises for putting his or her teachings to work for us.

In this exploration of life's big questions, why did we choose to focus on Greek and Roman philosophy?

First off, it's clear that the ancient Greco-Romans have already done a lot of the heavy lifting when it comes to developing a life philosophy. Thinkers ranging from the pre-Socratics to the Neoplatonists spent tons of time considering what they thought was the highest good in life and figuring out how to move toward it. Their insights can help us understand how to set our course through even the most treacherous existential waters.

There's another reason, too. As distant as this ancient period of history may seem, it's very present to the authors of this book. That's because we have all put philosophical principles from ancient Greece and Rome into practice in our own modern lives, in particular through our study and personal pursuit of Stoicism. Through our own experiences, we have found great value in this period of practical philosophizing and are eager to share these ideas with others in search of a coherent and meaningful way of life.

You may be wondering: If we practice Stoicism, why have we written a book called *Beyond Stoicism*? It's not because we think that Stoicism is incomplete or has fatal flaws. We believe that ancient Stoicism was mostly on the right track, but we disagree with one key aspect of it: that it is the only philosophy that fits human nature.

The Stoics were not the only ancient philosophers who thought they had a monopoly on the truth. This ancient viewpoint is most clearly represented in Cicero's *On The Ends of Good and Evil*, Book III, which grounds Stoicism in a particular theory of developmental psychology. In Book I, Cicero presents a similar argument, but this time, focused on justifying Epicureanism as the best candidate for the same role. These arguments offer evidence that many of the ancients believed that a single philosophy was the "correct" one, and that the best thought system should prove valid for every human in every situation.

But we don't think there is sufficient evidence to believe that a single philosophy of life is a natural fit for everyone. Rather, we believe that different philosophies are suitable for different people, based on their individual personalities and backgrounds. It's even possible that combining aspects of various philosophies could be the best approach for you.

In fact, the founder of Stoicism—Zeno of Citium—was one such person who curated his own philosophy of life out of preexisting ideas. He started out as a student of Cynicism, before studying with the Megarian teacher Stilpo, and he later attended Plato's Academy. Zeno united these three philosophies with his own innovations and other influences to create what we now know as Stoicism.

The spirit of bringing together wide-ranging ideas continued throughout ancient Stoicism's history, and this is also the spirit in which we present the philosophies in this book. If you're a practicing Stoic, we hope you'll find many new ideas and approaches that will enrich the way you live philosophically. If you're not a Stoic, we want to provide you with a constellation of philosophies to consider and explore. As the Stoic writer Seneca said in his Letter 33, the people "who have made these [philosophical] discoveries before us are not our masters, but our guides."

So let's meet the guides for our journey.

Greco-Roman philosophers in their historical context

The practice of philosophy in the Western tradition flourished from the period of classical Greece (beginning in the sixth century BCE) to the Roman Empire (through the fifth century CE), including the intermediate periods of Hellenism (323–30 BCE) and the Roman Republic (509–27 BCE).

While Plato and Aristotle are known to most everyone, some of the philosophers and schools that we discuss in this book aren't exactly household names and are correspondingly much less understood. Quite a few didn't leave a lot of written words that have been preserved to this day. And in many cases, they focused more attention on how to live in a practical sense rather than on bestowing on posterity a corpus of ideas fit for academic study—for instance, by outlining systemic changes to the way we think about government and metaphysics (like Plato) or creating broad taxonomies for categorizing the world (like Aristotle). The lesser-known thinkers of this period (like Aristippus, Carneades, and Stilpo, for instance) can be found on the dustier, under-explored corners of the ancient map; nevertheless, they provide intriguing clues to how we can wisely approach day-to-day life.

The ideas of the thinkers discussed in this book were articulated to help people cope with a world in turmoil and over which they had little, if any, control. And that's no coincidence. Much like our own turbulent times, the ancient world that gave birth to these philosophies was a period of unrest, war, and political and social upheaval. Philosophers in ancient Greece and Rome could rarely be found relaxing on long sofas drinking wine and nibbling on cheese (though they likely did a bit of that, too). By and large, they were out there in the real world, teaching others how to deal with the chaos. Many were subject to persecution and, in some cases, violent death at the hands of courts, mobs, or tyrants. As a result, their blueprints for thinking about how to live well are highly relevant to our modern angst during times characterized by major social changes and the accompanying challenges.

To understand the context even better, let's take a quick look at the historical period these thinkers lived through that set the stage for their often radical ideas.

In the political sphere, conquest and crisis were the norm in this period, oscillating from Athenian democracy to Alexander the Great's empire, and then from the Roman Republic to the Roman Empire. This unstable and often dangerous political milieu created a need for finding a way to live a good life in the midst of turmoil. Philosophy provided a solution.

Warfare was the source of unspeakable hardships in the Greco-Roman world, which clearly affected the philosophers we'll meet in this book. It included the wholesale destruction of cities and the enslavement of their citizens, and at least a couple of our philosophers, Aristotle and Stilpo, saw their own hometowns razed. Some of these thinkers were forced from their homes, schools, or jobs by political strife and tyrannical rulers. Plato was imprisoned by a tyrant he had tried to teach to be a better leader, and Socrates was executed on the orders of the Athenian assembly. Protagoras had his books burned, while Hypatia was brutally murdered by a mob. In addition, slavery was a universal practice; Epictetus was an enslaved man who was physically abused and left with a long-term injury.

It was also a period of enormous cross-fertilization among cultures and geographies throughout the Mediterranean. During this time of rampant colonization, Greek philosophers were born in places as far from Greece as modern Libya (Aristippus), and Roman philosophers came from far-flung areas of the empire, including what is now Turkey (Epictetus).

Observing culturally different ways of life and other spiritual traditions in distant lands had a powerful influence on our philosophers. When Alexander the Great traveled to India, new ideas and practices reached the Greek and later the Roman consciousness. That included fruitful interactions between Greeks and Indian sages, and possibly even early Buddhists in the case of Pyrrho. Persian Magi were said to have taught some of our philosophers, including Protagoras, and the Egyptians, too, contributed to the wisdom of Pythagoras and Hypatia.

Philosophy was not reserved for a handful of academics in this period. And for most thinkers, it was not a navel-gazing, esoteric exercise, but rather meant to be applied to common people's lived experience. Many of our philosophers—the influencers of their day—engaged with folks of varying walks of life, including regular citizens, to offer their ideas and guidance or to speak to crowds. Others, including Plato and Aristotle, focused on making their world a more secure and rational place by trying to educate political leaders, often with mixed results. Another philosopher, Epicurus, escaped the troubling world of politics to create a calming existence in a country garden, accepting women and slaves into a surprisingly inclusive community.

And despite the innumerable limitations placed on women in this period, there were a handful who were educated in philosophy and who grew to be respected for their ideas. Ancient sources give us insight into their lives and teachings, and we have included two women philosophers in this book, Hipparchia of Maroneia and Hypatia of Alexandria.

Later in the philosophical period covered in this book, Rome gained political and cultural dominance. The Roman general Lucius Cornelius Sulla laid siege to Athens, sacking and destroying Plato's and Aristotle's famed schools in 86 BCE, causing a cultural diaspora that shifted the center of philosophical teaching to Rome. Despite this setback, philosophy lived on and indeed flourished anew. One of our thinkers, Carneades, helped popularize Greek thought in Rome, regardless of the concerns of conservative Romans who didn't want their children influenced by the Greeks! As the Roman period continued, more people began to take on Greek-originated ideas and explore them further, as in the case of Epictetus and Stoicism.

But in Rome just as in Greece, philosophy could be a dangerous profession that did not always gain favor at the top. Roman emperors outlawed philosophers and expelled them from the capital, forcing Epictetus and others to flee. Later on, local rulers and Christian bishops oversaw the destruction of philosophical knowledge in Hypatia's Alexandria. Eventually the classical period came to a close in the fifth century CE, and philosophy went dark until the appropriately named Renaissance.

The quest for eudaimonia

To better appreciate one of the key reasons we chose to focus on the ancient Greco-Romans, we need to come back to the late twentieth and early twenty-first centuries. Our own time has seen a resurgence of interest in philosophies of life for reasons similar to those that prompted the originals: Like the ancients, we live in rapidly changing societies marked by major upheavals, without a shared understanding of how best to move forward.

Fewer people are involved in organized religion; the growth of extremist movements and the rise of new forms of technology have made many question long-held beliefs about ourselves and our place in the world. As individuals, we often feel we have a limited ability to act, and many of us long for some kind of guide to help us direct our efforts and navigate our existence. And while the details of our modern problems may differ from those faced by people in ancient times, fundamental human desires have not changed. We still want the same things (love, friendship, money, reputation, tranquility) and still fear the same threats (hatred, poverty, sickness, pain, death). That's why the instruments devised by the Greco-Romans still constitute a powerful tool kit to help us figure out how we want to live.

People have always wanted to be "happy" but have also had difficulty articulating what, exactly, happiness consists of and how to find it. Greek and Roman philosophers drew on three main concepts to craft their own compass for life in the quest for a happy existence: *telos*, living according to nature, and *eudaimonia*. Telos means goal or purpose. What is the purpose of a life well lived? To become rich and famous? To experience pleasure? To live serenely? To become a good person? To live according to nature means to seek guidance about the good life by solidifying an understanding of what sort of creature human beings are, what makes them tick, and why. Eudaimonia describes the "life worth living" that results from one's analysis of telos and human nature.

We believe that these concepts—properly updated—hold the key to living well in the twenty-first century. In this book, you'll read about useful ideas from a range of ancient philosophies that offer surprisingly fresh perspectives on how to live meaningfully in the world. By examining each of these, you can develop your own life philosophy, complete with your own telos, a sense of living according to nature, and the quest for eudaimonia. Bringing intentionality to making these choices—instead of merely falling into doing what feels easiest, most fun, or most stimulating at the time—is what defines a life philosophy, rather than just passively living. The Greeks and Romans used this approach to great effect, and so can you!

How to use this book

In the course of their search for the good life, the Greco-Romans converged on three major themes, and this book is a journey to three corresponding "ports" to which we will navigate and which we will take our time to explore through a discussion of several philosophical schools. The three ports are pleasure (Cyrenaicism and Epicureanism), character (Aristotelianism, Stoicism, Cynicism, and Platonism), and doubt (Socraticism, Sophism, Academic Skepticism, and Pyrrhonism). Or, to put it more straightforwardly: feeling good, being good, and thinking well.

These themes encompass much of what people think of when they consider a life well lived, so we've arranged the chapters accordingly, moving from the most intuitive (pleasure is good) to the most surprising (doubt will set you free). We'll also explore the far edges of the map with Here Be Dragons, a section that offers less opportunity for modern practice but which could leave you with some interesting ideas to ponder (Pythagoreanism, Megarianism, and Neoplatonism).

In addition to presenting such tools, we'll also guide you through practical exercises that can be applied to our lives today, a way to try out and "live" the relevant teachings of each philosophical school in real time. These exercises are separated over five days, so you can take each philosophy for a test drive over the course of a week. Feel free to go more slowly or quickly if you'd like. However, most of the exercises build off of one another, so we do encourage you to work your way through all the exercises for each chapter.

At the end, as befits any philosophical quest, we leave you with an invitation to continue questioning and exploring as you embark on your own philosophical journey.

Our advice: Don't feel obliged to pick one school or approach. A thoughtful and personal practice of Greco-Roman philosophy can incorporate a judiciously eclectic range of ideas taken from different schools. In the classical era, a variety of philosophies competed for people's attention, each one focused on different ultimate goals and a different emphasis on one of our three ports. What is important, in the end, is not the orthodoxy of one set of ideas but the process of seeking a philosophy of life that fits you as an individual.

Whether you select a specific life philosophy or create your own eclectic path, the Greek and Roman philosophies discussed throughout this book can provide you with an invaluable conceptual map for how to build a life worth living. Let's use them to make our journey the best it can be.

1

THE PORT OF PLEASURE

The first port we are going to call on our voyage through practical Hellenistic philosophy is perhaps the most obvious: pleasure.

Who doesn't want to have a pleasurable life? And who, conversely, objects to the avoidance of pain, except perhaps for a small number of masochists? Modern psychological research has accumulated a technical literature on "hedonism," that is, the pursuit of pleasure.[1] Indeed, psychologists have even identified a common problem with such pursuit, what they call the "hedonic treadmill."[2] This is the idea that we go after a particular pleasure, say, buying the latest shiny smartphone, because it gives us a thrill. The effect of the purchase, however, soon dissipates, and like drug addicts we resume the quest for another shiny object, in search of a repeated hedonic experience. In so doing, we put ourselves on a metaphorical treadmill that leads nowhere and that doesn't actually make us happy. All it does is line the pockets of our corporate overlords.

Hedonism, it seems, is a default mode for most human beings. This should not come as a surprise, since pain and pleasure are the two great motivators invented by natural selection to get animals to do what is conducive to their survival and reproduction. Think, for instance, about sex: Would you really go through all the trouble if it were not very—or at least mildly—pleasurable? As for pain, if a gash or a dislocated shoulder were not painful you might not notice before bleeding to death or finding yourself severely impaired when all of a sudden you need your arm to, say, catch a baseball.

Some of the ancient Greco-Roman hedonists were well aware of the pitfalls of "default" hedonism and crafted philosophies of life to circumvent the problems intrinsic in the instinctive, unreflective hedonism by which most people live. This effort produced two hedonistic schools: the Cyrenaics, which we cover in chapter 1, and the Epicureans, covered in chapter 2.

The two are profoundly different, as we shall see in a moment. The Cyrenaics thought that the only thing that matters is immediate physical pleasure, here and now. However, they came up with practices that allow us to own our pleasures instead of our pleasures owning us, thus attempting to bypass the hedonic treadmill. The Epicureans, by contrast, deployed a more sophisticated analysis according to which absence of pain is the real prize since it generates a smooth, calm mental pleasure that is far more desirable than any trifling joy physical pleasure may bring.

With those preliminaries in mind, let's set sail!

Chapter 1

SEEK PLEASURE WITH ARISTIPPUS

*I possess [Laïs the courtesan], but I am not possessed by her; since
the best thing is to possess pleasures without being their slave, not to
be devoid of pleasures.*

—Aristippus, in Diogenes Laërtius,
Lives of the Eminent Philosophers, Book 2

Dressed in finely woven linen robes and exquisite leather sandals, a confident man strode down the street with a striking woman on his arm, the famous courtesan Laïs of Corinth. All around the center of Athens, other men pointed and murmured to each other under their breath.

"There he goes—that royal dog," said one.

"Can you believe he'd show himself with that woman out in public?" another replied.

"What would Socrates think of him now?" said a third, his eyebrows raised, shaking his head.

The man they were pointing at was Aristippus. Born to a wealthy family around 435 BCE in Cyrene, a Greek colonial city on the coast of modern Libya, Aristippus had made his way to Athens to study with Socrates as a young man. That was before he became a philosopher himself—and a scandal.[1]

"Aristippus," one of the bystanders began, "why do you associate with that woman? She's been with countless men."

Aristippus turned to the questioner, looked him in the eye, and responded, "Is there any difference between buying a house where many once lived, and one where no one lived? Or a ship where many have sailed, compared with a ship on which nobody has sailed?"

The man scowled and said, "No."

"Well, there you have it. Laïs is an extraordinary companion—and the most beautiful woman in Greece," he said, smiling at her. "And we have plans for a fantastic banquet later this evening. We'll feast on partridges and fine wine. Laïs will play the flute and dance along with our friends. What a night it will be! And you, gentlemen, are not invited," he added with a laugh, turned on his heels, and left with Laïs.

It was to be one more night of pleasure for Aristippus, who considered pleasure his business—and the goal of life itself. And not just any type of pleasure, but that of the senses, which we can experience in the here and now. Aristippus enjoyed the company of women, fine foods and drinks, and nice things. In search of pleasure, he was not afraid to surround himself with courtesans skilled in the sensual arts, as well as associating with tyrannical rulers who could support his luxurious lifestyle. None of this would have been acceptable in the eyes of his teacher, Socrates.[2]

When taken to task by other Athenians, Aristippus used his sharp wit to defend his choice to privilege pleasure above all else—and to point out other people's logical inconsistencies (that, at least, would have made Socrates proud!). To Aristippus, other Greeks were just as keen on enjoying the finer things as he was but were simply unwilling to look foolish or to risk others' judgment in pursuit of them. As far as he was concerned, however, there was no shame in taking actions that subjected him to ridicule if they advanced his chosen lifestyle.

For example, Aristippus was known for accepting cash from King Dionysius I of Syracuse, in Sicily. Dionysius was a ruthless and capricious tyrant.[3] When he demanded that Aristippus and others at his court don purple women's robes and dance, Aristippus happily agreed, while his fellow philosopher Plato declined.[4] This kind of incident led other philosophers to label Aristippus a "royal dog."[5] But he was content to go with the flow and collect the king's money, allowing him to keep financing his pleasures.

Money wasn't a goal in and of itself, nor did Aristippus use it to accumulate power or influence. It was what money could buy that stimulated his interest, that is, particular pleasures. Aristippus was happy to spend money freely, or even toss it away. When another man criticized him for his extravagant spending on luxurious food, Aristippus asked, "Would you have bought this food for an obol?"[6] The man said yes. "Then it's not I who love pleasure, but you who love money."[7] In fact, he cared so little for money itself that he told his servant to "pour away" most of the heavy coins he was hauling and "carry only as much as you can."[8]

That's not to say that Aristippus thought we should heap pleasure upon pleasure without any sense of satisfaction. He made the point that a person who feels an insatiable desire to accumulate more and more things—such as couches, tables, or estates—suffers from a sickness that they're not even aware of.[9] The idea, he said, is to possess nice things that provide pleasures without being possessed by them.

In fact, Aristippus's life was not all fun and games. He also experienced hardship and handled himself according to the philosophical skills he had cultivated. Ancient sources tell us that while traveling near Rhodes, Aristippus's ship was wrecked. As he and his companions searched for anything that could help them survive on a wild-looking seashore, they discovered geometric figures drawn on the ground. Delighted at these "traces" of humans, he gamely marched toward the nearby city, where he found a gymnasium (center for sports and learning) and began talking philosophy with the locals. "There he fell to discussing philosophical subjects, and presents were bestowed upon him, so that he could not only fit himself out, but could also provide those who accompanied him with clothing and all other necessaries of life," the Roman architect, engineer, and writer Vitruvius later recounted in *De architectura*.[10]

Asked by his traveling companions what lesson he'd learned, Aristippus told them: "Children should be given property and resources of a kind that could swim with them even out of a shipwreck."[11] In other words, they should learn philosophy to know what to do in any situation and carry with them a sense of good judgment.

In some ways, Aristippus's lifestyle was strikingly modern. Like many people today, he sought out sensual experiences in the moment for pure enjoyment, including sex with no strings attached, fancy foods, and raging parties, without fear of shame. And despite what his compatriots said about his love of courtesans, Aristippus showed women more respect than the average Greek person of his day. That's evidenced by his long-term relationship with Laïs—whom he did not judge for being a courtesan—and his decision to educate his daughter, Arete ("Virtue"), who became one of his philosophical followers. Despite having two sons, Aristippus selected Arete as his preferred pupil. Aristippus did not leave behind any books that survive to this day. He likely returned to his birthplace, Cyrene, in his old age, and died in his late seventies, in 356 BCE.[12]

The original hedonists

When we think of a philosophy of pleasure today, we think of Epicureanism (see chapter 2). Epicureans have developed a reputation for being the advocates of a "sex, drugs, and rock 'n' roll" philosophy—which, as we shall soon see, couldn't be further from the truth. However, that description (except for the anachronistic reference to a type of music that became popular in the 1950s CE), would not be too misleading if it were applied to the Cyrenaics.[13] They were the true egoistic hedonists of the ancient world!

The school has a murky and short history. It was, allegedly, founded by Aristippus of Cyrene—a city in North Africa, in modern Libya, from which the Cyrenaics got their name. Aristippus was a contemporary of Plato. Like Plato, he was a student of Socrates, though it's hard to believe that Socrates would have recognized the sort of philosophy eventually espoused by his pupil as having any resemblance whatsoever with what he himself was preaching in Athens (see chapter 7). We say "allegedly" because it's more likely that Aristippus inspired only a broad precursor of what we call Cyrenaicism, and that the real work was done by his daughter Arete and her son, confusingly also named Aristippus (nicknamed *metrodidaktos*, "Mother-Taught," and born circa 380 BCE) about whom we don't know much.

Unfortunately, we don't know a lot about Arete either, except for a marble head that may or may not represent her, a fourth-century-BCE Roman copy of an original Greek version, currently at the Neues Museum in Berlin. Despite this dearth of evidence about Arete's own philosophy, she must have been remarkable, as she is mentioned by name in a number of ancient sources, including by Diogenes Laërtius, Strabo, the Christian theologian Clement of Alexandria, and in the tenth-century Byzantine encyclopedia known as the Suda.

More is known about Aristippus the Elder, who must have been a fascinating and somewhat paradoxical figure. He apparently fell in love, philosophically speaking, with Socrates upon hearing a description of him while attending the Olympic Games. Aristippus joined Socrates's entourage and stayed until shortly before Socrates's death in 399 BCE. But unlike Socrates, Aristippus was very much into the enjoyment of pleasures, as we have seen. He is reported to have been the first of Socrates's students to be paid for his teachings, to live in luxury, and often to avail himself of the favors of the previously mentioned Laïs of Corinth. Like Plato, Aristippus spent part of his life in Syracuse (Sicily) at the court of the tyrant Dionysius I (or his son, Dionysius II, or both). But we don't know what his specific purpose was other than to enjoy himself! (As we shall see in chapter 6, by contrast, we have a very good idea of what Plato was doing in the same place at around the same time, and it had little to do with fun and pleasure.)

Pleasure is the good

There are two fundamental, somewhat interrelated, aspects of Cyrenaic philosophy: its ethics—that is, how to live a good life—and its epistemology, or theory of knowledge. Both aspects had long-term effects, as Cyrenaic ethics influenced Epicurus (see chapter 2) as well as the founder of utilitarian philosophy Jeremy Bentham (1780), while Cyrenaic epistemology had strong similarities with some aspects of Sophism (chapter 8) as well as with Pyrrhonism (chapter 10).

Let's begin with the ethics. As true hedonists, the Cyrenaics believed that the highest good in life is pleasure and that everything else is therefore subordinate to it and instrumental to its attainment. Unlike the Epicureans, however, the Cyrenaics stressed physical pleasure in the here and now, forgoing both mental pleasures and the Epicurean emphasis on remembering past pleasures and anticipating future ones. The reason for these preferences probably has to do with the fact that physical pleasures are more intense than mental ones: Pause right now and think about enjoying a gelato; now actually go out and taste one. See the difference? Did you enjoy this impromptu exercise in practical philosophy?

Physical pleasures that we enjoy here and now are obviously more intense than the memory of similar pleasures from the past or their anticipation in the future. Why the difference in the case of the gelato? Because you are experiencing a physical pleasure only *while* you are actually tasting the gelato. Remembering past gelatos is a mental pleasure, hence an inferior one, from a Cyrenaic perspective.

The Cyrenaics thought that we should live "in agreement with nature." After all, we have instinctively (in other words, naturally) sought pleasure and avoided pain since we were toddlers. This, the Cyrenaics thought, must be Nature's way to tell us what is good and what is not. And who are we to argue with Nature?

From a modern perspective, the Cyrenaics (and the Epicureans) got things half right. It is indeed the case that instinctively seeking pleasure and avoiding pain are abilities that have evolved because they are good for us. However, they have been favored by natural selection not because they are the ultimate goods, but rather because they are instrumental to what Nature really considers the ultimate goods: survival and reproduction.

A further argument in favor of physical over mental pleasures advanced by the Cyrenaics was that we punish criminals by administering physical, not mental, pain. That's because the latter is not as bad as the former, which implies that their counterparts—physical and mental pleasures—are also similarly ranked.

The Cyrenaics made fun of the Epicurean idea that the highest pleasure was a static state in which we lack pain. They pointed out that that's the condition of a corpse, and that the Epicureans were implicitly equating being dead with being happy. (To be fair, the Epicureans would have vehemently objected to such characterization.)

Happiness itself was not the highest good for the Cyrenaics—pleasure was. The two are not the same thing, since the Cyrenaics defined happiness as being composed of past and present particular pleasures, like eating a gelato or enjoying a good swim.[14] For the Epicureans, the lack of pain is what brings happiness, whereas the Cyrenaics thought that happiness is an ill-defined and probably unattainable state of being. Pleasure, by contrast, is a goal that is easy to grasp and natural to pursue.

We should also not confuse the Cyrenaics with modern Utilitarians, despite the obvious connection and the historical influence of the former on the latter. Modern utilitarianism, originally articulated by Jeremy Bentham and John Stuart Mill in the late eighteenth and early nineteenth centuries, says that what is moral is whatever maximizes most people's pleasure and minimizes most people's pain. But the Cyrenaics were not concerned with *other* people's pains and pleasures, for the simple reason that we cannot *experience* them. All we can experience is *our own* pains and pleasures, and that's what we need to focus on. That is why their philosophy is not just hedonistic but also egoistic, meaning that it puts the individual—not other people or society at large—front and center.

Friendship and relationships

You may be wondering what the Cyrenaics, with such an egoistic philosophy, thought about friendship. It's a feature of human life that often brings pleasure, and accordingly, the importance of friendship for a good life is stressed by several Greco-Roman philosophies, including Aristotelianism, Epicureanism, and Stoicism. Here, too, the Cyrenaics are the odd ones out. Happiness for them is entirely instrumental, to be cultivated because of the pleasure that it brings *to us*. We hope that our friends also enjoy the pleasure of our company, but that's *their* experience, which is unavailable to us and therefore not our concern.

It makes no sense for a Cyrenaic to say that we should value friendship for its own sake, or that we should care about our friends regardless of the pleasure they bring us. In turn, this seems to imply the fungibility of friendships: If a friend no longer brings me pleasure, or if a new one brings me more pleasure, I should exchange the two, upgrading to the higher pleasure, so to speak.

Although the extant sources do not directly comment on other relationships (such as romantic ones), it would seem that what the Cyrenaics thought about friendship applies just as well to any other relationship, despite Aristippus's affectionate treatment of Laïs. The resulting picture may be unappealing to our modern sensibilities but, paradoxically, may more closely resemble our *actual* behavior as documented by psychologists. When people use dating apps, for example, they tend to "trade up" whenever a more desirable partner comes along.[15]

The future—or lack thereof

Another interesting aspect of Cyrenaicism, which follows from their focus on current pleasures, is their relative lack of concern for the future. This is very much at odds not just with what Epicurus taught but also with the ideas of Socrates, who was Aristippus's own teacher.

Socrates had used an interesting metaphor to make the point that a focus on current pleasure may be misleading. In the *Protagoras*, one of the Platonic dialogues, Socrates says that current pleasures loom large and future ones small as a result of something analogous to an optical illusion: Objects in the distance *appear* small, but they may not actually *be* small at all! Accordingly, we should mindfully correct our immediate perceptions, guided by our experience and wisdom.

By contrast with Socrates, the Cyrenaic bottom line was that we can we can experience pleasures only in the here and now, and that any calculation about the future is of much less concern because we cannot, now, experience future pleasures. Not only that: How do we know that what we consider pleasurable now will also be enjoyed by our future selves? As we age and accumulate experiences, what we value changes, so that we may be mistaken in thinking that twenty years down the road we will hold to the same preferences in terms of what we do or don't find pleasurable. Will my distant future self like gelato? Perhaps not! I cannot say, so I may as well enjoy the gelato now and let my future ego make whatever decisions will seem more appropriate at that point.

The whole idea of being concerned with our future selves implies one of the fundamental concepts of Greco-Roman philosophy, that of *telos*, or the ultimate goal for one's life. Later Cyrenaics actually denied that human life has a telos, arguing that it is just a succession of moments, each of which is enjoyable (or not) in its own regard.

Generally speaking, the Cyrenaics—like the Cynics (chapter 5), though for very different reasons—were unconcerned with standard morality. They thought that what most people regard as proper or improper is not the result of natural inclination (a concept popular in many other philosophies of the time) but is rooted in more or less arbitrary customs. What goes in Athens, so to speak, does not go in Corinth, and vice versa. Accordingly, there are all sorts of probably untrue stories about Aristippus, like the one in which he left a child to die because it was inconvenient to raise him. Such stories were likely concocted later on by his critics, but they nevertheless support the notion that he disregarded common morality.

It all comes from the senses

Let us now turn to Cyrenaic epistemology, their theory of knowledge. We can reasonably ask where the Cyrenaics got their system of ethics in the first place. How did they come to claim that physical pleasure in the here and now is the only goal in life, assuming that life actually has a goal? Cyrenaicism was a philosophy, not just a subjective expression of personal preferences, so its ethics must be connected to its epistemology. While ethics is concerned with answering the question "How should we live?," epistemology attempts to answer the question "How do we know?" Clearly the two are related, because for any given ethical claim, we can reasonably ask, "And how do you know *that*?"

The Cyrenaics were fundamentally empiricists who believed our source of knowledge is empirical data about the world, and that data ultimately comes from our sense experience. For instance, how do I know that there is such a thing as the Moon? Well, I can see it. Though to be precise, what I see is a disk in the sky of a certain size, color, and shape, which appears and disappears regularly and moves around in between appearances and disappearances. I then *infer* on the basis of these and other observations that the Moon is a planet-like object orbiting around our own planet.

Hold on a minute, however! How do I infer that it is a planet-like celestial body? Because I can look at it through a telescope, which allows different degrees of magnification, which in turn shows different surface details. Even though I am using an instrument, I am ultimately deriving what knowledge I have from my senses, specifically my eyes.

And how do I know that the Moon orbits the Earth? That's a more complicated inference, which requires the use of some theory and the deployment of mathematical tools. However, that theory and those tools are, at bottom, informed by empirical evidence that I gather through sensorial information—or so the broad empiricist account goes. There is, of course, an alternative one on offer, the so-called rationalist approach.

Rationalists, like Plato, think that the ultimate source of our knowledge is the human ability to think logically, as much as this is, of course, supplemented with empirical data. Plato took mathematics and geometry to be the ultimate models for how we can make progress, and those disciplines are independent of empirical evidence: The Pythagorean theorem is true regardless of whether there is any material object shaped as a triangle, because it applies to the *very idea* of triangles.

The debate between empiricists and rationalists[16] predates both Plato and the Cyrenaics and can be traced to some of the pre-Socratic philosophers of the sixth and fifth centuries BCE. The Milesians (Thales, Anaximander, Anaximenes), Xenophanes, and perhaps Heraclitus attempted to explain the world on the basis of empirical observations. By contrast, the Eleatic school (Parmenides, Zeno of Elea) championed the primacy of reason, which led them to conclusions that would appear to be contradicted by the senses. Most famously, they denied the existence of motion (as in Zeno's paradoxes).

The Cyrenaics were not just empiricists, they were radical ones. They thought that we are not licensed to infer anything about the world in itself on the basis of our sensorial data, anticipating Immanuel Kant's eighteenth-century distinction between phenomena (the world as we perceive it) and noumena (the world as it is in itself). Moreover, a Cyrenaic, would not say, for instance, "I see something red" but "I am experiencing a sensation that I'm perceiving as redness." This way of talking may not be practical, but it would be more accurate.

Why is it, exactly, that we cannot make inferences from our perceptions to the things in themselves? The Cyrenaics advanced two reasons. The first one is the relativity of perception: As we have all experienced, at least some of the time, the very same object is perceived differently by different observers. I see the sweater as green, you see it as blue. I think the Moon is larger than usual tonight and you don't think so. And so on.

That being the case, the Cyrenaics thought that the rational thing to do is what the Pyrrhonists (chapter 10) will also go with: suspend judgment. You and I have different perceptions of the sweater and the Moon, and those perceptions are truthful insofar each one of us is concerned. But we are not justified in thereby concluding that the sweater *really is* green (or blue), or that the Moon *really is* unusually large tonight (or not).

Not all the philosophers faced with the same facts about sensorial experience arrived at the same conclusion as the Cyrenaics. For instance, Protagoras, a Sophist, would say that the sweater is *both* green (to me) *and* blue (to you) because truth is always relative to the observer. By contrast, Democritus, an Atomist, would conclude that our discordant perceptions mean that the sweater is *neither* green *nor* blue. All three of these reactions are logically consistent with the empirical data, which goes to show why epistemology is a rather difficult subject. Incidentally, I (Massimo) am color blind. How is that bit of information going to change your understanding of what's going on with the sweater?

The second reason we can't tell how things are in themselves from our sense data is the privacy of experience. Let's say we agree on the color of the aforementioned sweater: We both say that it is green. How do you know that by "green" I mean the same thing you mean? We could be using the same word simply because we have been taught that sweaters of that color are "green," but in fact it is possible that our individual sense experiences are very different from each other and that you, for example, are really experiencing what I would call "red" whenever you say "green."

This is a problem that persists into modern metaphysics and philosophy of mind and is often referred to as the problem of other minds. It's rooted in the fact that we simply have no access to other people's minds and therefore, from a strict empirical perspective, have no way to tell what's going inside them. Not even if people tell us, because they could be using descriptors (green, red) that do not correspond to the same usage as ours.

Cyrenaics versus Sophists and Pyrrhonists

As we have seen, Cyrenaic epistemology connects the philosophy with both the Sophists and the Pyrrhonists. But there are still some major, if subtle, differences among the three approaches, which are worth making explicit.

For instance, while the Cyrenaics were subjectivists about truth, the Sophists were (broadly) relativists (see chapter 8). We have seen what this means in the case of sense perceptions: Cyrenaics can make truth statements only about their own perceptions, while for a Sophist, everyone's perceptions are true *for them*. However, some of the Sophists expanded their relativism well beyond sense perception. For instance, they would say that if you think stealing is wrong, that is true for you; but someone else may think stealing is not wrong, and that is true for them. The Cyrenaics would suspend judgment about such matters, because the truthfulness or falsity of ethical judgments cannot be ascertained via the senses.

That brings us to the similarities and differences between Cyrenaicism and Pyrrhonian skepticism (see chapter 10). Broadly speaking, there are three differences between Cyrenaics and Pyrrhonists. First, the Cyrenaics do not seem to doubt the existence of the external world, while the Pyrrhonists suspend judgment about this. The contrast stems from the fact that the Cyrenaics believed in cause and effect. If someone is having sense perceptions, these must be the effects of some cause or other, and that cause is what we mean by "the external world." For the Pyrrhonists, however, issues of ontology (the branch of metaphysics that concerns itself with what does and does not exist) are "non-evident matters," as they call them, and the Pyrrhonists are agnostic about all such matters.

Second, the Cyrenaics claim to have (limited) knowledge—specifically, knowledge of their own sensorial experiences. But for the Pyrrhonists, the term "knowledge" applies only to the world in and of itself, not to our perceptions, which means that, strictly speaking, we don't have knowledge at all.

Last, although the Cyrenaics seem to think that there is a world out there, they deny that we can have knowledge of it, as we discussed previously. The Pyrrhonists here are agnostic: Currently we do not seem to have knowledge of the world out there, but who knows, the future may reserve some epistemic surprise. . . .

Although Cyrenaicism lasted for only a few generations and was already considered extinct by the time of Cicero (first century BCE), the sort of hedonism championed by the Cyrenaics influenced later philosophers. Chief among them was the already mentioned Jeremy Bentham, the thinker who founded the modern approach known as Utilitarianism in 1780, a type of consequentialist philosophy (so termed because the criterion for judging an action morally good or bad is its consequences).

Perhaps most obviously, though, hedonism that focuses primarily on physical pleasures to be experienced in the moment is pretty much the default philosophy of most people, both in ancient times and in the modern era.

Live like a Cyrenaic

Just because Cyrenaicism is most people's default philosophy doesn't mean that modern Cyrenaics wouldn't make changes to their lives—especially their inner lives. As we mentioned in the Prologue, a philosophy of life should be lived with a sense of intentionality and purpose. That means that even if someone looks like they're living as a Cyrenaic from the outside, they're not practicing Cyrenaic philosophy if they're not intentionally crafting that lifestyle thoughtfully and on purpose.

A Cyrenaic philosopher not only had to craft an intentional life, they also had to put mental effort into maintaining that life through the use of spiritual exercises. Here, we'll offer a few of these exercises for you to practice over the course of this week. One such exercise that the Cyrenaics may have invented was made more famous by the Stoics, who we'll be covering later in this book. The exercise is often called "negative visualization" or *premeditatio malorum* in Latin.

The Roman statesman and philosopher Cicero tells us[17] that the Cyrenaics believed that distress was not caused by *all* bad things—only *unanticipated* bad things. This scrap of information hints at the idea that the Cyrenaics may have spent some of their mental time imagining bad future outcomes in order to reduce their future distress. It's interesting that these hedonists may have invented a spiritual exercise that the Stoics made famous!

You may have noticed an apparent contradiction at this point: in the last section, we said that the Cyrenaics didn't concern themselves with the future. If this were completely true, why would a Cyrenaic premeditate on future adversity? After all, wouldn't that cause some present-moment distress? Yes, it would. But the Cyrenaic philosopher was making a bet that a little bit of mental pain now could make for much less distress down the road. In that case, pondering future adversity is a rational exercise for someone embracing a hedonistic philosophy of life.

While mental pain was bad according to the Cyrenaics, it wasn't the worst possibility: that, to the Cyrenaics, was bodily pain. Conversely, its opposite—bodily pleasure—was the best thing in life. Part of Cyrenaic practical philosophy involves thinking through the implications of this belief, and then living in accordance with it. One corollary of this belief is laid out in Socratic Epistle 27, which is found in a manuscript called the *Codex Vaticanus Graecus 64*. There, Aristippus writes to his daughter Arete, whose property is under threat by rulers in Cyrene. He advises Arete that they can't take everything away from her and that a small amount of property is enough to live a luxurious life. Even a single tree is enough to bear sweet, delicious fruit!

While this letter was almost certainly not written by Aristippus,[18] it still conveys the spirit of Cyrenaicism quite well. Part of Cyrenaic training involved disdaining excess. Getting physical pleasure is great, but overindulging in physical pleasure yields diminishing returns. If you had a delicious gelato, how much more pleasure will two, three, or four give you? After a while, you won't get much satisfaction from eating it at all. Not only that, you'll likely cause present-moment discomfort in the not-too-distant future by eating too much. The physical pain that comes with the (uncertain, but still quite possible) diseases that result from constantly taking in too many calories also needs to be considered. More often than not, one gelato is enough for the practicing Cyrenaic philosopher.

Thus, twenty-first-century Cyrenaic life may look a bit different from how some people in rich countries live. The modern Cyrenaic philosopher may look down upon so-called "McMansions" (large, poorly built mass-produced houses found in many parts of the United States). But even urban dwellers in small apartments can find themselves eying the latest smartphone release while having several tablets and smartphones on their nightstand. Yes, the Cyrenaic happily partakes of the "good things" in life. But a big part of Cyrenaic practice is teaching yourself how much is "enough" when it comes to pleasure and comfort.

Over the course of the next week, you'll learn these Cyrenaic lessons for yourself.

Day 1: Balancing bodily pleasure and pain while managing mental distress

Jumping straight into exercises could be a touch stressful. So—in true Cyrenaic spirit—you'll start your journey into practical philosophy by getting a better understanding of how to balance bodily pleasure and pain from the comfort of your couch!

The main concern of a practicing Cyrenaic is to maximize physical pleasure while avoiding physical pain. Getting mental pleasure and avoiding mental pain is also good, but never as good as their physical counterparts. Over the next few days, you'll practice balancing these four aspects of the Cyrenaic hedonic calculus. But to do so properly, it will help to understand them a bit better.

The following are several simple scenarios that are suboptimal from a Cyrenaic perspective. In the space provided, write how you would go about solving these simple Cyrenaic puzzles by decreasing mental and physical discomfort and increasing physical and mental pleasure.

SCENARIO 1: You planned to cook a nice meal after work, but your feet and back hurt when you get home.

What would you do? _____

_____

_____

How does this increase bodily or mental pleasure or decrease bodily or mental discomfort? _____

_____

How does this improve your situation from a Cyrenaic perspective?

_____

_____

_____

SCENARIO 2: You're mocked for a lifestyle choice you take pleasure in, like seeking exotic cuisine or getting regular, expensive massages.

What would you do? _____

_____

How does this increase bodily or mental pleasure or decrease bodily or mental discomfort? _____

_____

How does this improve your situation from a Cyrenaic perspective?

_____

_____

SCENARIO 3: Your boss asks you to do something you think is beneath you, but you also think it'll increase your chances for a bonus.

What would you do? _____

_____

How does this increase bodily or mental pleasure or decrease bodily or mental discomfort? _____

_____

How does this improve your situation from a Cyrenaic perspective?

_____

_____

SCENARIO 4: You're having trouble finding what you're looking for in your cluttered closet for the umpteenth time.

What would you do? _____

_____

How does this increase bodily or mental pleasure or decrease bodily or mental discomfort? _____

_____

How does this improve your situation from a Cyrenaic perspective?

_____

_____

SCENARIO 5: You're bored.

What would you do? _____

_____

How does this increase bodily or mental pleasure or decrease bodily or mental discomfort? _____

_____

How does this improve your situation from a Cyrenaic perspective?

_____

_____

None of these questions has a single correct answer, but here are some possible solutions to these dilemmas.

Scenario 1's solution is straightforward: Don't cook, put your feet up, and order in! By doing this, you'll be avoiding physical pain (the main object to avoid as a Cyrenaic) while still eating something somewhat tasty. This minimizes the evil of physical pain while getting some physical pleasure from takeout. But this simple solution may not be so easy for people who can't afford ordering in. In that case, eating whatever's easy to obtain while staying off your feet is the way to go. You'll still be eliminating the physical pain of hunger while also avoiding the physical pain of standing up to cook. This still improves the situation from a Cyrenaic perspective! In 2.91 of his *Lives of the Eminent Philosophers*, Diogenes Laërtius tells us that the Cyrenaics thought that even the perfect Cyrenaic sage could not live pleasantly all the time. The goal of Cyrenaicism isn't to achieve constant pleasure: it's to maximize pleasure and minimize pain as often as possible.

Scenario 2 is something that you saw Aristippus handle at the beginning of this chapter, where he received scorn for being seen in public with the courtesan Laïs. Aristippus turned the tables through the use of sharp retorts and humor. He didn't let shaming stop him from indulging in physical pleasure, which he thought to be the highest good. And he even got some mental pleasure (which is lesser than bodily pleasure, but still good!) from the exchange by embarrassing the people who were harassing him. Finally, he didn't let the comments bother him, leaving his mental pain unchanged. Thus, Aristippus came away from the exchange with no more mental pain, the same amount of physical pleasure, and a bit more mental pleasure. He probably achieved this by training himself to endure mental hardships, which is something you'll have a chance to explore in future chapters.

Aristippus also modeled a way to solve Scenario 3 when he was asked to dance in purple robes at Dionysius's court. There was no present, clear pleasure or pain when Aristippus was asked to do this. Instead, he had to calculate the possible future (mental) embarrassment against the possible future (physical) pleasure that Dionysius's support would grant him if he agreed. Given his past experience with Dionysius and the fact that potential physical pleasure always outweighs possible mental discomfort, Aristippus danced up a storm. The Cyrenaic solution to the third scenario would be similar as long as you were pretty certain that you'd get the bonus and that you could use that bonus to effectively increase future physical pleasure. If you don't need the money or you're very uncertain of the bonus, then perhaps your hedonic calculus would be different.

The cluttered closet in Scenario 4 suggests you have too much stuff or at least need to organize better. If the things that are taking up space aren't useful for reducing physical discomfort or improving physical pleasure, it may be best to toss them. If not, a reorganization is in order. It's not fun, but a small amount of discomfort is worth it to the Cyrenaic if it provides more physical comfort down the road.

Scenario 5 is simple to solve in theory but can be hard in practice. The clear answer is to find something pleasurable to do, since boredom arises from the fact that nothing pleasurable is available or comes to mind. Finding pleasure in unlikely places is a skill that the Cyrenaic aims to cultivate. Aristippus demonstrated this when he was shipwrecked. He experienced joy when seeing signs of civilization, enjoyed mental pleasure through conversing with the locals he tracked down, and won them over so much that they provided him with all he needed for a pleasant time there.

Day 2: Introduce more pleasure into your life

Now that you've tested your understanding of Cyrenaic philosophy in theory, it's time to put it into practice in your own life by exploring how, in three simple steps, you can make something you already do more pleasurable or less of a pain (literally!).

Step 1: Think about one thing in your life that you get physical comfort or pleasure from that could be done more easily or bring more pleasure. This could be something you already do that brings you pleasure but could be made better or easier (for instance, getting a massaging shower head: You already bathe, so why not make it more pleasant!). Or it could be something that's missing from your life that could bring pleasure. Remember that the Cyrenaics believed physical pleasures and pains were the main focus in life, so try it for yourself!

_____

_____

_____

_____

_____

_____

_____

Step 2: Think of ways to increase physical enjoyment, decrease physical discomfort when obtaining it, or both. This could be bringing something new into your life or trying to make an existing aspect of your life easier. For example, if you enjoy cooking delicious meals but have trouble digging through your pots and pans, you could plan to reorganize your kitchen to make it easier to cook.

_____

_____

_____

_____

_____

_____

Step 3: Execute your plan and enjoy! The final step is to try it out and see how it goes. It's not a problem if it takes a few days to execute your plan. You'll be prompted to collect your thoughts about all these exercises at the end of the week.

Day 3: Remove some pain from your life

This exercise will help you explore the flip side of Day 2: The steps are the same, but in this case, explore something that causes you physical discomfort that you have a good chance of alleviating, and put it into practice. The trick here is to also give up as little physical pleasure as possible in the process.

Step 1: Think about one thing in your life that causes you physical discomfort that would be relatively easy to mitigate. Our days are filled with minor difficulties that lead to unnecessary physical discomfort. Daily routines and chores are two such examples for a lot of people.

Perhaps there's something you can do to make them less uncomfortable. Keep in mind that we're focusing on physical discomforts, not mental ones!

_____

_____

_____

_____

_____

_____

Step 2: Come up with ways to mitigate physical discomfort while not forgoing much—if any—physical pleasure. An expensive new couch may be a bit more comfortable, but going into unmanageable debt could lead to a lot more future discomfort, so go small and double-check your hedonic calculation! Some examples of mitigating discomfort are hiring someone to mow your lawn or breaking up physically demanding chores into smaller, less taxing chunks.

_____

_____

_____

_____

_____

_____

_____

_____

Step 3: Do it and see how it goes!

Day 4: Trim the excess

So far, the exercises we've suggested had the straightforward goal of removing pain and increasing pleasure when possible. It's not exactly rocket science! However, there are some subtle aspects to this philosophy, which you'll be exploring over the next couple of days.

One of the finer points of Cyrenaic hedonism was exemplified by Aristippus in the court of Dionysius of Syracuse. Diogenes Laërtius tells us that on one occasion, the king offered Aristippus his choice of three courtesans with whom to spend the night. Instead of choosing one, he walked away arm-in-arm with all three. Not surprising!

What's more baffling is what Aristippus did next. Once he was out of sight of Dionysius, he dismissed all three courtesans and went to bed alone. Why would the paradigmatic hedonistic philosopher choose not to engage in a night of pleasure? Diogenes Laërtius suggests that it was an exercise to train his temperance. That's one possibility that you'll have the opportunity to practice in future chapters. However, there's another possibility: that Aristippus knew that he had had his fill of pleasure for the moment, so there was no need for anything further. His main goal wasn't a night of passion: it was to make a powerful impression on his chief benefactor.[19] With that goal accomplished, he didn't need to do any more.

This ability to know when enough is enough is a key Cyrenaic skill. As we said earlier, Aristippus firmly held that an insatiable desire was a sign of an ill mind that doesn't truly understand what's needed for a pleasant life. Having ten comfy couches is pointless, since you can only lie on one at a time! Not only does having too much not add anything to one's pleasure, it may lead to future physical and mental discomfort. Having a nice car would probably be fine for a Cyrenaic. Having a garage full of them is a different matter. You have to labor to maintain them, and there is more to worry about in terms of theft or damage. Since you can you can enjoy driving only one car at a time, the cost of owning lots of them would likely not be worth it.

You may not have a car collection as big as Jay Leno's, but it's likely you can find some excessiveness in your own life, owning or doing too much of something when you'd get just as much physical pleasure with less and while having less to fret over. Today's exercise aims to uncover a small thing you can change to trim some of the excess in your life without sacrificing pleasure.

Step 1: Take two minutes to make a list of things you do or own that make your life harder. Don't focus on events that happen to you or circumstances you find yourself in. Instead, list activities you engage in and stuff you own that make your life more difficult than it needs to be, either because you worry about them or because they make you work harder than you have to. They can be large or small, ranging from a cluttered drawer you always find yourself digging through to your new fancy car you're afraid will get dinged.

_____

_____

_____

_____

_____

_____

_____

_____

_____

Step 2: Take another couple of minutes to review your previous list, then cross out anything that does *not* bring you any bodily pleasure or relieve bodily pain. Remember that the Cyrenaics were much more concerned with physical pleasure and pain, so focus on the physical for now! We'll be tackling mental pleasure and pain in the next chapter.

The things that you crossed off are excessive from a Cyrenaic perspective. Aristippus would advise you to train yourself to eliminate these things entirely. But given that you're just taking Cyrenaicism for a spin, we don't recommend making huge changes based on this exercise alone! That said, if there are small items or activities that jump out at you, drop one of them and see how it feels over the rest of the week as your exercise for today. If nothing jumps out at you, move on to the final step.

Step 3: Look at the items from Step 1 that aren't crossed out and ask yourself if there's any way you can make them physically or mentally easier to do or own; if there is, implement your plan. The remaining items from Step 1 give you pleasure, but also some mental or physical discomfort. Your goal is to see if there's any way to make them easier so you can get just as much pleasure from them with less mental or physical stress.

Day 5: Discover the easy pleasures

One of the main skills that helped Aristippus live his version of the good life was the ability to take pleasure in what's easily available without striving painfully to achieve it. Recall Aristippus's joy at seeing the geometrical figures in the ground after he was shipwrecked near Rhodes and the delight he felt while conversing with the locals. These are simple pleasures that Aristippus didn't have to work hard to obtain, yet he still exhibited the ability to find joy in what was present. A big part of maximizing pleasure is not enduring too much discomfort along the way.

Your final exercise for this chapter is simple: Do whatever you'd normally do, but try to enjoy it more by savoring the little things you encounter during your day.

It bears repeating that a Cyrenaic savors life by focusing on the physical pleasures first and foremost. But if none are available, mental pleasures will do (hence Aristippus's joy when conversing with the locals after being shipwrecked). This requires a shift in attitude, knowing where to direct your attention, and a little mental energy. Here are some ideas on how to savor whatever comes your way during the course of your day.

Physical savoring by focusing on the senses

- Pay attention to the taste of the food you're eating. Chew more slowly and focus on the flavor.
- Take a relaxed position when sitting or lying down. Occasionally tune in to the relaxed sensation of your muscles.

- Turn your attention to pleasant sights, sounds, and smells you encounter throughout your day, be it interesting street art, the sleek design of a car, the smells wafting from a bakery, or the greenery along the sidewalk.

If you have difficulty focusing on the physical, or if physical pleasures aren't easily available, then feel free to cultivate some mental pleasures by striking up an interesting conversation, reading, or simply contemplating things for which you're grateful. Again, according to the Cyrenaics, mental pleasures aren't as good as physical ones, but they're still good!

Finally, take it easy! Remember, your goal today is to get more pleasure out of what you normally do.

REFLECTION

Now that you've dipped your toes into Cyrenaicism, take some time to reflect on its fruits. You've explored four types of Cyrenaic exercise: getting more bodily pleasure, minimizing bodily pain, trimming things from your life that don't produce pleasure, and learning to enjoy what easily comes your way. Which of these worked best for you, and which didn't? Which do you think you'd like to practice more in the future? And what's your impression of Cyrenaicism as a life philosophy in general?

_____

_____

_____

_____

_____

_____

_____

_____

_____

_____

_____

_____

_____

_____

_____

_____

_____

_____

_____

_____

_____

_____

_____

_____

In the next chapter, we'll continue our pursuit of pleasure from a very different angle. Instead of focusing on bodily pleasures, we'll explore the viewpoint of Epicurus, who thought that the best kind of pleasure was the absence of pain, particularly of the mental variety.

Chapter 2

AVOID PAIN AND STRESS
WITH EPICURUS

Don't fear god,
Don't worry about death;
What is good is easy to get, and
What is terrible is easy to endure.

—Philodemus, from the Herculaneum Papyrus

It was a warm spring morning at the Garden, a property near the Dipylon gate, just outside Athens. The sun filtered through the branches of tall oak trees and dappled the fig, almond, and apple groves watered by streams from the Eridanus River. Bees buzzed around flowering shrubs. In the courtyard, the Garden's inhabitants were setting up their simple breakfast. Bread with olive oil, barley-meal, and pitchers of water graced the tables.[1]

Epicurus, the Garden's founder, took his place. A middle-aged man dressed in a simple cloak and leather sandals, he had a full, curly beard, a long nose, and a warm but serious gaze. "Another beautiful day living in beautiful obscurity," he said, prompting smiles and gentle laughter from those gathering for the meal. He scanned the benches, now filling up with his closest friends, people he had welcomed to join the Garden's experiment in group living.

"Good morning, friends," Epicurus continued, nodding to those sitting around him. "Remember this day as all days: Friendship reminds all of us to wake up to happiness! And now, let's eat. Our simple meal will relieve our hunger and thirst, and our conversation will lighten our souls."

Astonishingly, the friends who broke bread together under the cypresses were not exclusively high-born Athenians but included women and former slaves. Epicurus made a point to admit women to the Garden not as a rare exception but as a general principle. His was the first Greek philosophical school to do so. Even women who had been courtesans were welcomed by Epicurus, including his friend Leontion,[2] along with many other students and companions, such as Epicurus's favorite servant, Mys ("Mouse").[3]

Epicurus himself came from a family of Athenians who had sought out opportunities in Samos, an island colonized by the city until the settlers were abruptly expelled for political reasons. After leaving Samos, Epicurus eventually returned to Athens to complete his obligatory military service. But he was already questioning the world he grew up in, one that couldn't adequately explain how things worked and why things were the way they were. Even as a young student he talked back to teachers who couldn't tell him how the universe was born out of chaos.[4] His interest in the nature of the cosmos and in the human condition continued to grow, and around the age of fourteen he took up philosophy.[5]

Epicurus told his followers he was self-taught, though he most likely studied with established philosophers at first. What he may have meant was that he came up with his own ideas about science, nature, and ethics. Epicurus called other thinkers "confused." He concluded that humans are fully in charge of their own destinies, unbeholden to distant gods. He thought that the world is composed of atoms and void, just as Atomists like the philosopher Democritus had argued a generation earlier. And in the course of his reflections, Epicurus came to believe that to seek pleasure and to flee from pain is at the heart of human nature.

He professed that people should withdraw from the pressures of society, avoid physical and mental pain and discomfort, and aim for a state of peace and well-being. Epicurus believed that the good life was to "live in obscurity,"[6] setting aside the stress-inducing pursuits of wealth, power, influence, and fame, and he even cautioned against marriage and having children. Instead, people should focus on enjoying simple pleasures and the camaraderie of friends, without fear of death or punishment in a nonexistent afterlife.[7]

Epicurus worked steadily to teach his ideas, writing numerous books and treatises (almost all of which have now been lost), and he lived by them alongside his closest friends. That's what the Garden was all about.

At the Garden, no one talked about politics, business, or the gods. It was a place of serenity and escape in a time when the wars among Alexander's successors raged on for decades. The later Roman writer and politician Seneca tells us that Epicurus's Garden had this motto carved on the front gate: "Stranger, here you will do well to tarry; here our highest good is pleasure."[8]

This doesn't mean that the Garden-dwellers caroused in gluttonous feasts. Epicurus said a pot of cheese would be his biggest luxury, and he advocated for a down-to-earth yet pleasurable existence. Instead of rich, expensive foods, Epicurus and his friends enjoyed cheese and bread. Rather than racing around acquiring the latest fashions, they relied on basic tunics and cloaks. Instead of debating the most recent war, they spoke calmly about the nature of the cosmos. Rather than engaging in frequent sexual relationships and marriage, they cultivated close friendships and deep conversations. Their late-night philosophy seminars were legendary.[9]

At the Garden, Epicurus remained cheerful and kept sharing his ideas until the end, even when riven with pain from ailments, including kidney stones, that slowly destroyed his health. True to his ideas, he was unafraid of death and passed away calmly in his bathtub, surrounded by friends, in 270 BCE.[10]

For generations to follow in the Greek and Roman world, Epicurus was celebrated as the *heros ktistes* ("founding hero") of the Garden, with commemorations held in his honor during his birthday month.[11] Bronze statues were erected in his memory, and several of his followers named their children Epicurus. As the ancient biographer Diogenes Laërtius put it, Epicurus's friends were "so numerous they could not be measured by entire cities," and "all who knew him [were] captivated by the siren spells of his doctrines."[12]

Sophisticated hedonism

Contrary to what you may have heard, Epicureanism is *not* the philosophy of sex, drugs, and rock 'n' roll, though this misconception has been around for a while—ever since the time of Epicurus, in fact! There is even some doubt that Epicureanism qualifies as a hedonistic—that is, pleasure-seeking—philosophy. For Epicurus, the highest "pleasure" is lack of pain, something that would have hardly satisfied the Cyrenaics (see chapter 1), who most certainly *were* hedonists.

Rather, Epicureanism is about reaching two goals in life: *aponia* and *ataraxia*. The first means that you are in no physical distress at all. We reach aponia when we are not thirsty or hungry, nor lacking anything else that the human body requires. Ataraxia means tranquility of mind, which is achieved when we no longer have fears, unfulfilled desires, or any of the mental states that otherwise disturb us. You may be inclined to think that there is more to life than not being hungry or fearful, but Epicurus would beg to differ, and he put forth some pretty good reasons that are worth entertaining.

The basic Epicurean argument in favor of finding pleasure and avoiding pain is simple; that's what Nature very clearly tells us. Think about human infants and how they behave. At bottom, they are drawn to comfort and withdraw from unpleasantness. And who are we, say the Epicureans, to think we can do better than Nature itself?

Epicurean philosophy identifies three kinds of desires: natural and necessary, natural but not necessary, and unnatural and unnecessary. The first category is satisfied by things like the acquisition of clothing, shelter, food, and water. The desire we have for these things is natural, meaning that we seek them instinctively, without having to justify why or think too much about it. This desire is also necessary, because without clothes, shelter, food, and water we'd be dead or lead a very uncomfortable life. The good news is that such needs are also easy to satisfy, all things considered.

The second category—desires that are natural but not necessary—is in a sense an elaboration of the first group. Consider things such as designer clothes, gourmet meals, fancy wine, and a large house. Desiring these is natural because they are the same types of items we have already encountered in the first group, and they are still about satisfying basic human needs. But they are unnecessary because those desires can be met by simpler versions of the same things. The problem with this second group of desires is that they are more difficult to procure, and hence potentially undermine our happiness, because we suffer pain whenever we can't get them.

The last category—desires that are both unnecessary and unnatural—is the most troublesome. These include such things as fame and wealth, which are inherently limitless. Once we start accumulating money and possessions there is no logical stopping point. We want more and more. Once we start caring about what some people think of us then we want an increasing number of people to admire us, or simply to "like" our posts on social media. Because these desires are open-ended, they will constantly cause us pain—the pain of not having enough wealth or enough fame, because there is no such thing as "enough" of this category of things.

And that's why the Epicurean life is one of simple pleasures. Because the corresponding desires are natural, necessary, and easy to satisfy. Anything beyond that is not worth the pain that it is guaranteed to bring.

The Epicureans have a lot more to say on the subject of pleasure. For instance, they make a distinction between pleasures of the body and pleasures of the mind. Unlike their forerunners the Cyrenaics, Epicureans valued pleasures of the mind more than those of the body. But that's not because they were snobbish. As any good philosophers would, they had an argument to defend their position. They explained that we are capable of experiencing sensual pleasures (food, sex, and so on) only in the here and now. Pleasures of the mind, by contrast—say, the pleasure induced by a conversation with a friend, or by the reading of a good book—extend to both the past and the present. I may recall such pleasures anytime I want—for instance, by going over the content of my conversation, or reciting a book passage from memory. When it comes to physical pleasures, by contrast, I can recall *that* I experienced pleasure but not the pleasure itself. That's why mental pleasures are preferable to physical ones, though it doesn't mean we shouldn't also experience the latter, with moderation.

Epicureans realized that some pleasures are dynamic (*kinetic*) and others are static (*katastematic*), and that the static ones are more valuable than the dynamic ones. A dynamic pleasure can be physical or mental—for instance, the pleasure of satisfying your hunger with good food, or the joy you may experience at seeing an old friend. By their very nature, however, kinetic pleasures are transitory, and thereby generate corresponding pains. You may be happy with your recent meal, but you will get hungry again. You are glad to see your friends, but you will then be sad to see them go, and so on. By contrast, katastematic pleasures are here to stay. For example, we can gain enduring pleasure from conquering our fear of dying, as we will no longer have to suffer the pain of worrying about it. We naturally seek both kinds of pleasures, but we ought to care particularly for the katastematic ones, because they get us closer to the ultimate goals of aponia and ataraxia.

Trust your senses

As in the case of the other Hellenistic philosophies, the Epicureans' take on ethics (how to live the best life) is intimately connected to their epistemology (how we know things) and their metaphysics (how the world works). We have already seen, for instance, that the fundamental Epicurean idea that what is important in life is to seek pleasure and avoid pain is based on empirical observations of the behavior of human infants. The underlying epistemological principle is that empirical data perceived by our senses are our major source of knowledge about the world, while the underlying metaphysical principle is the idea that Nature itself tells us what is good and what is evil—a notion known as ethical naturalism in modern philosophical parlance.

More generally, the Epicureans were fairly radical empiricists, valuing what our senses tell us while being distrustful of our reasoning abilities. In this way, they differed dramatically from other schools that we'll examine later on, such as the Platonists and the Stoics. For example, imagine partially submerging a stick in water. It will look to you as if it were distorted, and this would seem like an obvious case where reason corrects our senses, as the Stoics would argue. But the Epicureans actually blame reason in assuming that the sensorial data are not distorted. In reality, they think, our senses are giving us an accurate picture of the situation, not because the stick is really distorted, but because *its image* is, due to some different property of air and water. In a way, this is correct, as modern physics tells us that the apparent distortion is the result of differences in how air and water bend light. Only additional sensorial information will give us the correct result: if we touch the stick directly, we will feel—firsthand, as it were—that it is not, in fact, bent.

Metaphysically speaking, the Epicureans were Atomists, meaning that they thought the world is made up of indivisible particles of matter (the literal meaning of "atom"), characterized by various shapes, sizes, and weights. These particles move within a void, combining to yield the macroscopic objects that we perceive—including human bodies. So everything is made of matter and decays according to the laws regulating the behavior of matter. This includes the human soul, which is why the Epicureans were not concerned with what happens to us after death. After all, there will be no "us" capable of having any concerns. As Epicurus puts it in his letter to his friend Menoeceus: "Death, therefore, the most awful of evils, is nothing to us, seeing that, when we are, death is not come, and, when death is come, we are not."

The fourfold remedy

The Epicurean views on ethics, epistemology, and metaphysics arguably culminate in the so-called *tetrapharmakos*, literally meaning the fourfold remedy (for a happy life). As introduced in the epigraph to this chapter, it consists of the following four precepts.

> *Don't fear god,*
> *Don't worry about death;*
> *What is good is easy to get,*
> *What is terrible is easy to endure.*

This articulation of the tetrapharmakos is attributed to the Greek philosopher and poet Philodemus of Gadara (110–35 BCE) and is found in a famous papyrus retrieved at Herculaneum, near Pompeii. We do not need to fear the gods because they are simply not concerned with human affairs, being busy doing whatever gods do (contemplating themselves in the act of contemplating the cosmos, or something like that). Think about your utter lack of concern for an ant living nearby; the relationship is similar. As we have already seen, there is also no sense in fearing death (as distinct from the process of dying), because we will not be "there" when it arrives. Our analysis of the natural and necessary pleasures tells us that what is truly good is relatively easy to get and what is terrible—mostly, for an Epicurean, pain—is relatively easy to endure.

You may not find the last bit particularly convincing, but this was an attitude shared by other schools as well. For instance, the Stoic emperor-philosopher Marcus Aurelius writes in his *Meditations*: "Pain is neither intolerable nor everlasting if you bear in mind that it has its limits, and if you add nothing to it in imagination."[13]

The idea is that what makes pain apparently intolerable is our mental conception of it—the story we tell ourselves about it—and this elevates physical pain to mental suffering. Pain is unavoidable but (mostly) endurable, whereas suffering is avoidable because it is a matter of how we *think* about our experience of pain. A similar approach to pain management is found in the meditative practices of some Eastern traditions, like Buddhism, and is also at the basis of modern approaches such as cognitive behavioral therapy.

The tetrapharmakos is linked to the famous Epicurean epitaph that is often used at secular humanist funerals today: *Non fui, fui, non sum, non curo* ("I was not; I have been; I am not; I do not mind"). It's not a bad message to leave for posterity.

One important and controversial aspect of Epicureanism, which stems directly from the philosophy's view of what is good (pleasure) and what is evil (pain), is that Epicureans are discouraged from getting involved in social and political issues, on the reasonable ground that these bring pain. Even though some Epicureans—like Julius Caesar—clearly flouted this recommendation, it makes perfect sense within the framework of the philosophy. But this makes Epicureanism into a somewhat inward-looking approach to the good life, focused on cultivating the friendship of a select few while rejecting a broader involvement with society at large.

Still, the Epicureans put their approach very much into practice, with great success. At one point there were more than four hundred Epicurean "gardens," or communes, as we would call them today, scattered throughout Europe. After the collapse of the Roman Empire, many of these locations were taken over by Christian monks and turned into a not entirely dissimilar form of communal living: monasteries.

Live like an Epicurean

The glimmers of an Epicurean lifestyle seen in Christian monasteries eventually escaped their walls in part through the Protestant Reformation of the sixteenth century, and found their way into nineteenth-century utopian communal movements such as the Shakers[14] and the Oneida Community in New York,[15] as well as nineteenth-century philosophy through the transcendentalist notion of plain living. These threads continued into the twentieth century in some of the communal living models of the 1960s and 70s.

Today, some quasi-Epicurean forms of living can be seen in a wide variety of settings. Practicing minimalists are one example: They wish to declutter their lives for aesthetic or environmental anti-consumerist reasons. Another example is that of rationalist group houses, where people with similar worldviews and an interest in improving their applied rationality skills form communities to achieve both practical and social goals. There are also organizations such as the Foundation for Intentional Community[16] that allow people to find and join a wide range of worldwide like-minded communities. But if you search the foundation's website for an Epicurean community to join, you'll get no hits. This is indicative of the current state of Epicureanism as a lived philosophy: While shards of it have survived to the present, no full-blown Epicurean communities exist nowadays, to our knowledge. There are, however, some organizations such as the Society for the Friends of Epicurus that are attempting to bring a new form of the philosophy into today's world.[17] There are also a couple of books on modern Epicurean practice.[18]

A full-blown modern Epicurean community would be very different from the contemporary experiments mentioned previously. Sure, they'd be organized with intention—but not around ecological or religious ideals. Rather, people would get together for mutual philosophical support, with the ultimate goal of attaining ataraxia (tranquility of mind). Instead of the ideals of free love found in hippie communes of the 1960s, you would find little sex going on in an Epicurean garden, since sexual attraction was considered one of the natural but unnecessary desires. These types of desires are allowed to be satisfied by the practicing Epicurean, but only if they don't get in the way of ataraxia. And—as your own experience or a random sampling of pop songs will tell you—this is an unrealistic expectation for many romantic relationships. Instead, practicing modern Epicureans would train themselves to be content with intellectual conversations with their housemates while tempering their sexual desires.

Epicureans may work just enough to be physically comfortable in order to avoid aponia (physical distress), perhaps at a job, or maybe living off the land and earning enough money for essentials by selling their excess produce. And unlike small-"e" epicureans, who relish fine cuisine, the modern Epicurean would be satisfied with simple greens, bread, and—if they want to get fancy—an occasional nibble of cheese.

This broad picture of a modern Epicurean lifestyle paints a life that goes against the hustle and bustle of modern culture in many industrialized countries, especially the United States. Those of us with full-time jobs, those who juggle several gigs, or who are entrepreneurs would have to radically change our lives in order to fully embrace an Epicurean lifestyle.

This is in stark contrast to the Cyrenaic philosophy that we covered in the last chapter, which is essentially a well-thought-out version of the default life philosophy many of us actually live. Becoming a modern Cyrenaic would require thought and effort, but it wouldn't require a dramatic lifestyle change for many people. Epicureanism is different: Becoming an Epicurean would necessitate a sea change in both thought and deed for many of us.

This is an important point that you'll see in many of the life philosophies we cover in this book, so it bears repeating: Many of the philosophies the Greeks and Romans practiced were full-time endeavors that required constant attention and effort. They were not simple life hacks to achieve a specific goal. They required a radical shift in priorities to align one's life with their precepts. That's a big commitment, and the point of this book is not to convince you to drop everything and become an Epicurean, a Cynic, or the next Socrates. Instead, our aim is to provide you with a taste of what these philosophies would be like if you were to live them, and to give you a chance to explore the shores before setting sail for your favorite philosophy's port. So let's turn our attention to how you may dip your toes into the waters of Epicureanism for just a week.

Day 1: Get more comfortable with Epicurean theory

To prepare, let's go through a pop quiz to help you wrap your head around how to put the Epicurean framework into practice in your modern life. We've written out a few pleasures and desires in the following table. See if you can categorize them according to Epicurus's three types of desires (see page 42) and on the basis of being kinetic or katastematic pleasures.

If you need tips for classifying your desires, recall that unnatural and unnecessary desires have no limit—they can never be satisfied; you'll just keep wanting more and more over time. Natural and unnecessary desires tend to be fancier versions of natural and necessary desires. Finally, kinetic pleasures tend to be immediate, whereas katastematic pleasures are the relief and peace you get by removing something painful or uncomfortable. The answers are on page 53.

Goal	If you wanted this, it would be a _____ desire	If you achieved this, you would get _____ pleasure from it
To have sex		
To lower stress		
To consume a delicious meal		
To get a lot of "likes" on a recent social media post		
To eat to satiety		
To put your aching feet up after a long day of hiking		
To have close friends		
To get a large bonus at work		
To be satisfied with your current income		

Now that you have some sense of the Epicurean framework of desires and pleasures, let's see how much of these desires and pleasures occupy your day-to-day life.

Days 2 and 3: Cataloging your current life

Take two days this week to create your own table similar to the previous one, but apply it to the specifics of your life. Each day, reflect on a few things you desired or got pleasure of any kind from, and try to categorize them according to the three types of desire and the two types of pleasure, just like we did previously. The goal during these two days is *not* to change what you do and how you live your life. Instead, it's simply to go about your normal day, observe how you live your life, and write your observations in the table that follows.

	Desire or pleasure	Type of desire (natural/unnatural + necessary/unnecessary) or type of pleasure (kinetic/katastematic)
First day		
Second day		

You can fill out the table at the end of each day, but we suggest taking quick notes during the course of a day whenever you pursue a desire or indulge in a pleasure, so you don't have to rely on your memory at the end of the day.

This exercise will not only help you get a better understanding of the Epicurean framework but may also allow you to notice any patterns in the desires and pleasures you have. Do you tend toward unnatural, unnecessary desires, or are natural, unnecessary desires more your thing? Or perhaps most of the pleasures you pursue are already katastematic? The only way to know is to observe yourself honestly.

Now that you've spent part of your week observing your own desires and pleasures, it's time to act.

Days 4 and 5: Pursue proper pleasures

Over the course of the final two days, you'll engage in one small Epicurean practice each day that either cultivates and strengthens a natural and necessary desire, or one that reduces and weakens an unnatural and unnecessary desire, depending on the data you collected earlier in the week. An example of the former would be to call a good friend you haven't talked to in a while. An example of the latter is not to buy anything besides basic necessities.

Take a look at your observations over the last few days, focusing on kinetic pleasures you indulged in or unnecessary desires you pursued. Unnatural and unnecessary desires are prime targets for change, but it will also be useful to try to quell natural and unnecessary desires, especially if you find that you frequently engaged in specific ones.

Plan your next two days in the table that follows.

	Instead of ___	... which is a ___ [type of desire or pleasure]	I will ___	... which is a ___
Example	Eating a tasty dinner	Kinetic pleasure	Eat a simple salad and plain bread to satiety	Katastematic pleasure
Day 1				
Day 2				

While you probably won't attain ataraxia with a week's worth of practice, you'll at least begin to get a feel for the philosophy, and you'll get to know yourself a bit better in the process.

REFLECTION

Once you're done, take some time to reflect on your experience of dabbling in Epicureanism. What did you find challenging? How do you think it might fit into the life you want to lead?

_____

_____

_____

_____

_____

_____

_____

_____

_____

_____

_____

_____

_____

_____

_____

_____

_____

_____

_____

_____

_____

_____

_____

_____

_____

_____

_____

In the next chapter, we'll learn even more about how philosophy can help you balance your life from one of the most important philosophers in the Western canon: Aristotle.

Here are the answers to page 49. To have sex: natural and unnecessary, kinetic. To lower stress: natural and necessary, katastematic. To consume a delicious meal: natural and unnecessary, kinetic. To get a lot of "likes" on a post: unnatural and unnecessary, kinetic. To eat to satiety: natural and necessary, katastematic. To put your aching feet up: natural and necessary, katastematic. To have close friends: natural and necessary, katastematic. To get a large bonus: unnatural and unnecessary, kinetic. To be satisfied with your current income: natural and necessary, katastematic.

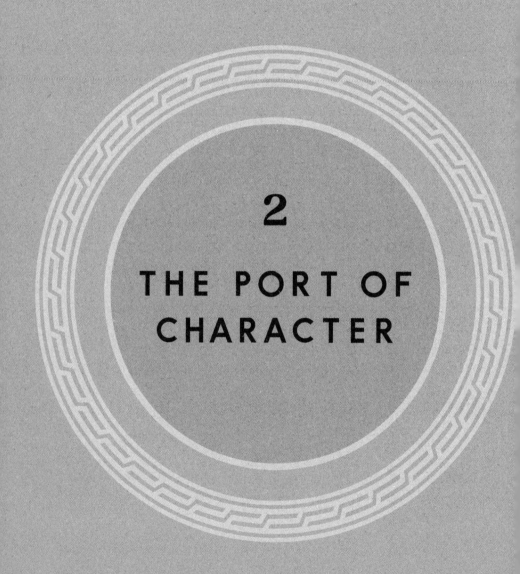

2

THE PORT OF CHARACTER

We are now leaving the relatively small Port of Pleasure (two philosophies) and entering the massive Port of Character, represented here by four approaches: Aristotelianism (chapter 3), Stoicism (chapter 4), Cynicism (chapter 5), and Platonism (chapter 6). These are some of the biggest guns in Hellenism, and they will offer us an interesting variety of perspectives on the very concept of character, why it is relevant, and how to improve it.[1]

In approaching this port, keep in mind that Aristotelianism, Stoicism, and Cynicism form a continuum with respect to one of their crucial tenets: the importance of virtue (which is regarded as a character trait). Aristotle took what is arguably the most commonsensical position: Happiness, in the sense of eudaimonia (that is, a life worth living) requires both virtue (which depends on character) and a number of "externals," such as health, education, wealth, reputation, and even a bit of good looks.

The Cynics, by contrast, adopted the most radical stance: Virtue, by itself, is both necessary and sufficient for eudaimonia. Not only that, but externals actually get in the way, and so we should renounce them as much as is feasible. Hence the Cynics' famous "dog-like" minimalist lifestyle.

The Stoics ended up striking a middle ground in this conceptual space: Virtue is both necessary and sufficient for a good life, just as the Cynics said. However, externals have some (indirect, secondary) value, and they are preferred, all else being equal, especially insofar as they make it possible for us to actually exercise virtue and thus improve our character.

The fourth philosophy encountered in this port, Platonism, is a very different kind of animal. In fact, it is so broad and complex that we limited ourselves to one aspect only: how to build a just society. As we will see, for Plato, this cannot be done unless we work on justice as an internal virtue. So, it all goes back, once again, to character.

There are at least two possible problems with all of these approaches that you should keep in mind. First, there's the question of what improving your character *actually* gets you. Pleasure is obviously desirable for most people. But the advantages of a good character are not as plain to see. To paraphrase a familiar New York saying, "Virtue and $2.90 will get you on the subway!" Having a good character doesn't have the immediate psychological payoff for most people that pleasure does. Modern philosophers have tried to argue that cultivating virtue is a "reliable bet" for flourishing, but even then they sometimes admit that you can lose that bet.[2] Why should you take a gamble when pleasure bears immediate fruit? (Because it's the virtuous thing to do, would reply Plato, Aristotle, the Cynics, and the Stoics.)

A second potential issue is that some modern social psychologists argue that "character" is a fiction; the empirical evidence, they say, does not support people having stable character traits, such as being "brave" or "compassionate."[3] Instead, situations and contexts that people find themselves in are the main drivers of human behavior. If this is true, it's no way to build character, since there's no such thing as character in the first place. But the issue is not settled, and defenders of the reality of character seem to be on the upswing.[4]

With those caveats in mind, let's weigh anchor and set sail for the port of character.

Chapter 3

STRIKE THE RIGHT BALANCE
WITH ARISTOTLE

One swallow does not make a summer, nor does one day; and so too one day, or a short time, does not make a man blessed and happy.
—Aristotle, *Nicomachean Ethics*, 1.1098a

Aristotle walked alone through the wooded garden of the school he'd founded, the Lyceum, heading toward the enormous plane tree with its giant roots extending fifty feet all around. Arriving at the tree, he sat down and picked up a still-green leaf that had fallen on this beautiful June day in 323 BCE, studying its veins intently for a moment.

He needed to think.

The sixty-year-old philosopher had spent the morning teaching students at the school, which he had named for Apollo Lyceus, "the wolf god." For the last twelve years, it had been his classroom, library, garden, and home, and he'd lectured while ambling back and forth along a covered walkway, the *peripatos*. That practice inspired the common name for Aristotle's philosophical school: the Peripatetics.[1] As Aristotle was speaking to his pupils that morning, Theophrastus, another lecturer, rushed over to tell him the stunning news: "King Alexander is dead."

Aristotle's eyes widened. "Dead? Killed in battle?" he asked.

"No," came the answer. "They say the Macedonian king died of a fever in Babylon."

Aristotle quickly ended his lecture and walked off into the trees. "Alexander always acted as if he were immortal, but the rest of us knew better," he said to himself. Nevertheless, he was shocked by the news that the thirty-three–year-old ruler had been taken by a fever. After all, Aristotle's personal history connected him tightly to the king who would soon become known as Alexander the Great.

Aristotle was born in 384 BCE in the Greek city of Stagira, situated near the border with Macedonia, a kingdom of Greek-speaking towns in the south and non-Greek tribes in the north. Before Aristotle's birth, his father, Nicomachus, served as physician to King Amyntas III of Macedonia.[2] Later, Amyntas's son, Philip II, took the throne. Philip was Alexander's father.

Aristotle moved to Athens and began studying philosophy at Plato's Academy at age seventeen. A wealthy young man, he enjoyed dressing well, wore rings, and curled his hair; yet his real energy went into reading, researching, writing, and, later, teaching. Plato nicknamed him "the Reader" for his voracious consumption of books.[3] Aristotle stayed at the Academy for twenty years, pursuing ethics, metaphysics, and politics, as well as mathematics, astronomy, medicine, and more. He eventually became a lecturer.

After Plato's death, Aristotle—passed over as head of the Academy in favor of Plato's nephew Speusippus[4]—left town for Asia Minor, where he took on the role of court philosopher for Hermias, a ruler who had once been a slave and who was enamored with the idea of becoming a philosopher-king. (Perhaps this was a more successful, if short-lived, effort at bringing philosophy into government than Plato's attempts with Dionysius II, which we'll look at in chapter 6. It would end when Hermias was killed by the Persians.) Aristotle married Hermias's niece and adoptive daughter, Pythias. While in Asia Minor, Aristotle also nurtured his interest in animals and biology, researching the fauna in a sea lagoon.[5]

One day in the winter of 343/342 BCE, a messenger arrived from King Philip II of Macedonia: Aristotle was invited to tutor his thirteen-year-old son, Alexander. It was an opportunity not to be missed, Aristotle thought—a chance to shape the mind of a future leader of an increasingly powerful empire, to usher him into a life of good habits and virtues. It would also be a way to build bridges with influential people who could support his work. Aristotle decamped to Pella, the capital of Macedonia, with his wife and daughter (also named Pythias, like her mother).[6]

As Aristotle sat under the plane tree at the Lyceum, he recalled his arrival at Pella, the court of King Philip, a brilliant, imperious fellow full of pride for his teenage son. Philip started their conversation by announcing, "I want Alexander to be able to command his men with honor—and to be capable of dealing intelligently with any other leader in the world. After all, his lineage extends back to Heracles through me, and to Achilles through his mother, Olympias.[7] I won't bring him up as an ignoramus, Aristotle. That's why I want you here to teach him."

Aristotle felt the power of his position: an established philosopher in demand by a king. It was a chance for him to demonstrate his own courage. If he meekly took on the job without asking for anything in return, he'd be cowardly; if he asked for too much from this ruthless ruler (who had killed and enslaved many), he'd be foolhardy.

The philosopher thought carefully, and, walking the line between those two extremes, came up with a proposal: He would do the job but had two requests. "First, rebuild my hometown of Stagira—you razed it after you conquered it. Second, provide a spot outside court for me to teach Alexander, along with some of his noble peers. In the right environment, I'll be able to give him the best education," Aristotle said.

Philip gave Aristotle an appraising look. Having studied with Greek thinkers and political and military strategists during several formative years spent in Thebes, Philip knew the benefits of a philosophical education. "This is turning into quite the negotiation," Philip said finally with a laugh. "But I have heard good things about you, and I know your father served my father well. I'll give you a fine location now, outside town, at the Sanctuary of the Nymphs at Mieza. As for Stagira, I'll see what I can do."

Philip's workers set up the Macedonian boys' school in a flash, replete with shady walkways and stone seats. There, Aristotle began working with the young Alexander, a boy with a mane of curly blond hair, one brown eye and one blue, and a handsome face, who seemed in constant physical movement. For three years, Aristotle served as teacher to Alexander, who proved stubborn but smart. The philosopher taught the boy ethics, politics, and literature (especially Homer), and attempted to instill in him new habits and ways of thinking, means to help him develop a good character.[8]

After Aristotle saw Alexander drinking so many goblets of wine that he passed out one night with his friends, he said to him the next day, "Every virtue sits in-between two vices, Alexander. For example, it is virtuous to be temperate with drink, and to show self-control. If we're too given to indulging, we'll suffer from dissipation. If we never enjoy a drink, or good food, we'll suffer from being insensible to those pleasures. The goal should be to find the middle way between excess and deficiency, to build a good character and a beautiful, virtuous life." Aristotle explained, "We seek out a mean that falls somewhere between the two extremes, depending on our own situation. That's true of every virtue. Another example is courage—it's between rashness and cowardice. Or pride—between ambition and humility. Or modesty—between shyness and shamelessness. We can use our reason to find the path. Do you see?"

Alexander nodded, and in this peaceful campus in the countryside, it seemed he might even be learning. But rather than following moderation, Alexander always wanted to push himself to his limits, in search of the kind of glory his father respected, glory in keeping with a warrior king.

Soon enough Philip pulled his son out of school and installed him as the regent of Macedonia when Philip went campaigning, ending the boy's schooling at around age sixteen. In battles, Alexander demonstrated a kind of fearless bravado that went far beyond courage—always (like his father) leading from the front into increasingly dangerous fights. Alexander took on the mantle of king at the age of twenty when his father was killed by one of his bodyguards.[9] That was the beginning of his meteoric rise as he conquered territory after territory.

Aristotle left Macedonia after ending his tutoring role to help rebuild Stagira. Later, in 335 BCE, when Alexander captured Athens—and with the Macedonian king's protection—Aristotle returned to the city, still the capital of Greek philosophy, and organized his new school at the Lyceum.[10] He shared with his students what he'd learned over a lifetime of inquiry, not only philosophy but also physics, cosmology, meteorology, psychology, and the newer disciplines of biology, zoology, and anatomy. He wrote some two

hundred books on a wide range of subjects, making him the most knowl-
edgeable man of his time.

As the years passed, Aristotle continued to develop the discipline of the
virtuous mean and encouraged his daughter Pythias and his son Nicomachus
to cultivate it as they grew older, even if Alexander had gone down a different path. Alexander's distance from virtue was confirmed for Aristotle
when, in 327 BCE, the king had the philosopher's nephew Callisthenes, a
court historian, arrested for treason. (Callisthenes died while imprisoned.[11])
Alexander let suspicions fall on Aristotle's head, too.

Now, in 323 BCE, sitting in the Lyceum's woods, Aristotle saw just one path
forward after Alexander's sudden death: he'd need to leave Athens. The
Athenians were filled with suppressed anger at living under Macedonian
control. Their hostility would now boil over into harsh anti-Macedonian
action. Aristotle, as a former employee of Macedonia's royal house, was
inextricably linked to its patronage, despite the anti-imperialist teachings
he promoted.[12] Without royal protection, it was time for Aristotle to end
this chapter in Athens before it was too late. He rose from under the tree
and made his way back to Theophrastus and his students, who gathered
around the peripatos.

"I will deny the Athenians the opportunity of sinning twice against philosophy," Aristotle said. The men began to talk among themselves. They
could see the danger to Aristotle and understood what he meant—that he
could end up just like Socrates, executed for political reasons.

As he packed, Aristotle reflected: The Athenians weren't able to find
the mean when it came to their rampant anger. They were swayed by
anti-Macedonian rhetoric and would go to extremes rather than finding
the middle ground that would make them virtuous people. Their rashness
and rage had caused so many tragedies in the past, so many needless wars
and deaths.

Aristotle left with his family, retiring to the island of Euboea (the modern
Evia in central Greece), his mother's native land. He died a year later, in 322
BCE. His work was later edited by the scholar Andronicus of Rhodes, who
compiled Aristotle's manuscripts and lecture notes.[13] For centuries afterward, his work was celebrated by philosophers and Christian theologians,

as well as Jewish and Muslim thinkers, turning Aristotle into a figure so prominent he was known in the Middle Ages as "*the* Philosopher."[14] The Italian poet Dante Alighieri called him "The Master of those who know."[15] Aristotle launched many new fields of study in the sciences, and is still considered today among the most influential thinkers of all time.

The nature of virtue

What is virtue, exactly? Virtue is a not-too-great translation of the Greek word *arete*, which we think is better rendered as "excellence." One of the reasons virtue is a bad translation is that the word applies to a lot of things: human beings, animals, plants, and even inanimate objects. All of these can be "excellent." For example, an excellent horse is one that is healthy and can run fast. But it sounds a little weird to call that horse virtuous!

Each different type of thing has its own way to be excellent. The characteristics that make a tomato plant excellent would not be the same as those that make a human excellent. Since we presume that all of our readers are human, the aspect of arete we should focus on is what makes for a virtuous (or excellent) human being. There are a number of ways to render this concept, and different Greco-Roman philosophers had a distinctive understanding of how to unpack the idea of virtue, and even of how many virtues there are.

Aristotle, in particular, thought that every virtue is defined in relation to opposing vices. For instance, gluttony is a vice because the glutton is enslaved by his craving for rich food. But at the opposite end of the spectrum we find an ascetic who barely eats and does not enjoy his food. The virtuous middle lies in developing the right attitude toward food, appreciating that it is a source of both nourishment and pleasure, but that too much (or too little) nourishment affects our bodily health, while too much (or too little) pleasure affects the health of our soul.

Famously, Aristotle claims that virtue is a mean.[16] Don't think of a simple arithmetic mean, though. We can't just assign numbers on a dial to virtue and vices and define virtue as sticking to the middle range of the dial. Aristotle is also not calling for mediocrity, as in "let's shoot for the average."

To better understand the idea of the Aristotelian mean, consider an illuminating example provided by Aristotle himself: Milo the wrestler. Because

Milo is an athlete, he needs to eat a lot more than a normal person does, since his training has him burn a lot more calories than the average person. For Milo, therefore, achieving moderation at the table—which is a virtue—doesn't imply the same thing as for most of us. If he used one of us (Massimo) as a point of reference, he would probably starve. And if one of us used him in the same fashion, we would rapidly balloon to obesity.

Massimo has experienced firsthand the difference between an average person and the kind of athlete Aristotle is talking about. Years ago, he went to Osaka, Japan, and spent a whole day watching a sumo competition. He watched as the wrestlers came into the arena in the morning and could appreciate at close quarters that their bodies needed a lot more nutrition than his did. Just as in the case of Milo, what is virtuous for a sumo wrestler, in terms of appetite, is definitely not what is virtuous for Massimo. And vice versa.

Aristotle thinks that the virtuous person is the one who sees things the right way, who understands, for instance, that neither gluttony nor asceticism are conducive to human flourishing and, crucially, acts in accordance with this understanding. Aristotle says that most of us are not actually virtuous even when we do manage to strike the right balance. If the way to achieve that balance is through a constant struggle—say, having to tear ourselves away from delicious treats—then, at best, we are continent, not virtuous. (Aristotle calls those people *enkratic*, meaning "those who have control.") That is, we show self-restraint, which is better than nothing, but we do not have true temperance. The difference is that the wise person achieves an equilibrium that is stable and effortless, while the continent person is always in turmoil, and the equilibrium achieved is unstable, maintained only at the cost of constant vigilance and effort.

It could be worse, though. We could be willfully vicious. According to Aristotle, there are people who engage in vice not because they momentarily lose their virtuous balance and make a mistake they are going to regret, but because they have decided that's what they want to do, all talk of virtue be damned. Some people behave like gluttons because they have a hard time restraining themselves; others truly are gluttons because they choose to prioritize bodily pleasures, thinking that that's actually the right thing to do (think of the Cyrenaics we encountered in chapter 1!).

There is, finally, yet another group of people who know what is right and yet cannot bring themselves to do it, regardless of how much they may struggle to achieve even a precarious balance. They suffer from a peculiar condition, which Aristotle called *akrasia*, often translated as weakness of the will. Consider your stereotypical couch potato, who realizes that he should get up and go for a walk, if not to the gym, and who certainly understands that eating junk food while watching television is not good for either his body or his soul. And yet, he can't manage to get his posterior off the couch, nor can he summon the willpower to throw the potato chips where they belong: in the garbage can.

Overall, we have four categories when it comes to virtue: the vicious person, the *akratic* one (whose will is deficient), the one who makes an effort (enkratic), and finally, the rare truly virtuous individual. Which one are you?

According to Aristotle, truly virtuous individuals benefit from a congruence of right reason and right desire. This means that virtue lies not in the action but in the doer of the action. The same action may be virtuous or not, depending on the reasons and desires that led the agent to act in that particular way.

For instance, let's say that I volunteer at the local soup kitchen. On the face of it, this may seem like a virtuous thing to do, as it is helping people in need. But is it really? That depends. If I do it because I genuinely want to alleviate the suffering of others, then my action is virtuous—even if what I do may not really change the overall situation. What matters is my intention. But if I do it because I need an extra line on my résumé that says I have performed community service so that I'm successful with my next job application, then no, my action is not virtuous, even though it does, practically, benefit others.

This is a major difference between virtue ethics and most modern approaches to ethics. A modern deontologist—someone who thinks that ethics is about duties and following rules—might say it doesn't matter what my intentions are; volunteering is the right thing to do.* Similarly, a modern

---

* Interestingly, though, the father of modern deontology, Immanuel Kant (1724–1804), felt strongly that our motivations are pertinent to whether our actions are moral or not. He went so far as to say that if I feel good about doing good, then I'm not actually acting morally. Moral duties, for Kant, aren't supposed to generate pleasure. He was a rather stern kind of guy.

utilitarian, whose philosophy is that what is ethical is what increases most people's pleasure (or decreases most people's pain) would approve of the act of volunteering regardless of the motivations of the volunteer. But virtue ethics is about improving our own character, and when it comes to character, intentions matter very much.

How to become (more) virtuous

Now that we have a better understanding of what virtue is—at least, according to Aristotle—the obvious next question is: How do we become more virtuous? It is often said that Aristotle thought the road to virtue is through habit. It's a bit more complicated than that, depending on exactly what we mean by "habit."

Moral virtue denotes an active state of mind, not a passive or mindless routine. Accordingly, an action is virtuous when it is carried out knowingly, mindfully, and for its own sake. This ability to purposefully act virtuously, in turn, is the hallmark of a virtuous character. So, when Aristotle writes that "it makes no small difference to be habituated this way or that way straight from childhood, but an enormous difference, or rather all the difference,"[17] he does not mean "habit" in the sense of a passive propensity to act one way or another.

Aristotle tells us that children learn not by passive acquisition of knowledge from their teachers but through an active, mindful involvement.[18] The same goes for learning virtue. Habits, by contrast, originate passively, and sometimes even in response to conditioning imposed from the outside that flows below the radar of conscious awareness. The contemporary philosopher Joe Sachs, in a brilliant article on Aristotle's ethics,[19] mentions a story told about the psychologist B. F. Skinner, one of the leading exponents of what was called behaviorism, a school of thought in psychology that flourished during the first part of the twentieth century. The story goes that, unbeknownst to Skinner, his students trained him to teach more often from one corner of the classroom. They did that by nodding approvingly whenever he approached the target corner and frowning when he moved away. They instilled a habit in Skinner, but it certainly wasn't a mindful one! (And they should all have gotten an A in that class for demonstrating in practice such a subtle understanding of operant conditioning, a crucial concept of behaviorism.)

Aristotle tells us that "the virtues come about in us neither by nature nor apart from nature,"[20] meaning that we are not naturally virtuous, and yet we become virtuous by deliberately building on the gifts that nature gives us (in other words, our social instincts). In a sense, (human) nature makes it possible for us to become virtuous because we innately care about each other, and this possibility is enhanced and developed by the proper use of another of nature's gifts: reason. We can alter our own perceptions and desires by thinking through them rationally, reflecting on our choices, and deliberately acting in certain ways. The adult, mature human being is the result of the initial conditions set by nature and further shaped by our parents and our society, all mediated by our own deliberations and decisions. Our character is partly determined by external factors and partly coauthored by us.*

Virtue is beautiful

Another fascinating aspect of Aristotle's take on virtue is that it is beautiful. He says that the virtuous person sees virtuous actions and desires as beautiful, and that perception is a true reflection of the state of things, meaning virtuous actions and desires truly are beautiful. At first glance, it may seem strange to make a connection between virtue and beauty, but if we reflect for a moment we see that we use expressions like "that was a beautiful thing to do," or "that was an ugly thing to do" when talking about moral or immoral actions, respectively. Similarly, we talk of beautiful and ugly thoughts, again applying beauty in an ethical sense.

The expression that Aristotle uses, *to kalon*, means "the beautiful." Courage, magnanimity, and all the other virtues are for the sake of the beautiful, which is what all virtues have in common. Following this thought, a virtuous act is analogous to a well-made work of art. They are both beautiful.

We can put this into a broader context when we remember that according to Aristotle there are three categories of goods: what is beautiful, what is pleasant, and what is advantageous. The first two are for their own sake, while the third is instrumental, ultimately done for the sake of one of the other two.

---

* This is another point of contact between Aristotelianism and Stoicism. Both Cicero (who was sympathetic to the Stoics) and Seneca write that nature gives us both the beginning of wisdom, by instilling in us strong prosocial instincts, and the means to expand such beginnings, by way of reason.

For instance, a painting by Michelangelo is beautiful, and we want to see it because it is beautiful, and for no other reason. A fine bath at the end of a long day is pleasant, and again, we seek it for that reason and that reason only. By contrast, having money in our bank account is advantageous because it allows us to do other things, such as buying a ticket to Rome to see a Michelangelo painting in person, or affording us the ability to take a nice bath in the privacy of our home. But nobody, except perhaps a compulsive hoarder, accumulates money for its own sake, or because it is beautiful or pleasant in its own right.

An advantageous good is always for the sake of something (or someone) else and therefore cannot possibly qualify as the highest category of good. Pleasure is a good, but—according to Aristotle—is never ultimately fulfilling, as it provides only temporary satisfaction. (Of course, the Cyrenaics and Epicureans would disagree, as we've seen in chapters 1 and 2.) It is only seeking the beautiful that truly fulfills us, and that is why it's the highest good. That also explains why we would carry out a virtuous action for its own sake: Because the action itself is beautiful.

There is a parallel between Aristotle's treatment of what is good and friendship. He suggests there are three types of friendship, which neatly mirror his classification of the three types of goods: friendships of utility (instrumental), friendships of pleasure, and friendships of virtue. We all have friends of utility—that is, people we associate with primarily because they perform a useful function. Consider, for instance, your colleagues at work. The chief reason you frequently interact with them is because they are colleagues, helping you (just as you help them) carry out your duties at whatever job you have. This doesn't mean that you don't genuinely enjoy the company of (some of) those people. You really do like going out for drinks after work. But chances are that if either you or they move on to another company you will not keep in touch.

Friends of pleasure are buddies with whom you share a particular interest. You all get together, say, to watch football, or to hike, or to participate in a book club, because that's what you have in common. Again, this doesn't mean you don't genuinely like their company. But it does mean that should your or their interests change, you will likely shift to other friends.

Finally, we have the highest and most precious (and rare) type of friendship: that based on virtue. A friend of this kind will genuinely care for you and stick by you through thick and thin. They will not be afraid to hold a mirror to your soul, as Aristotle puts it, and even point out—if necessary—that perhaps you are not doing the right thing just now. It is through this type of friendship that we improve as human beings. And it is this friendship that is truly beautiful.

Live like Aristotle

By now, you may have gotten the sense that your journey to the Port of Character will be quite a bit different from your previous focus on pleasure. The last two chapters were conceptually straightforward; both Aristippus's and Epicurus's philosophies are about maximizing one simple thing: pleasure. Of course, their approaches to pleasure were somewhat different: Cyrenaicism's focus was attaining as much bodily pleasure as possible, while the main aim of the Epicureans was to get pleasure through peace of mind.

However, Aristotle doesn't paint as simple a picture of what the good life is. On its face, aiming for "virtue/excellence" sounds straightforward, but it's a tricky concept to pin down. Aristotle defines it through a series of heady, theory-laden relationships to many aspects of a person's character. On top of that, what's virtuous varies from person to person, as the example involving Milo the wrestler's diet plan demonstrated. All of this leads to a theory of the good life that's a lot more complicated than "just go for pleasure."

Not only is the theory more complicated than what you've already encountered, it's also less practical. Astute readers may have caught a glimpse of this sentiment previously, when we quoted Aristotle as saying that how we are habituated in childhood makes "all the difference." What if your upbringing wasn't a particularly good one? Is a good life still attainable? According to Aristotle, no. While Aristotle would suggest that virtue is worth striving for, if we lack external goods like a nurturing upbringing, health, or being physically attractive, our happiness will be "impeded" even if we are virtuous. And if the misfortunes we suffer throughout life are too great, happiness is essentially impossible, even for the virtuous.[21] According to Aristotle, virtue is necessary for a happy life but it's not sufficient (meaning, even if you are virtuous, it might not lead to happiness). You'll need luck and virtue put to the correct use in order to live the happiest life possible. And how does one put it to the correct use? By living a life of the mind—the life Aristotle mostly led.[22] The life of a nerdy philosopher.[23]

This week, you'll learn to use Aristotle's sharp analysis of virtue in order to get a better handle on what virtue actually is in your life, with a bit of practice at the end. This will lay the groundwork for explorations of virtue in future chapters.

Day 1: Take an Aristotelian moral inventory

Traveling successfully requires at least three ingredients: a starting point, a destination, and directions for getting there. This section of the book assumes a destination: building character. Whether that's a destination worth traveling to is something you'll figure out for yourself by the end of this book, but for now, we'll take it as a given. In a few days, you'll begin crafting your own directions for how to make progress toward that destination. Today, your goal is to find out where you're starting from. You'll do this by taking a "moral inventory" of yourself (to borrow a phrase from twelve-step programs) through an Aristotelian lens. Before we lay out the specifics of today's exercise, it's worth going over the spirit in which you should perform it.

The goal of this exercise is not to make you feel bad about yourself by dwelling on your negative aspects. Instead, think of it as discovering the most impactful way to make yourself a more beautiful human being. If you're feeling down when doing the exercise, you can also take a moment to think about and dwell on the positive aspects of your character in order to appreciate the ways in which your character is already beautiful.

Keeping this attitude in mind, turn your attention to the table that follows, which contains a list of several Aristotelian virtues—aspects of character that strike a balance between deficiencies and excesses.[24] Your assignment today is to rate yourself in each area according to the four categories when it comes to virtue.

- Vicious (as in having vice, not being brutal, cruel, or violent): You often intentionally and willfully try to act in a way that Aristotle would consider "deficient" or "excessive" in this area, or you act mindlessly because you've never thought about what's right or appropriate.

- Akratic: You know in your head where the "golden mean" lies but can rarely bring yourself to act in accordance with what you think is right.

- Enkratic: You can do what's right in this area, but only with a lot of effort and struggle.

- Virtuous: You frequently do what's right in this area, consciously and willfully (not out of simple, mindless habit), with little effort and for its own sake (not out of any promise of other rewards).

If you have trouble rating yourself, try to think of several specific instances in your life where you were faced with an opportunity to exercise the virtue. Did you do so successfully? If so, was it hard, or did it come easily? If it came easily, was it done out of mindless habit, or intentionally? If you're still having trouble, just skip that virtue and move on.

Virtue (the mean)	Extremes	Self-rating (vicious, akratic, enkratic, virtuous)
Justice: Giving others exactly what they deserve (mostly in relation to nonmaterial things like time, praise, or honesty and information).	**Excess:** Giving people more than what they deserve. **Deficiency:** Giving people less than what they deserve.	
Temperance: Moderately enjoying pleasures.	**Excess:** Overindulging in pleasure. Profligacy or gluttony. **Deficiency:** Not enjoying even simple pleasures or avoiding them out of fear or self-punishment. Anhedonia, asceticism, or insensibility.	
Courage: Enduring fear or discomfort and acting in spite of it in appropriate situations.	**Excess:** Rushing into dangerous situations regardless of necessity or consequence. Rashness. **Deficiency:** Avoiding things that make you uncomfortable even if it's necessary or worthwhile. Cowardice.	

Generosity: Giving others material things or money in appropriate amounts.	**Excess:** Spending too much on others or spending lavishly. Prodigality. **Deficiency:** Spending too little on others. Being stingy.	
Ambition: Striving for external excellence for its own sake; for example, in your career.	**Excess:** Striving for external reward or pushing yourself too far. Over-ambitious. **Deficiency:** Not striving hard enough. Under-ambitious.	
Gentleness: Having a balanced, even temper while still being able to be firm when needed.	**Excess:** Being too hot-headed and prone to getting angry or upset with others. Irascibility. **Deficiency:** Not standing up for oneself or others, even when appropriate. Being a doormat.	
Self-truthfulness: Being truthful and sincere about yourself and your accomplishments.	**Excess:** Exaggerating or lying about your good qualities to others while ignoring your bad ones. Boastfulness. **Deficiency:** Severely de-emphasizing your good qualities to others or intentionally focusing on your bad qualities when describing yourself. Self-deprecation.	
Wittiness: Being able to be appropriately playful and funny with speech.	**Excess:** Being overly vulgar or slapstick when it comes to wit and humor, or being humorous all the time regardless of circumstance. Buffoonery. **Deficiency:** Being sour, grumpy, crude, or unable to apply wit and humor well. Boorishness.	
Friendliness: Being pleasant and easy to get along with in your interactions with others.	**Excess:** Overpraising, especially for the sake of winning someone's favor. Obsequiousness. **Deficiency:** Being overly harsh or combative with people in general. Quarrelsome.	

Day 2: Target the most important domains

Your goal today is to cull the list of virtues from the previous exercise and choose the three most important ones for you to tackle. We recommend that you consider tackling the virtues that offer a combination of ease and impact for you. You're more likely to succeed at easy improvements, so those are more worth pursuing, all else being equal. However, some aspects of your character may improve your life and the lives of those around you more than others and may be worth pursuing even if they're a bit harder.

To help you choose the three most important domains, fill in the table that follows and assign the specified point value to each column, then add them up in order to get a score for each domain.* Briefly write out your reasons for your ratings to make sure you rated them correctly, and feel free to change your score if it feels off after setting your reasoning down in writing. The three highest scores will be the three virtues you'll focus on in the coming days . . . and the next months or years, should you find the Port of Character a worthwhile destination!

Virtue	How *easy* would this be for you to improve on, and why? 1 = Hard 2 = Moderate 3 = Easy	How *impactful* would improving in this domain be both to yourself and those around you, and why? 1 = Not very impactful 2 = Somewhat impactful 3 = Quite impactful 4 = Extremely impactful	Total score The top three scores will be the areas you focus on for the rest of this week. Break ties in whatever manner you see fit.
Justice			
Temperance			
Courage			
Generosity			
Ambition			
Gentleness			
Self-truthfulness			
Wittiness			
Friendliness			

* This algorithmic selection process would probably make Aristotle turn in his grave, since he was pretty adamant about ethics being more an art of living that defies hard and fast rules.

Write your top three virtues to work on here.

Virtue 1: _____

Virtue 2: _____

Virtue 3: _____

Day 3: Explore right desire

As you learned in this chapter, Aristotle held that virtuous action comes about through the confluence of two factors: right reason and right desire. You'll tackle right reason tomorrow. For now, let's focus on right desire. What right desire means at a theoretical level is straightforward: It is simply desiring virtue for its own sake, not for any other side benefits it may provide. Right desire can also be seen as the wish to perform virtuous actions because the action is beautiful (kalon), and not for any other reason. Today's exercise—journaling about what makes your top three virtues beautiful—will help you get a better grip on what "right desire" means for you at a personal level.

Take five to ten minutes per virtue to try to convince yourself that becoming more virtuous in the specific domain would be good and beautiful in and of itself, regardless of its side benefits. You can do this in any way you see fit. If you have trouble, here are some questions you can attempt to answer to get unstuck. Respond to as many or as few as you find useful.

- Think of someone who is good at the virtue you're considering. Why do you find them admirable or inspiring? Why do you find that aspect of their personality beautiful?

- How would improving in this domain make your life less "ugly" (the opposite of the beautiful, which Aristotle thought the virtuous person has an aversion to[25])?

- Why would you feel proud of yourself if you were perfectly virtuous in this domain?

- How would perfecting this virtue allow you to be the best caregiver, parent, or friend you could be?
- How would others' lives improve because of your self-improvement in this domain?

Virtue 1: _____

_____

_____

_____

_____

_____

Virtue 2: _____

_____

_____

_____

_____

_____

Virtue 3: _____

_____

_____

_____

_____

_____

Day 4: Exploring right reason

Out of the two ingredients that make up virtuous activities, right reason is a much trickier one to understand than right desire. The ultimate goal of right reason is to find the mean between excesses. However, as you saw in the example of Milo the wrestler, the mean can vary from person to person: A good-size meal for Milo is not a good-size meal for everyone! But things get even more complicated: The mean also varies from situation to situation, even for the same person. For example, if Milo needed to lose weight in order to make a certain weight class, he'd cut out a lot of liquid before the weigh-in, which is appropriate in his situation. However, after the weigh-in, he'd take in a lot more to get a weight advantage before the bout.

Right reason is what guides Milo to the conclusion that what he's consuming is the mean between excesses. Unfortunately, Aristotle does not clearly lay out what right reason actually is! This is probably because Aristotle didn't think that there was an algorithmic, clear decision-making procedure in order to get to the mean. It requires fluid, constant practice of trying to find the mean for yourself in different situations.[26] With that in mind, today's goal is to practice exercising your right reason with regard to your top three virtues.

In the table that follows, exercise your right reason by giving two different virtuous actions for the same virtue that differ because of the situation. For example, listing all your accomplishments honestly at a job interview hits the mean of the virtue of self-truthfulness. However, it falls into excess if you're around a friend who you know feels insecure about their own accomplishments; in that case, the mean lies in holding back and not talking about your successes. Both actions approximate the mean of self-truthfulness but are very different from each other because of the particular situation.

Virtue	Situations	Virtuous actions	Why does the action avoid excess & deficiency in this situation?	What about the situations makes the virtuous actions different?
Virtue 1:	Situation 1:	Action 1:	Reason 1:	
	Situation 2:	Action 2:	Reason 2:	
Virtue 2:	Situation 1:	Action 1:	Reason 1:	
	Situation 2:	Action 2:	Reason 2:	
Virtue 3:	Situation 1:	Action 1:	Reason 1:	
	Situation 2:	Action 2:	Reason 2:	

Day 5: Plan a step toward virtue

Although Aristotle was quite theoretical in his approach, he did lay out some ingredients for what makes for an effective Aristotelian practice. In short, he said that it requires behavioral repetition: "We become just by doing just acts, temperate by doing temperate acts, brave by doing brave acts."[27] But we can't do so mindlessly. Instead, we must do these acts knowingly, for their own sake, and in a "stable condition"—that is, consistently.[28] Getting to a stable condition requires repeated practice, so it isn't completely up to us. However, the first two are more in our control. If Day 3's exercise did its job, you've become more convinced that virtue is worth pursuing for its own sake. That leaves mindfully acting as the final ingredient of cultivating virtue. That's the ingredient you'll be tackling today by creating an outline of a conscious practice plan for one of your top three virtues.

You're welcome to choose one of your top three on your own, but we have a suggestion: Pick the one that you strongly believe is good for its own sake. Recall that right desire is an essential ingredient of virtue. If you don't strongly believe that the virtue is worth cultivating in itself, all the practice in the world won't help. So, we suggest briefly revisiting Day 3's exercise in order to remind yourself which of the three virtues you find most worthwhile in and of itself.

Now that you've chosen a virtue, let's create an action plan for practicing it mindfully. Your plan should have three key ingredients.

1. A specific, clear type of circumstance or a specific time and date where you will practice the virtuous action.

2. The willingness and ability to pay attention while you're in the midst of the action.

3. A way to remind yourself that you're doing the action for its own sake, and not for any by-product of the action.

The first two ingredients will help you perform the action consciously, intentionally, and mindfully. The last ingredient will help you perform the action using right desire.

Let's go through an example to see how this works. Suppose you're hesitant to praise your child on their academic performance, even though it's quite good. This could be taken as a deficiency of justice, since you are not giving your child due credit when it's deserved. An action plan such as "I'll compliment my child more" doesn't meet the three criteria, since it's not specific as to when you'll give the compliments. It also contains no checkpoints to increase the chances you'll give the compliment consciously and for its own sake. However, the following plan checks all the boxes: "When my child gets their report card next week, I will find at least one specific subject to compliment by praising their constant dedication and hard work. I'll set a reminder on my phone to pay attention that day. I'll also write a quick journal entry the night before reminding myself of the importance of being just when it comes to my child."

Now it's your turn. In the space that follows, plan a simple step toward a virtue that's important to you.

The virtue I will be practicing is: _____

Specific circumstance or time/date I will act:_____

_____

I will increase the chances I'll act intentionally and mindfully by:

_____

I will remind myself of right desire for the action by: _____

_____

Once you've done your activity, write about how it went here.

_____

_____

_____

_____

_____

_____

REFLECTION

Now that you've set sail for the Port of Character, take some time to reflect on your experience with Aristotle in the space that follows. Do you find his approach to virtue clever and nuanced, or overly complicated and hard to act upon? Was it easy or hard for you to value virtue for its own sake? What's your take on virtue versus pleasure as a way of life?

_____

_____

_____

_____

_____

_____

_____

_____

_____

_____

_____

_____

_____

_____

_____

_____

_____

_____

Chapter 4

FOCUS ON WHAT'S UP TO YOU
WITH EPICTETUS

The operations of the will are in our power; not in our power are the
body, the body's parts, property, parents, siblings, children, country
or friends.

—Epictetus, *Discourses* 1.22.10

T he waters of the Ionian Sea lapped the shores of Komaros as the boat
carrying Epictetus and his companions neared the harbor. They had
arrived at the western coast of Greece and soon would take the road up to
Nicopolis, the city built to commemorate the victory of the first Roman
emperor, Augustus, over his foes Antony and Cleopatra.[1]

Epictetus arose and picked up his crutch with a sense of determination.
The bearded man in his late thirties was ready to embark on a new path that
he had chosen in the wake of a tough setback—the latest in a long series of
such choices in the face of harsh circumstances outside of his control. It was
the year 89 CE, and Emperor Domitian, fearful of opposition to his rule, had
banished the Stoic thinker—along with all the other philosophers—from
Rome. So, Epictetus packed his few belongings and set course for Nicopolis
in Epirus (northwest Greece).[2]

Epictetus didn't complain about the difficulty of walking on his perma-
nently injured leg as he slowly moved off the boat, the Mediterranean sun

shining down on the small group that included his students and friends. It was an obstacle he was used to coping with daily. He said to his companions with a sideways smile, "I won't be competing in the Olympic games anytime soon. But I tell you, the Olympics of how to live well is my constant study. In that, I hope one day to find myself emulating Socrates."

From his birth in approximately 50 CE as a slave in the Greco-Roman city of Hierapolis in Phrygia, in modern southwestern Turkey,[3] to his rise to fame as a Roman Stoic philosopher, Epictetus used his own power of choice—his *prohairesis*—no matter what he was up against. Even living as a slave, when nearly everything was outside his power, he could still choose his own opinions, motivations, and values. He could still decide how to respond to the circumstances he found himself in, answering with reason and aiming for virtue. Despite the chaos around him, he could act with wisdom, justice, courage, and temperance—the four primary Stoic virtues.

The origin of Epictetus's leg injury was one example of a situation beyond his control. As an enslaved boy he served Epaphroditus, a rich man who himself had once been a slave of Emperor Claudius and who now worked for Emperor Nero as his secretary in charge of petitions. In fact, Epictetus's very name indicated his status: it meant "acquired."[4] One day, Epaphroditus became angry with Epictetus and viciously twisted his leg. With complete calm, the young Epictetus warned him that if the older man kept twisting, his leg would break—and it did. Instead of crying out, he said, "There, did I not tell you that it would break?" The injury remained with him for the rest of his life.[5]

Epictetus's circumstances also came with unexpected opportunities that he used as a springboard to a better life. His choices eventually led him to practice philosophy, and later teach others. When Epictetus was young, it was fashionable in Nero's court to possess slaves who were poets, grammarians, musicians, and—you guessed it—philosophers.[6] So Epaphroditus allowed Epictetus to learn from the prominent Roman Stoic philosopher Musonius Rufus, whose work focused on practical ethics.[7] That experience turned the student into a lifelong Stoic.

Later, after Nero committed suicide with the help of Epaphroditus, another opportunity arose. Epictetus gained his freedom, and he rose from student to teacher in Rome, eventually becoming the most recognized philosopher of his time.[8]

Epictetus placed high expectations on his students. He often called them out for their hypocrisy and questioned whether they were capable of taking Stoic teaching seriously, which required its adherents to give up more conventional ways of thinking. Like the Cynic thinkers who inspired the first Stoic, Zeno, Epictetus and his followers rejected the idea that material possessions and outward achievements were the keys to a good life.

In his lectures, Epictetus pointedly asked his students: Why even try to become a Stoic if you are not willing to set aside the pursuit of worldly things that should not be goals in themselves, like wealth, power, status, beauty, and property? After all, those things are only good if you use them with virtue, and you can do that only if you understand how to use your judgment properly. If worldly things are what you care about, you'll remain a servant to those things all your life. Instead, he told his followers, you need to train yourself to make rational judgments about the world, and to use your Nature-given power of choice wisely to cultivate your character and grow your ability to act with virtue. This, for him, was at the core of human flourishing.

Epictetus lived simply. One day, he was awakened in the middle of the night by a noise at his window. He realized that his iron lamp, kept by the altar of his household gods, had been stolen. Epictetus chose to replace it with a simple lamp of clay, since expensive objects were of no real value to him. He commented that the man who had stolen it had been willing to become "a wild beast" and "a man of bad faith"—paying a price in debasing his character far higher than the monetary value of the lamp.[9]

With his no-nonsense attitude, Epictetus gathered many followers. His school in Nicopolis attracted the sons of wealthy Romans, and Emperor Hadrian paid him personal visits. Epictetus's teachings would later influence people throughout the Roman Empire, including the future emperor Marcus Aurelius, whose *Meditations* drew upon the former slave's teachings. Epictetus's interactions with his students were recorded by Flavius Arrian, who captured what he heard in *The Discourses*, and summarized it in a shorter volume, *The Enchiridion* (The Handbook).[10]

Near the end of his life, Epictetus—who had never married—decided to raise the child of a friend who lacked the means to bring up a baby.[11] It was a final act of choice to help another human facing hardship and uncertainty.

After his death in around 135 CE, Epictetus's followers kept his name and teachings alive. Rather ironically, given the master's teachings, a wealthy fan paid a small fortune for the famous earthenware oil lamp, no doubt wanting a tangible connection to the celebrated philosopher.[12]

Live in accordance with Nature

You may or may not have heard of Epictetus before reading this chapter, but it's a good bet you've heard of Stoicism. The philosophy has seen a dramatic comeback in the twenty-first century, and for good reason. Far from counseling us to go through life with a stiff upper lip and suppress our emotions, Stoicism is a philosophy of resilience and universal compassion, a system of ideas that has turned out to be useful to people from all levels of society, from the slave-turned-teacher Epictetus to the emperor Marcus Aurelius.

Stoicism begins with a fundamental idea: We should do our best to live in agreement with Nature. This doesn't mean to strip naked and run into a forest to hug trees, though there certainly isn't anything wrong with that. Rather, it means that we should get our cues about how to live a good life from Nature—specifically, human nature. Here is how the commentator Diogenes Laërtius puts it in his *Lives of the Eminent Philosophers*.

> Zeno was the first (*in his treatise* On the Nature of Man) *to designate as the end "life in agreement with nature" (or living agreeably with nature), which is the same as a virtuous life, virtue being the goal towards which nature guides us. (7.87)*

The Zeno in question is Zeno of Citium, a Phoenician merchant who, near the end of the fourth century BCE, lost everything he had in a shipwreck, arrived in Athens, fell in love with philosophy, and eventually began his own school. Since Zeno taught under an open public colonnade known as the Stoa Poikile (painted porch), his philosophy soon became known as Stoicism.

Why did Zeno think that living according to Nature is the same as living virtuously? To understand this, first consider a very different situation. Imagine that you have just moved into a new apartment and your best friend brings you a house-warming present: a cactus. (Don't ask us why, ask your friend.) If you wish to take care of the cactus there are a few details you need to know about the nature of cactuses. They are, of course, plants. More specifically, they are desert plants, which means they need a lot of light but relatively little water. If you water them too much, they'll die. A Stoic (as well as any botanist) would say that for a cactus to live according to Nature means, among other things, to receive the ideal combination of light (a lot) and water (little).

So, too, for a human being. After all, we are members of a biological species, *Homo sapiens*. Our species evolved, just as cactuses and every other living organism did. It follows that there is such a thing as human nature, and that if we understand what it consists of then we will be able to live a good life, as Nature intended. The Stoics realized that we have much in common with other animals, such as the need for food, water, and shelter, as well as a desire for sex to leave offspring for the next generation. All of those elements are in agreement with nature. The Stoics also thought there are two characteristics that distinguish human nature from that of any other animal, and are therefore specific to the human (as distinct from the cactus's) conception of a good life: the ability to reason and the fact that we are highly social.

Perhaps other species have an ability to reason, for instance, chimpanzees or dolphins; and certainly there are other species of social animals, from several kinds of primates to social insects like ants, bees, and termites, but no species on the planet has the reasoning ability of human beings. And no other has such complex, hierarchical societies characterized by a highly specialized yet flexible division of labor. The Stoics argued that, if this observation about human nature is correct, it follows that a good human life is one in which we use reason to solve problems and live prosocially, that is, in harmony with other people.

It is important to understand that living according to Nature is *not* the same as saying that whatever comes naturally to a human being is therefore good. All sorts of things are natural and yet not good. For a cactus, it is natural to get infected by a number of parasites, including bacteria, fungi, and insects. (Incidentally, many of these parasites thrive when one overwaters a cactus.) What's good is that which helps the thing in question to be the healthiest, best version of itself. Sure, it's natural for a cactus to wilt because of disease. But that doesn't make for a flourishing cactus.

Similarly, certain mind states come naturally to many humans but aren't good for them. An important example, according to the Stoics, is anger. The Roman Stoic Seneca the Younger wrote an entire book on the topic. Here is his take on anger.

> Anger [is] a short madness: for it is equally devoid of self-control, regardless of decorum, forgetful of kinship, obstinately engrossed in whatever it begins to do, deaf to reason and advice, excited by trifling causes, awkward at perceiving what is true and just, and very like a falling rock which breaks itself to pieces upon the very thing which it crushes. That you may know that they whom anger possesses are not sane, look at their appearance. (On Anger, 1.1)

Remember: A flourishing, healthy human is rational and prosocial. Accordingly, Seneca calls out anger as destroying those two key characteristics of human beings when he says anger is a "madness" that makes us "forgetful of kinship" and "deaf to reason." That is why anger is natural, yet bad for us.

Let us now return to Zeno and the basic Stoic principle of living according to Nature. We still have not explained why this is the same as living virtuously. To understand the point, we have to remember that the ancient Greek word for virtue is *arete*, which best translates as "excellence." Arete applies to human beings and their activities, to animals, plants, and even inanimate objects. Consider, for instance, what arete means in the case of a knife. The proper function of a knife is to cut, so an excellent knife will be one that cuts very well. The proper functions of human beings, according to the Stoics, are to think rationally and behave prosocially. So, a human being characterized by arete—that is, a virtuous human being—is one who does those two things well. Conveniently, those are the same two things that are typical of humanity as a species (again, according to the Stoics), which is why living according to Nature translates into living virtuously. We are virtuous when we "function" in the best possible way for whatever purpose Nature designed us for.

Incidentally, the ancient Stoics thought that Nature is the same as God, and that God made human beings in a certain way for our own benefit. A contemporary view might simply substitute natural selection and evolution for Nature/God and arrive at the same result: *Homo sapiens* evolved, and we have been equipped by natural selection with the ability to reason and an instinct for cooperation in order to survive and reproduce.[13]

From the general notion that we should live according to Nature, the Stoics derived a number of specific conclusions that shaped their worldview and their behavior. For instance, cosmopolitanism, which is the notion that all of humanity is a brother/sisterhood and that we ought to behave toward other people in the way we behave toward our kin. Here is how Epictetus puts it: "Do as Socrates did, never replying to the question of where he was from with, 'I am Athenian,' or 'I am from Corinth,' but always, 'I am a citizen of the world.'"[14]

If we agree that we should aspire to be cosmopolitans, then a number of other important practical consequences immediately follow. Among these are that national boundaries are arbitrary and ultimately undesirable and that war is an irrational waste of resources, because human beings flourish when they cooperate with each other, not when they slaughter each other. You can begin to see why this two-and-a-half-millennia-old philosophy retains a strong appeal for the modern mind.

The fundamental rule of life

Epictetus is also famous for a practical insight: what he called the fundamental rule of life. According to Epictetus:

> *Some things are up to us, while others are not. Up to us are opinion, motivation, desire, aversion, and, in a word, whatever is of our own doing; not up to us are our body, our property, reputation, office, and, in a word, whatever is not of our own doing.*[15]

The idea is found in other traditions as well, from the writings of the eighteenth-century Buddhist scholar Shantideva to those of the eleventh-century Jewish philosopher Solomon ibn Gabirol. You might have come across it in the form of the Serenity Prayer, written around 1934 by the American theologian Reinhold Niebuhr and often recited at the beginning of meetings of twelve-step organizations like Alcoholics Anonymous. Niebuhr's version is:

> *God, grant me the serenity to accept the things I cannot change,*
> *Courage to change the things I can,*
> *And wisdom to know the difference.*

Let's unpack Epictetus's rule carefully, because every word is important. First, the terms "opinion," "motivation," "desire," and "aversion" are only approximate and somewhat misleading English translations of the original Greek.

"Opinion" is really *hypolepsis*, which means grasping or taking up. In this context the word refers to the sort of deliberate judgments we make about things, especially the judgment of whether something is good or bad. For instance, the only things that are truly good are my own correct judgments, and the only things that are truly bad are my own incorrect judgments. A correct judgment, broadly speaking, is one that improves us as human beings, making us more reasonable and prosocial; an incorrect judgment, by contrast, is one that undermines our quest to become better human beings.

"Motivation" is *horme*, which is the intentions we have to act in some way or other. For instance, "I am going to try to act in agreement with Epictetus's fundamental rule as much as I can manage."

"Desire" is *orexis*, meaning something we consider good or desirable and are therefore prone to want. For instance, "I want to act virtuously (in other words, reasonably and prosocially) because that makes me a better person."

"Aversion" is *ekklisis*, the opposite of *orexis*—that is, something we consider bad or undesirable and are therefore prone to stay away from. For instance, "I am averse to lying and cheating because those are unvirtuous activities and they go against my goal of becoming a better person."

So, what Epictetus is saying is that what is up to us are only our considered judgments, intentions to act, and endorsed values (or disvalues). And in fact, all three are forms of judgment, which is why Epictetus thought that the whole point of Stoic training was to refine our faculty of judgment, or *prohairesis*.

What, then, is *not* up to us? Pretty much everything else, including but not limited to our body (health), wealth, reputation, career, relationships, and so on. A typical objection to this central idea of Stoicism, especially when it is misleadingly labeled as a dichotomy of "control," is that surely my judgments are influenced by other people and external factors, and just as surely I can influence my health, career, and reputation, which is obviously true, but misses the point.

That's why Epictetus speaks of matters being "up to us" or "not up to us." If I arrive at a particular judgment—say, that cheating on my partner is bad—my conclusion may have been influenced by others, but ultimately I own it, it is mine in the sense that the buck stops with me. I am the one ultimately responsible for that judgment, regardless of how many external factors contributed to form it.

Conversely, when it comes to what Stoics call "externals," sometimes I can influence them, but the ultimate outcome depends on a lot of factors that are not up to me, and therefore the buck does not stop with me. Consider health: Of course I have plenty of opportunities to influence it positively. I can decide to go to the gym regularly, eat healthy foods in moderate quantities, drink less, practice preventive medicine, follow the advice of my doctor, and so on. All of these things are the result of my judgments—and therefore up to me—but I may still fall sick and even die as a result of accident or disease.

The Roman writer Marcus Tullius Cicero, who was not a Stoic but was highly sympathetic to Stoic philosophy, used the metaphor of an archer to get this point across.[16] If the archer's goal is to hit an enemy soldier on the battlefield, what is and is not up to him? Up to him are the choice of bow and arrow, practicing archery before the battle, the choice of where to position himself to take the shot, the choice of the moment when to shoot, and the aim. Notice that these are all the results of the archer's judgments. Not up to him is whether the arrow hits the target or not—in other words, the outcome of all the judgments listed previously. That's because the enemy soldier might turn at the last minute and duck, or perhaps a sudden gust of wind comes into play and ruins the shot, or maybe the bow's string unexpectedly breaks. Epictetus advised his students to always, no matter what the situation, "apply the rule"[17]: Is this up to me? If yes, then let's focus our attention on it; if no, then let's take it for what it is and not worry about it. As we shall see next, the practice of applying the rule is very useful to us denizens of the twenty-first century, as it pertains to pretty much all we do in our busy lives.

Live like a Stoic

A modern Stoic life isn't that hard to imagine. In fact, there are quite a few people who are attempting to live one in the modern world. Modern practitioners of Stoicism tend to fall into two camps depending on how essential they think ancient Stoic "physics" (a broader concept than our use of the term covers, roughly encompassing science, metaphysics, and theology) is. The first camp—the modern secular Stoics—discards almost all of ancient Stoic views of physics, particularly the pantheistic notion that the universe is a conscious, rational being evolving toward its own good. They see ancient Stoic physics as incompatible with modern science and not essential to living a Stoic life. The other camp—the traditional Stoics—believe that Stoic ethics is difficult, if not impossible, to practice without equating the universe with a rational, good living organism. Since the universe is evolving toward its own good and we're a part of the universe, then everything that happens is good. If practicing traditional Stoics realize this in their heart of hearts, they can embrace whatever happens, whether pleasant or painful. The traditional Stoic would claim that without a belief in a rational, good cosmos, it's impossible for modern, atheistic Stoics to hold such an attitude toward their fate. They can bear it, but they can't *love* it.[18]

Unlike some ancient philosophies like Epicureanism (which you've seen previously) or Cynicism (which you'll encounter next), a modern Stoic life does not necessarily imply drastic external changes to your way of living. Stoicism doesn't require that you form a commune or become homeless. Instead, modern Stoics engage in practices to temper their desires and aversions and do more good in the world in order to become better human beings and better versions of themselves. This could necessitate major life changes for some people (for example, an aspiring Stoic who engages in highly unethical business practices may need to look for a different line of work), but not for all modern practitioners.

Many modern Stoics choose to focus on applying Epictetus's rule as a form of spiritual exercise. The rule is easy in theory, yet not so easy in practice, as you may discover as you try to live like a Stoic over the next few days! But don't worry, the difficulty of a task is not up to you; only your reaction to it is. So let's jump in and explore Epictetus's rule slowly but steadily. As a reminder, here is the rule.

> *Some things are up to us, while others are not. Up to us are opinion, motivation, desire, aversion, and, in a word, whatever is of our own doing; not up to us are our body, our property, reputation, office, and, in a word, whatever is not of our own doing.*

Day 1: Getting familiar with Epictetus's rule

Let's start simply by taking a quiz on what is and is not up to you in order to get a handle on how you'll be applying Epictetus's rule over the next week. The answers are on the next page.

Situation	Up to you or not up to you?
1. An unusually bad traffic jam makes you late for work even though you left home with plenty of time to spare.	
2. Your boss yells at you when you arrive late.	
3. You're very upset that your boss yelled at you for being late, even though it wasn't your fault.	
4. Your (apparently very mean!) boss chastises you publicly for some sloppy work you know is your fault.	
5. You get injured.	
6. You hate getting injured.	
7. Wanting to speak up against injustice.	
8. Failing to speak up against a specific injustice because you were afraid.	
9. Wanting to move your finger.	
10. Moving your finger.	

Here are the answers.

1. Not up to you. The traffic jam was unusual, and you allowed a reasonable amount of time to get to work.
2. Not up to you. You can't control what other people think of you, although you can influence it.
3. Up to you. The Stoics would claim that your opinion that being yelled at is bad, coupled with your aversion to being castigated, directly led to being upset. Since you can change your aversions and opinions, you can change your reactions, and so your reactions are indeed up to you.
4. Not up to you. Although it's your fault, your boss's reaction is still not within your control. Not all bosses would act the same way, or even be upset. Of course, your actions coupled with your boss's personality both played a role in their reaction. But their reaction is still not up to you entirely.
5. Not up to you. While you can influence injury risk, it's not ultimately up to you if you get injured.
6. Up to you. You don't have to like being injured, but it doesn't have to make you upset, either.
7. Up to you. This is a desire and a motivation, both of which are on Epictetus's list of things that are up to you.
8. Up to you. The Stoics would say that the fear stemmed from an aversion to the consequences of speaking up. This may or may not have been a wise decision depending on the details of the situation. But the Stoics urge us to focus on the motivation in addition to the action. If it was indeed wise not to speak up in the specific instance, then it would have been better if the lack of action was driven by wisdom, not fear!
9. Up to you. Motivation is on Epictetus's list of things that are up to us, and wanting to move your finger is a motivation.
10. Not up to you. Healthy people can wiggle their fingers as much as they want. But there is no guarantee you will be healthy. This small act is painful or impossible for some. It takes quite an advanced Stoic to not be upset at losing basic bodily functions, but at the end of the day, even the simple act of moving one's finger is not up to us.

Day 2: Journal about someone else's passion

Today, you'll continue to explore Epictetus's rule by journaling about what happens when someone else cares too much about what's *not* up to them. According to Epictetus, when we focus on what's not up to us, we suffer from a passion. A passion (*pathos* in Greek) is a type of unhealthy emotion that has two traits: It temporarily destroys our ability to reason, and it makes us less social. Recall that our rationality and sociability are the two major characteristics of human nature, according to the Stoics. Thus, being in the throes of passion literally makes us less human.

This is why the Stoics advocate for the complete elimination of passions (which are one type of emotion, but not all emotions!). Not because doing so makes us feel better—some passions such as righteous anger or lust can feel quite good—but because passions harm our human nature. And the goal of Stoicism is to be the best human being you can be. This means thinking clearly and caring about others as often as possible.

The Stoics readily admitted that completely eliminating passions isn't easy. Only the fully wise Stoic sage has achieved that goal, and as Seneca says in his Letter 42 to Lucilius, the Stoic sage is as rare as the mythological phoenix, which rises from its own ashes once every five hundred years. Stoics also emphasized that being passionless doesn't mean being emotionless; Epictetus explicitly tells his students that Stoics should not be "unfeeling like a statue."[19] Instead, they should cultivate healthy emotions that don't get in the way of thinking clearly or of caring about others' well-being.

Examples of passions include jealousy, fear, lust, anger, schadenfreude, and greed. According to Epictetus, passions are caused by a strong desire for, or aversion to, something that is not up to us. That's why his rule is so important: By internalizing and clearly seeing what is up to you and what isn't, you will be able to reduce your passions over time, becoming a better human being in the process.

Since it can be difficult to see your own passions well, we ask that you pay attention to other people's passions today and notice when and why someone is in the throes of a passion. These can be people you encounter during your day, people you see in the news, or even a fictional character in a television show you watch.

At the end of the day, take some time to write about how the passion arose from their caring too much about things that aren't up to them. Your goal is to try to explain how the passion you witnessed in someone else could have been caused by their focus on externals. Here's an example.

> Today I saw my husband get angry with a customer service rep on the phone when they said his broken smartwatch was out of warranty and couldn't be returned for repair. The fact that the watch broke outside of warranty and that the rep wouldn't make an exception isn't up to him (and probably isn't up to the poor rep, either!). Caring about these things that aren't up to him probably caused his anger. If he focused on what was up to him—using kind words or maybe taking a deep breath—perhaps he wouldn't have snapped at the rep.

In summary, look for examples of other people's passions over the course of your day. At the end of the day, take some time to write in the space that follows about how focusing on what's not up to you could have caused these passions.

_____

_____

_____

_____

_____

_____

_____

Day 3: Journal about a passion of your own

You spent yesterday noticing others' passions and thinking about how they could have arisen by not applying Epictetus's rule well. Today, you'll do the same thing with yourself.

Throughout the day, notice when a passion such as fear, greed, or anger arises. At the end of the day, use the space that follows to journal about the situation, as well as how it could have arisen by focusing on what wasn't up to you.

_____

_____

_____

_____

_____

_____

_____

Days 4 & 5: "Apply the rule" to your own passions throughout your day

---

Over the past two days, you've explored how passions arise in yourself and others through failing to apply Epictetus's rule. This has hopefully given you a better understanding of how focusing on what's not up to us can lead to passions. However, this understanding isn't enough to combat your own passions. Epictetus tells us that we have to constantly remind ourselves of the rule and purposefully not dwell on what's not up to us if we're to improve ourselves.

> As soon as you leave the house at break of day, examine everyone whom you see, everyone whom you hear, and answer as if under questioning. What did you see? A handsome man or beautiful woman? Apply the rule. Does this lie within the sphere of choice, or outside it? Outside. Throw it away. . . . You met a consul? Apply the rule. What kind of thing is a consulship? One that lies outside the sphere of choice, or inside? Outside. Throw that away too, it doesn't stand the test. Away with it; it is nothing to you. If we . . . practiced this exercise from morning until night, we would then have achieved something, by the gods.[20]

Being beautiful or powerful is not up to us. Nor is winning the favor of the beautiful or powerful. The only thing that is up to us are our desires, aversions, motivations, and opinions. Epictetus tells his students that as they go about their day they should constantly divert attention from thoughts around how things outside their "sphere of choice" are good or bad. Practicing this consistently throughout one's entire day is the main way to make progress as a Stoic. Over the course of the next two days, we suggest you do the same.

Every time you feel a desire for or aversion to something external, ask if it's up to you or not. If it's outside your sphere of choice, divert your attention from it and move on. We advise that you do this through a terse inner dialogue with yourself, just like Epictetus does in the previous quote. For instance, if you're worried you're running late for work, ask yourself, "Is this up to me or not? Not. Forget about it." You see someone attractive and your eyes glance in their direction. "Is this internal or external? External. Glance away." You notice a really nice car and feel a pang of wanting. "Is that in my sphere of choice or outside? Outside. Move on." For everything external that pushes or pulls your attention, apply the rule. And if it's not up to you, briefly coach yourself to divert your attention and move on.

This is simple, but not easy. You may forget to apply the rule throughout the day. It may help to set a few reminders on your phone, or put reminders elsewhere in your environment (such as a sticky note on your desk) so that you don't forget.

We've provided some space here to write about your experiences with this exercise each day. For your first day of practice, take note of what was particularly hard about the exercise, and write about ways you can improve on your second day of practice.

REFLECTIONS ON YOUR FIRST DAY OF "APPLYING THE RULE"

_____

_____

_____

_____

_____

_____

REFLECTIONS ON YOUR SECOND DAY OF "APPLYING THE RULE"

_____

_____

_____

_____

_____

_____

_____

_____

_____

Now that you've had some practice with focusing on what's up to you, use the space that follows to reflect on your experience with Epictetus's rule. What did you find challenging? If you continuously applied the rule, do you think it would improve your life? If so, how?

_____

_____

_____

_____

_____

_____

_____

_____

_____

_____

Chapter 5

BE A REBEL LIKE HIPPARCHIA

*Do you suppose that I have been ill advised about myself, if instead
of wasting further time upon the loom I spent it in education?*
—Hipparchia of Maroneia, in Diogenes Laërtius,
Lives of the Eminent Philosophers, Book 6

As evening fell, men gathered for a drinking party at Lysimachus's home. They reclined on sofas as their cups were filled with wine, and the conversation flowed just as freely. Then, as the party was really getting started, a strange couple dressed in tattered cloaks swept over the threshold It was Crates, the Cynic philosopher, already hunched with age, and Hipparchia, his young wife, who had decided to adopt the Cynic lifestyle.[1]

All eyes turned toward Hipparchia, a person so unusual that outrageous stories were being told about the "lady philosopher." Hipparchia was not just the sole wife at this get-together (the only other women included in symposia were courtesans hired to play flutes, dance, or be intimate with the male guests). She was also the rare woman who pursued the highly non-conformist life of a Cynic—one that consisted of living an austere existence devoted to following Nature's laws, freeing oneself from social conventions, and drawing upon reason to speak boldly to the powerful.

Soon, a man raised his chin toward the Cynic couple. It was Theodorus the Atheist, challenging Hipparchia. "Married women should stay at home, weaving on their looms and tending children," he remarked. He, too, was a philosopher, a member of the Cyrenaic school, and he had little use for Cynicism.

"What's wrong with focusing on my education, instead of wasting time making more cloth?" Hipparchia countered as she turned toward Theodorus. "I'll give you a taste of how rationally my mind works," she said. "Anything Theodorus does that is not wrong would also not be wrong for Hipparchia to do, yes?" she began. He nodded grudgingly.

"Well, Theodorus is not wrong to strike himself, if he chooses. Then it follows that Hipparchia would not be wrong to hit him, either," she said while completing the syllogism with a half-smile. Theodorus stood up suddenly, angry that a woman had taunted him so cleverly. He thrust out his arms toward Hipparchia to pull up her dress and violently expose her body.

But Hipparchia did not care if he revealed her nakedness to the crowd. She stayed calm and kept making her arguments, adhering to the Cynic belief that nothing natural should bring shame—and that humans are natural without clothes and the physical paraphernalia of society.

It was clear: Hipparchia was a Cynic who fought for a seat at the table and got it. Her outside-the-box actions made her one of the few ancient Greek women philosophers to be taken seriously in her own time.

She sacrificed the comforts of wealth and position to take on this role. Her noble parents had surely picked out at least one well-heeled suitor for her to marry as she turned seventeen. But by the time these men were being considered in her hometown of Maroneia, Hipparchia had already met the Cynic Crates.

Earlier, Crates had become her brother Metrocles's mentor under unusual circumstances. A prominent young man from Thrace, Metrocles experienced ill-timed flatulence during a public speech rehearsal. His response was dramatic: His sense of shame provoked him to go into seclusion with a plan to starve himself to death. When Crates heard about the incident, he decided to visit Metrocles after deliberately ingesting gas-producing legumes, to show him that anyone could naturally fart in front of others without shame. Metrocles became Crates's student.[2]

Not long after, when Metrocles's sister Hipparchia met the Cynic, she encountered a very different kind of man from those her parents wanted her to settle down with. It was she who decided she must marry Crates—and after she'd made her choice, she told her parents she would do so or die. While her philosopher brother may have approved, Hipparchia's parents were not pleased. The Cynic would certainly not offer their daughter a comfortable, conventional married life. In a typical ancient Greek marriage, she would have spent her days at home practicing domestic arts such as weaving, alongside giving birth to and raising children. But that was not Hipparchia's vision of her future.

After Hipparchia expressed her wish to marry Crates, her parents urged him to talk her out of the union. Crates attempted to do so. He dropped his threadbare cloak to reveal to her all she'd gain through the marriage: an old, decrepit husband's body, and no other fortune. "This is the bridegroom, and this is his property. Think it over! You'll be no companion for me unless you adopt my way of life," said Crates.[3] (Indeed, he "was ugly to look at, and when exercising used to be laughed at," according to the biographer Diogenes Laërtius.[4])

Undeterred, Hipparchia stuck with Crates. More than to Crates's physical body, she was drawn to the life of the Cynic and embraced the Cynic way of thinking. Though still a teenager, she persisted in adopting Crates's Cynic practices and married him, becoming his lifelong companion. The couple had two children together.[5]

It was far from a conventional marriage. Cynic thinking freed Hipparchia to go to public places that typically excluded married women, such as dinners and symposia, and liberated her to challenge men's arguments. And that's just what she did with Theodorus.

Ultimately, Hipparchia is remembered as a woman who defied her upbringing, her parents, and her society to pursue Cynicism by the side of her companion, Crates. Her choice gave the followers of this school of thought a clear picture of how anyone—even a wealthy, respectable woman of marrying age—could chuck all social conventions to become a dedicated Cynic, a rebel for life.

A dog's life is a good life

If you wanted to learn philosophy in ancient Athens, you had a bewildering number of options. You could go to Plato's Academy, Aristotle's Lyceum, Epicurus's Garden, or simply listen to the Stoics at the Stoa Poikile, just off the Agora, Athens's main marketplace.

But if you were attracted to the Cynic school, finding it would be a bit more challenging, because there was no Cynic school, only individual Cynics practicing their philosophy in the streets of Athens. Practice—*askesis* in Greek—was in fact all the Cynics did, paying little if any attention to the sort of abstract theorizing that was so important to the other schools.

The Stoics, close cousins of the Cynics, argued that to live a good life one ought to reason well, and therefore study logic. In addition, one ought to have a grasp of how the world works, which translated into studying natural philosophy (what we now call science).

But for the Cynics that was all a waste of time. The only way to learn how to live virtuously was to practice virtue, all the time, everywhere. As a result, their lifestyle was more than a bit unorthodox. As a matter of course, they did not marry or have children (Hipparchia and Crates were an exception). They didn't own property, and they ate, slept, and had sex in the streets. Diogenes of Sinope was once rebuked for masturbating in public, to which he responded: "If only it were as easy to banish hunger by rubbing the belly!" No wonder they were referred to as *kunikos*, meaning dog-like.

The Cynics wrote about their way of living, but none of their books survived. According to the commentator Diogenes Laërtius, Diogenes of Sinope authored a number of treatises, including *On Virtue*, *On Good*, and *On Love*. Presumably, they were all practically oriented. Interestingly, a number of Cynic writings were satires, so much so that the third-century-BCE Cynic Menippus of Gadara (in modern-day Jordan) started an entire genre still known today as Menippean satire. Menippus used comedy to discuss serious subjects, making fun of some of the other Hellenistic schools, especially the Stoics and Epicureans. In antiquity, Menippus influenced the Roman writers Varro, Horace, Petronius, Seneca, and Lucian, among others. His impact can also be detected in a huge range of authors across the centuries, including Erasmus, Rabelais, Cervantes, Swift, Voltaire, Lewis Carroll, and Monty Python's Terry Gilliam. Cynicism has influenced our culture for millennia!

Satire turned out to be a major contribution of Cynic philosophy to the world's literature—and likely a reason for the contemporary English understanding of the word "cynic," meaning someone who always questions people's motives. It's easy to find examples of satirical or sarcastic remarks in Cynic lore, particularly when it comes to Diogenes of Sinope. One day, Plato saw Diogenes washing lettuce, a lowly occupation for a philosopher. Plato approached, and—referring to Diogenes's refusal to do as Plato had done and pay homage to Dionysius, the tyrant of Syracuse—said, "Had you paid court to Dionysius, you wouldn't now be washing lettuces," to which Diogenes calmly replied, "If you had washed lettuces, you wouldn't have paid court to Dionysius." It's all a matter of priorities: avoid washing lettuce, a perfectly normal activity, or be obliged to a tyrant, an ethically compromising situation?

Like many Hellenistic philosophies, Cynicism began as a development of Socraticism, and specifically of the notion that virtue is the chief good in life. Perhaps the first Cynic was Antisthenes of Athens, who was a student of Socrates and is often featured in Xenophon's *Memorabilia*, a book about the life of Socrates that inspired Zeno of Citium, the founder of Stoicism, to turn from commerce to philosophy.

Antisthenes thought that the best way to walk the path of virtue was to adopt an ascetic life, even more so than Socrates himself had done. (After all, Socrates did have a job, a wife, and children.) Accordingly, Antisthenes started a school that catered to the less well-to-do classes and adopted what later became the typical costume of a Cynic: a coarse cloak, a staff, and a sack containing minimal personal effects.

Nature, not nurture

But what does Cynicism consist of, philosophically? Beyond the antics of colorful exponents like Diogenes of Sinope, and the conscious embrace of a minimalist and provocative lifestyle, Cynic philosophy was quite revolutionary.

To begin with, the Cynics thought that Nature, not society—as argued, for instance, by the Sophists—should be our guide for how to live well. They spent a lot of time making fun of Athenian customs precisely to highlight how arbitrary and ridiculous they were. For instance, when Diogenes's friends asked him how he wished to be buried after he died, he replied that he didn't care, and they could simply throw his body outside the city walls. His shocked companions pointed out that he would become lunch for wild beasts, to which Diogenes replied that if that bothered them they could put a stick next to his body so he could fend off the animals. The friends, naturally, commented that he would not be able to use the stick, being dead and all. Exactly. By the same token, he retorted, he wouldn't feel his body being eaten. Diogenes had just exposed yet another contradiction between the pious beliefs of the Athenians and the way the world works—that is, the way Nature works.

More broadly, a life according to Nature is characterized by two fundamental aspects: the rejection of social norms and the exercise of freedom. Human beings are capable of making their decisions in accordance with their own nature and do not require social norms or religious rituals. Religious authorities are then social parasites, and sure enough, Diogenes referred to temple priests as "big thieves" who go unrecognized as such, while society is busy carrying off the "little thieves" who sometimes steal from the priests.

This line of reasoning leads to the conclusion that the Cynics were the first, in the Western tradition, to articulate a theory of anarchy. According to them, the ideal human society is an anarchic one in which every person is capable of thinking on their own and making decisions about how to live. Of course, this assumes that all members of society act virtuously because they think rationally, which means that Cynic anarchy was not an actual political project but rather an idealized aspiration. Idealized or not, every human being ought to want to aspire to virtue, which is why when someone told Diogenes that they were not good at philosophy, he replied, "Why then live, if you do not care to live well?"

Cynic ethics is not a kind of "your opinion, my opinion" relativism, because Nature speaks clearly and unambiguously to those who use reason to understand it. One of the clearest messages that Nature sends us is that what is valued by most people—like wealth or fame—actually gets in the way of our happiness, and is definitely not needed for it. So, praying to the gods to be granted wealth, fame, and all the rest is foolish in the extreme.

Three kinds of freedom

The second element of a life lived in agreement with Nature—that is, freedom—in turn had three components for the Cynics: liberty from restrictions imposed by society (*eleutheria*), self-sufficiency (*autarkeia*), and freedom of speech (*parrhesia*). The last was especially prized. When Diogenes was asked what was the most beautiful thing in the world, he answered "parrhesia," freedom of speech.

The three components of freedom were tightly interconnected, as is evident from the actual behavior of those who practiced Cynicism. When Diogenes is described as repeatedly ignoring social conventions, he is exercising eleutheria. When he tells Plato that he would rather wash lettuce than pay homage to the tyrant of Syracuse, he is practicing autarkeia. And when he tells Alexander the Great to "move out of the way because you are blocking the Sun," he is (dangerously!) engaging in parrhesia.

Freedom as understood in this way is linked with the first element of a life according to nature: reason. It is by way of reason that we arrive at the value of freedom. It is also reason that tells us we want to live a life of virtue—understood as moral excellence—because it is only this kind of life that guarantees our freedom as social animals.

Perhaps the most stunning and influential consequence of the way the Cynics built their philosophy was their invention of cosmopolitanism—again a first, not just in the Western tradition, but worldwide. National boundaries are arbitrary and irrational, and national identities are the result of chance, according to the Cynics. It was again Diogenes of Sinope who, when asked where he was from, replied, "I am a citizen of the world" (*kosmopolites*), a response that the second-century Stoic Epictetus later attributed to Socrates.

Note that Diogenes did not say that he was *apolis*, that is, without a society. Rather, he felt that he belonged to the entire *kosmos*, meaning the world, and therefore nature. This is a revolutionary step that is just as important for us to ponder as it was for the ancients. As is the case today, citizenship was fundamental in the Greco-Roman world. To be a citizen of Athens or Rome carried enormous practical advantages, and was a highly guarded privilege.

The Athenians, even at the height of their power, actually restricted citizenship such that even a son of the statesman Pericles could not claim it, because their mother, Aspasia, was not Athenian. (That said, Pericles made an exception to the law by decree in the case of his own son. It always pays to be the guy in charge.)

By contrast, the Romans kept expanding the right of citizenship—not without internal controversy and resistance—until 212 CE, when the emperor Caracalla granted the privilege to every free inhabitant of the empire. It was this approach that contributed to making the Roman Empire last so long: even conquered peoples quickly assimilated and became proud to be "Romans."

Cosmopolitanism, like anarchy, was not a political program for the Cynics, but an aspiration. As such, it was inherited by the Stoics and it began to be articulated as an actual political program by the Roman statesman Cicero, who offered the democratic Roman Republic as a potential practical model for how to implement cosmopolitanism. We still aspire today to the cosmopolitan ideal, attempting to move closer to it by way of creating supranational organizations like the United Nations.

How did the Cynics practice their radical philosophy? Their askesis was rigorous, arguably even more rigorous than the Stoic version, which is why Epictetus admonishes his students not to embrace the Cynic lifestyle casually, as it requires a special calling. Most of us will have enough difficulties behaving like a Stoic, let alone raising the bar all the way to Cynicism!

Cynic practice was the soul's analog of physical training in the gym. When we go to the gym we don't do it for its own sake, but because we want better aerobic capacity, more muscle mass, and a heightened physical fitness. The same goes for the Cynic philosophical gym: We "go" there to become better human beings, better trained in reason, virtue, and the exercise of freedom.

How do we do that? Crates, Hipparchia's husband from our earlier story, was a student of Diogenes and, in turn, the teacher of Zeno of Citium (the first Stoic). He was very wealthy, but he got rid of his possessions in order to become a Cynic. Diogenes, in turn, was famous not just for his sarcasm and flouting of social conventions, but for his askesis. He went barefoot in the snow during the winter, rolled in scalding sand during summer, and hugged statues to, as he put it, "practice rejection." As the teacher, so the student.

Live like a Cynic

As you can imagine, living the life of a modern Cynic would be very demanding. It would require discarding pointless theoretical pursuits, most—if not all—of one's possessions, and extreme physical training in order to endure hardship. The purpose of this chapter isn't to convert you to full-blown Cynicism. Instead, it's to help guide you through a key aspect of the philosophy to see how different facets of the Cynic concept of freedom can be useful today.

The three components of Cynic freedom outlined earlier provide a useful starting point. Again, they are as follows.

- Autarkeia: self-sufficiency
- Eleutheria: liberty from social conventions
- Parrhesia: frank speech

While autarkeia is a critical feature of Cynicism, we won't encourage you to explore it this week since you've already tasted it through your exploration of Epicureanism in chapter 2. Crates would probably roll over in his grave if he heard us say this, but the practice of minimalism involved in Epicureanism resembles how the Cynics achieve autarkeia: One achieves self-sufficiency through reducing possessions and wants as much as possible. Epicurean autarkeia was milder than the Cynic version—the Epicureans were still okay with having a roof over their heads, for instance—but the spirit was similar. Since we don't think it's wise to immediately throw away all your possessions as Crates did, let's move on to eleutheria.

The author David Foster Wallace started his commencement address to Kenyon College's 2005 graduating class by telling a joke about fish swimming in water. Two young fish run into an older fish, who asks, "How's the water?" The two young fish swim on for a bit, then one turns to the other and asks, "What the hell is water?" They didn't know what water was because they were surrounded by it 24-7. It's hard to see what you're constantly immersed in. Social conventions are a lot like water was to the young fish in Wallace's joke: We spend our lives mired in them, and they can be hard to see.

How can you better see the social conventions that you automatically follow? Here are some characteristics that may help you identify them.

- They're implicit rules governing acceptable behavior in specific situations.

- They tend to come naturally and are usually followed without much thought.

- They're often arbitrary.

- You or people around you tend to be shocked, disgusted, or upset when others don't follow these rules.

- You may feel embarrassed or ashamed if you unintentionally break such a rule, even if it didn't hurt anybody.

- People around you tend to scorn or shame others for not following them.

Social conventions take many forms, from the relatively harmless, such as saying "bless you" when someone sneezes, to the significantly harmful, such as the sexist expectations Hipparchia experienced and that persist today. Some social conventions are not of much use, while others—like driving on the correct side of the road—are arbitrary and yet still serve an essential purpose.

Let's take some time to list a few social conventions *you* follow. You'd probably be able to fill the rest of this book with this task, so let's focus on social conventions you think are somewhat harmful and that don't serve any apparent purpose. In the space that follows, make a list and check whether each entry is harmful and/or useless, and in the final column rate how hard it would be for you to overcome these social conventions.

Social convention I follow	Is it harmful? (✓ if yes)	Is it useless? (✓ if yes)	How hard would it be to act against? (1 to 5, from very easy to very hard)

Keep this list on the back burner for now while we briefly turn our attention to the final aspect of Cynic freedom: parrhesia.

On its face, parrhesia looks like funny, irreverent witticism. However, the Cynic practice involved much more than that. You can see this for yourself by looking at two of the examples of parrhesia we gave earlier in this chapter: Hipparchia's barbed syllogism leveled at Theodorus (page 98), and Diogenes's request that Alexander the Great stop blocking the sun (page 103). The two instances have a common theme: They are both aimed at people of higher status by a person of presumably lower status (in the former case, the lone woman philosopher at a symposium of men, and in the latter case, a homeless street philosopher targeting the most powerful person in Greece).

As the scholar Ansgar Allen points out in his book on the history of Cynicism, parrhesia was actually a social norm in ancient Greece.[6] However, it was a norm reserved for free male citizens and was meant to be accompanied by mutual respect. Both Hipparchia's and Diogenes's use of parrhesia stretched this norm to the breaking point. According to the norm, Hipparchia had no right to parrhesia in the eyes of her society because she was a woman. Whereas Diogenes flouted the norm by attempting to deflate a powerful ruler.

These examples illustrate that the Cynics weren't just being snarky. They "punched up" to bring the haughty down a peg while highlighting the absurdity of social conventions through their bold, harsh speech. Thus, parrhesia and eleutheria are two sides of the same coin: They are both philosophical acts meant to highlight the absurdity of useless and harmful social hierarchies and conventions. The former achieves this through speech; the latter, through deeds.

Now it's your turn to dip into Cynic practice by returning to the table you filled out earlier. Over the next five days, choose at least one social convention that you listed and plan a small act of rebellion each day. You're welcome to focus on a single convention, or choose several different ones to practice over the course of the next few days.

We recommend that you start with a convention that would be easy for you to flout. If you didn't rank any conventions as a "1," then choose one that you ranked a "2." If all the ones you listed would be hard, go back and choose another that would be easy for you. You can work your way up to more difficult tasks over the next few days, but we suggest that you don't tackle anything too hard, since the goal is to test the waters of Cynicism, not to become a full-blown Cynic in the course of a single week!

To help plan your activities, fill in the table that follows. The final two columns are important safety checks. Full-blown Cynic practice has an excellent chance of alienating you from others, and could even be physically dangerous. Remember that Epictetus warned his Stoic students that Cynicism requires a special calling. Your objective is to get a taste of Cynicism over the next few days, not to cause harm. If you answer "yes" in either of the last two columns, nix the plan and think of another way to test the waters!

Your acts don't have to be grandiose: They could be as simple as wearing a shirt inside out or knocking a haughty politician down a peg on social media. Jut remember to punch up, not down!

	Social norm to be flouted (from previous chart)	How will you flout it (speech or behavior)?	When specifically will you do it (time, circumstance, etc.)	How hard will this be for you to do? (1 to 5, from very easy to very hard)	Could this put you in physical danger?	Could this harm your relationships or others around you?
Day 1						
Day 2						
Day 3						
Day 4						
Day 5						

At the end of each day, write about your experience in the spaces that follow. Focus on how you felt at the time, how you felt afterward, any effects your act achieved (or didn't), and whether it gets easier over time.

Day 1: _____

_____

Day 2: _____

_____

Day 3: _____

_____

Day 4: _____

_____

Day 5: _____

_____

Finally, once you've completed this exercise, take some time to reflect on your mild acts of Cynic rebellion in the space that follows. Did it get easier or harder over time? How effectively were you able to highlight the absurdity of social conventions to yourself or others? Do you feel freer? What aspects of this philosophy—if any—do you think are valuable in crafting your own life philosophy going forward?

_____

_____

_____

_____

_____

_____

_____

Chapter 6

WORK TOWARD A JUST SOCIETY WITH PLATO

The human race will have no respite from evils until those who are really philosophers acquire political power or until, through some divine dispensation, those who rule and have political authority in the cities become real philosophers.

—Plato, Letter 7, 326a–b

It was Plato's last chance—his one remaining opportunity to test his political ideas. Now in his sixties, he had long ago given up on the democratic government of Athens, which had been responsible for the execution of his mentor and friend, Socrates. But as he landed once more on the shores of Syracuse, a Greek city on the coast of Sicily, in 362 BCE, he saw a glimmer of possibility to establish a just government by educating a philosopher-king. He dreamed of a leader who could govern using philosophical principles, becoming a role model for all of Greece. And although he'd been burned by Syracuse's fickle regime on a previous sojourn, he was willing to try one more time. After all, the city's ruler, Dionysius II, had sent a trireme, a large ship, to pick him up in Athens to bring him to his court.

The imposing limestone citadel rose above the harbor of Syracuse as Plato disembarked from the ship that had transported him across the Mediterranean. The philosopher had suffered through a week-long journey across the choppy sea from Athens in the Syracusan trireme—rowed by 170 heavily muscled men. Plato was glad to make landfall, despite the city's hostile reputation toward Athenians.[1]

Dionysius claimed to be interested in learning philosophy, and since Plato was the most celebrated philosopher of his day, it seemed to make sense that Plato would become his teacher. Plato pinned his political hopes on this man, though he was an unusual candidate to become a virtuous ruler. His father, Dionysius I, was a brilliant military leader who had taken power at the end of the fifth century and managed to build Syracuse into the dominant state in Magna Graecia (Greater Greece), controlling not only portions of Sicily but also territory in Italy extending to the southeastern coast of the Adriatic.[2] He also wrote plays and earned honors from an Athenian festival for one of his works.

Dionysius I was worried, however, that his own son might dethrone him, and he raised the boy in seclusion, without a solid education. The younger Dionysius was filled with wine and constantly exposed to pleasurable company to distract him from the real business of leadership. Nevertheless, when the aging father died in his sleep, the younger man took control of Syracuse.

It seemed that Dionysius II* felt ambivalent about tyranny itself. He stated publicly, at a palace sacrifice, that the tyrannical style of government was a sort of curse.[3] Plato, during an earlier visit to Syracuse along with his friend and student Dion, had helped Dionysius work on a draft plan for a new constitutional monarchy. Unfortunately for Plato, the plan was scrapped when Dionysius fell under the sway of factions in his court who disliked Plato's influence. Dion was banished, and Plato was virtually imprisoned in the citadel—a bird in a cage, he recalled—until Dionysius finally let him leave.[4]

But now, five years later, Dionysius seemed determined to walk a better path. He invited intellectuals, including the philosophers Archytas, Archedemus, and Aristippus of Cyrene—the founder of the hedonistic Cyrenaic school we explored in chapter 1—to surround him at court. Plato's communications with these philosophers had led him to believe that Dionysius might be willing to adopt a philosophical approach to leadership.

---

* Dionysius and his father shared the same name and the two men were known as Dionysius I and II. From this point forward, Dionysius II will be referred to simply as Dionysius.

Plato imagined that his approach could usher in a constitutional monarchy and the rule of law, with philosophically minded advisers playing an important role. Hopeful about Dionysius's potential and trusting the court philosophers' reports, Plato sought out the possibility to build a better polis based on justice and freedom from capricious executions and exiles. Syracuse under Dionysius could be his chance. Plato was no longer the young man he had been when he started out as Socrates's student in Athens, but he still cultivated the hope of making a difference despite the chronic uncertainties in Syracuse's political situation.

As a scion of a rich and powerful Athenian family, Plato in his youth had come to understand that those wielding political power don't always do the right thing. As a young man, he had entertained the notion of entering politics himself, but he became disillusioned after Athens experienced the upheaval of defeat by Sparta and the subsequent rule of the Thirty Tyrants, a puppet government that engaged in the execution of political rivals. Following the tyrants' demise, the reinstatement of Athenian democracy led to the trial and execution of Plato's teacher Socrates in 399 BCE. Plato was about twenty-five years old at the time. After all that, Plato came to believe that trying to shape Athens's politics was a lost cause. Sparta, the other powerful Greek city-state, seemed even more impervious to political change because of its fiercely entrenched oligarchy.[5] So when it came to political reform in the Greek world, if one sliver of optimism remained for Plato, it was focused on Syracuse.

Deeply disappointed by the death of Socrates and the state of Athenian politics, Plato had withdrawn from the political sphere, and for more than thirty years, he focused on philosophy and teaching rather than leadership and the exercise of power. While removed from politics, he founded the Academy in 383 to 387 BCE just outside the city walls of Athens, attracting many of Greece's brightest minds, including the polymath Aristotle. All the while, Plato was writing a series of philosophical dialogues featuring Socrates as the main protagonist in conversation with his students and associates. These volumes of philosophical dialectics introduced many people to Socrates's quest for wisdom. Some of Plato's dialogues dealt with political philosophy, including the multibook *Republic*, in which he imagined what an ideal government would look like. Plato's reputation spread far and wide in the Greek world, even to Dionysius himself. And that's what prompted his return visit to Syracuse, to try once again to help create a just law-giver—a philosopher-king.

That is how Plato found himself back at Dionysius' court in 362 BCE. As he was escorted by Dionysius's armed guards into the ruler's inner chamber in the Syracusan citadel, a sumptuous meal was in progress—which came as no surprise to Plato in the land of pleasures that was Sicily. The acrid smell of oven-cooked sea bream covered in hot cheese and vinegar pierced the air, and copious amounts of wine graced the table in fancy goblets.[6] There was no want for anything in a court supported by taxes, gifts, war booty, and royal estates.

To Plato, these Italian feasts and nightly luxuries seemed to have no end. In this court, no one went to bed alone. How could a man indulging in all this be interested in self-control of any kind, let alone philosophy? And yet, Plato's friends had assured him that Dionysius loved philosophy more than ever and wanted to learn.[7]

Plato had grown skilled in assessing potential students for his school, to see if they had what it took to adopt the study of philosophy as a way of life. So, as he stood in Syracuse's inner citadel that day, Plato had already devised a way to gauge Dionysius's progress in philosophy and his willingness to reform both his personal life and the way he governed. The results of this test would reveal the path that Plato would take in Syracuse. He would decide whether to fully commit to shaping a new type of leader, or retreat into damage control for himself and his friends.

As Plato was escorted in to see the ruler, Dionysius rose from his cushioned seat—wobbly on his feet—to greet the philosopher. Plato's stomach sank immediately. Clearly the man was drunk again, just as he had been the last time he'd seen him years before. His posh robes framing his flushed face, Dionysius called out a hearty, "Welcome to Syracuse, Plato! Glad to see you've taken us up on our invitation at last!"

"I must thank you for sending your ship to bring me here, and it is good to see you again," Plato replied politely. "May we have a moment to talk privately?"

"Of course! All of you—out!" Dionysius said forcefully, ordering everyone else in the room to leave.

Plato then began peppering Dionysius with pointed questions, not so much about philosophical concepts but about his lifestyle and his willingness to learn. Was he aware of what he was committing to change about himself and his way of governing? Could he go without drinking for a time, to have a clear head to learn the basic ideas of the Academy? Would he be able to devote himself to a wide-ranging course of study? Would he be amenable to being guided by a teacher—Plato at first, and later, others?

Between swigs from his goblet, Dionysius smirked and shook his head. "Well, Plato, you see, I'm the ruler of this city—and I cannot be beholden to any teacher to tell me what to do. I'm sure you understand?" he drawled. "Anyway, I already know your most important doctrines. I've heard them from other philosophers at court."

"Then why did you send for me?" Plato asked, dumbfounded.

"Oh, I like having you here. You're so very wise," Dionysius replied, practically winking in Plato's direction. He clearly enjoyed including Greece's most celebrated philosopher in his menagerie of thinkers.

Plato grew angry. Dionysius seemed willing to absorb soundbites of philosophical principles and to use those ideas to burnish his reputation, but he was clearly not inclined to change his ways or exercise the self-control needed to study philosophy. Dionysius had no intention of putting himself under the sway of anyone, not even a highly respected teacher.

It took just this short conversation for Plato to realize the depths of his miscalculation. This man would never change. Once again, Plato had allowed himself to be lured in by this tyrant who had simply made a show of loving wisdom in order to gain the admiration of others and keep up with the current fad for philosophy among Syracusans.

Plato refused to take part in the tyrant's game. The final insult came when Dionysius went so far as to publish his own book of Platonic philosophy, to show off his supposed brilliance. How the tyrant could have actually learned anything of substance, Plato told his friends, was beyond him.

Dionysius released Plato at the urging of the philosopher's friend Archytas of Tarentum, a Pythagorean teacher and mathematician, and Plato sailed back to Greece. He could do nothing to prevent a later rebellion in the city that brought down Dionysius and left Dion, Plato's friend, temporarily in charge. That is, until Dion was betrayed by Callipus, one of his allies, and assassinated.

The experiment in Syracuse was the nail in the coffin of Plato's desire to create a real-world polis ruled according to philosophical principles. He returned to Athens and continued to teach and write. He died in 347 BCE, and his work has been studied ever since as the foundation of Western philosophy. In his last years, Plato wrote a lengthy work, *Laws*, that focused on the practical importance of good laws, rather than rulers, to build excellence in government.[8] He may have died thinking he failed to create a new form of government, but he had, in fact, laid the foundations for many discussions of the nature of government far into the future.

The daring philosopher

Plato visited Syracuse a total of three times, in 387 BCE, 367 BCE, and 362 BCE, at the ages of forty-one, sixty-one, and sixty-six, respectively. Although he died in 348 BCE, when he was about seventy-six years old, it was quite a feat for someone in his sixties to cross the Mediterranean and visit a generally unfriendly city. After all, Athens had launched a naval expedition against Syracuse during the Peloponnesian War, less than three decades before Plato's first trip. Although the expedition ended in disaster for the Athenians, one might have expected feelings to still run high on the part of the Sicilians.

Yet Plato took the risk, more than once. His first visit (during the reign of Dionysius I) might simply have been an opportunity for tourism, as he wanted to see Mount Etna, the active volcano on the island. But he came back twice more (under Dionysius II) with the express purpose of testing some of his ideas in political philosophy in the real-world laboratory of human affairs that was Syracuse. This is a remarkable example of hands-on philosophy for a thinker who is often criticized for being all about theory and utopia.

The decision to get involved in Syracusan politics was even more surprising given that Plato had pointedly turned away from public involvement after his mentor and friend Socrates was put to death by the Athenian democracy in 399 BCE. Indeed, Plato had actually left Athens in disgust and only returned to it several years later, to establish his famous Academy shortly before his first voyage to Italy. His adventures show an enviable degree of resilience after failure and an exceptional willingness to get back up on his feet and start again.

Perhaps it shouldn't be surprising that Plato was destined to both write about politics and attempt to put his ideas into practice. After all, on his father's side he was descended from Codrus, one of the early kings of Athens, while on his mother's side he was related to Solon, a major reformer of the Athenian constitution and one of the Seven Sages whose sayings were featured at the Temple of Apollo at Delphi.

The story of Solon is particularly pertinent to understanding Plato's political philosophy. Solon (630–560 BCE) was entrusted with the difficult task of mediating between the aristocracy and the people, who at the time were on the verge of a civil war rooted in the existence of profound inequality. He then passed a series of laws that likely represented a fair compromise, based on the fact that they managed to displease both sides in the dispute.

Solon's laws achieved the desired result, in part by way of constitutional reforms that put into place safeguards guaranteeing a balance of power between the factions, so that neither could gain the upper hand. The resulting arrangement was based on what we would today call checks and balances, taking into account the various interests at stake. It is important to note that Solon's system was not rooted in the modern concept of distributive justice, but rather on a notion of fairness based on acknowledging and respecting the differences between classes. As we shall see, Plato proposed something very similar in his political treatises.

The nature of political philosophy

Plato wrote forty-one dialogues[9] on pretty much every imaginable philosophical subject—so much so that the twentieth-century philosopher Alfred North Whitehead famously quipped, "The safest general characterization of the European philosophical tradition is that it consists of a series of footnotes to Plato." Nevertheless, only three of these dialogues are devoted to what we would call his political philosophy: *Republic*, *Statesman*, and *Laws*.[10] Interestingly, *Republic* is considered a "middle" Platonic dialogue, while the other two are classified as late dialogues, meaning that all three reflect Plato's mature thought, not the early influences by Socrates—even though "Socrates" is the major character in *Republic* and appears in *Statesman* (but not in *Laws*).

According to Plato, political philosophy is defined by three tasks, which are especially evident in *Republic*. It begins with a conceptual analysis, for instance, an inquiry into the nature of justice; it continues, on the basis of such analysis, with the articulation of a critical evaluation of different beliefs pertinent to the structure of good society; and it culminates in the formulation of a framework according to which a desirable and just society might be achieved.

Let's take a look, for instance, at the conceptual analysis of a crucial idea informing *Republic*: justice.[11] In the course of the dialogue, we are given four different definitions, beginning with "speaking the truth and repaying what one has borrowed."[12] Socrates isn't buying it, pointing out that sometimes returning what is borrowed—such as giving back a knife to someone who is now depressed and suicidal—is not a good thing.

Well, then, how about "treating friends well and enemies badly"?[13] This, too, is a nonstarter, as Socrates remarks that one may be mistaken in judging others, thus ending up harming good people. But perhaps one can take this criticism under consideration and modify the definition of justice, arriving at: "To treat well a friend who is good and to harm an enemy who is bad."[14] Here Socrates replies that it cannot be just to harm anyone, friend or enemy. The only definition that is not rejected in the course of the discussion is that justice is "to render to each his due,"[15] which is pretty close to modern conceptions of justice as fairness.[16]

At this point, one of the most obnoxious characters in all Platonic dialogues jumps in: Thrasymachus, a sophist who lived between 459 and 400 BCE. He is angry at Socrates and all his talk of justice, which Thrasymachus dismisses by saying, "Justice is nothing else than the interest of the stronger."[17] The challenge is one that takes much of the rest of *Republic* to address, and which still hangs at the forefront of modern discussions in moral philosophy: How do we reject moral relativism, specifically, the notion that might makes right?

The ultimate answer, provided by both Plato and most other Greco-Roman schools, is that human beings are naturally prosocial animals, and that their own well-being depends on cooperation and harmony with other human beings. As Plato puts it, "Injustice causes civil war, hatred, and fighting, while justice brings friendship and a sense of common purpose."[18] "Justice"

The way this works in practice is this: We usually have preliminary information about any given impression. For instance, we have basic knowledge of viruses and vaccines. That background information is quantified as the "prior" in a Bayesian framework. Let's say, for instance, that the current prior for vaccines working, as a general prophylactic tool, is 80 percent, analogous to Carneades's "convincingly true."

Now we look at the new evidence specifically concerning COVID-19 vaccines and it seems to go in the direction of the conclusion that they do, in fact, work. That is, their likelihood is high. This means that our posterior probability, obtained by combining the prior and the likelihood, will be higher than the prior itself, say, 95 percent. Our assessment of the notion that vaccines are effective has moved from "convincingly true" to "undiverted" territory. Had the likelihood, by contrast, been lower, the posterior probability may actually have gone down when compared to the prior probability, and we would have lost a bit of confidence in the effectiveness of vaccines. Graphically, it looks something like this.

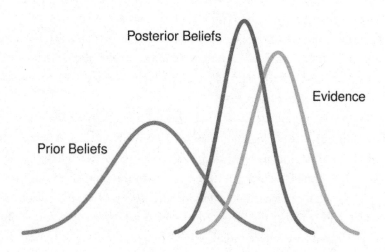

You can see that evidence "drags" posterior probabilities (or beliefs) higher (or lower) than the prior probabilities (or beliefs), as it should. That is, it stands to reason that evidence and argument change our assessment of the persuasiveness (pithanon) of a particular notion, just as Carneades suggested.

academics, but rather wise men and women who are trained for leadership and who exercise their role in society not because they enjoy it or even less because they want to accrue power and material advantages, but because it is their duty.[19] Accordingly, Plato prohibits his ideal political leaders from owning property because he is worried by the possibility of corruption. Think of it as an extreme version of our modern laws aimed at decreasing the influence of power and money in politics. The reason for the existence of a government, according to Plato, is to benefit citizens of all social classes, which requires mediating between potentially conflicting interests. He was famously critical of our most cherished form of government: democracy.

But we have to keep in mind a number of considerations for this perspective. First, at a personal level, democracy had unjustly killed his friend and mentor, Socrates. Second, and more substantially, Plato specifically criticized the Greek model of democracy, which stipulated that a simple majority of votes would decide the fate of individuals or of the entire society (as when the Athenians voted to embark on the disastrous Sicilian expedition). That's more akin to mob rule, or a tyranny of the majority, and pretty far from our modern concept of representation in a republic founded on a constitution. (The modern conception is, if anything, much closer to the Roman Republican model, which had developed in parallel with the Greek one on the other side of the Ionian Sea.)

One way to think about Plato's criticism of democracy is that it is based on two cardinal ideas. To begin with, while Plato explicitly values freedom, Greek-style democracy brings, in a sense, too much freedom, with the danger of descending into anarchy. Equality, one of the fundamental tenets of democracy, asserts that everyone—no matter their education, means, and so on—has the right and is assumed to have the capacity to govern, which Plato thought easily opens the way to demagogues and, eventually, to tyranny. As unpalatable as such ideas are, he has been shown to be correct a number of times in recent history.

Moreover, being a politician requires a particular skill set, rooted in virtue and good judgment, which not everyone possesses.[20] We can see this at work in a dialogue attributed to Plato, the *Alcibiades Major*, which also makes very clear in what sense aristocracy is a government by the best people ("best" meaning those who possess wisdom). Put that way, who *wouldn't* want the "best" people in charge? Let's take a quick look at the dialogue.

For context, Alcibiades (450–404 BCE) was a friend and student of Socrates and a very, very ambitious man.[21] Right before beginning his political career, when he was twenty years old and Socrates was about forty, Alcibiades went to his mentor to ask for advice: Should he pursue his dream of becoming a leader, politically and militarily, of Athens?

The young man certainly thought so. He pointed out that he was strong, handsome, rich, brave, and descended from one of the most noble and ancient families in the city. Socrates had to make an effort not to laugh at his young companion, replying that those are not the qualities that matter for the job. What's crucial is the one thing that Alcibiades did not possess: wisdom. Indeed, Socrates berated his friend rather harshly:

"Then alas, Alcibiades, what a condition you suffer from! I hesitate to name it, but it must be said. You are wedded to stupidity, best of men, of the most extreme sort, as the argument accuses you and you accuse yourself. So this is why you are leaping into the affairs of the city before you have been educated."[22]

The word often translated as "stupidity" in the previous passage is more properly rendered as "un-wisdom." In fact, Socrates went on to say that it wasn't just Alcibiades who suffered from this particular malady, but most politicians (except, perhaps, he added, the famous Athenian statesman Pericles). Here we see the stark contrast between the two versions of the concept of "best" embedded in the word aristocracy, which is rooted in the Greek *aristos*, meaning "best of its kind, noblest, bravest, most virtuous."[23]

Alcibiades thinks of himself as an aristocrat—one of the best men—in the way in which most people still interpret the concept: of "noble" descent, which usually also implies rich and powerful. Plato and Socrates, conversely, think of the best people as those who are most wise. And who would object to having things run by the wisest among us?

It is important to note that one of the most intriguing aspects of Plato's political philosophy is the direct connection he makes between a just society and a just individual. *Republic* begins with the question of what justice is and what makes a person just. At some point, Socrates suggests that perhaps they would make inroads if they looked at the big picture, that is, society at large. After all, societies are made up of individuals, one macrocosm encompassing a number of microcosms.

Live like Plato

All of the chapters in this section have been laying the groundwork for helping you to create a more just society. Chapter 3 focused on Aristotle's concept of virtue, where you practiced applying the "golden mean." Chapter 4's exercises focused on resilience by applying Epictetus's fundamental rule in the service of "living according to nature," which means being rational and—equally important—prosocial. And chapter 5 explored the concept of Cynic freedom in the service of demonstrating the absurdity of useless and harmful social conventions while bringing the haughty down a peg. While the skills you've practiced in this section can benefit you, they come to full fruition only when used to strengthen and benefit society along the way, just as Plato attempted to do.

We've focused on Plato's political excursions rather than his full philosophy because his philosophy is vast and sometimes impractical. So, let's jump right in and explore how you can apply the lessons from the Syracusan chapter of Plato's life to take a small step in working toward a more just society by dipping your toes in the realm of political action.

Day 1: Find a political cause

The first step you'll be taking this week is finding a cause. This likely came easily for Plato through his firsthand experience of the flaws of government. He saw tyranny take hold in post-war Athens, only to find the democracy that replaced it would execute his friend and mentor. Societies outside of Athens seemed little better to Plato, who believed that almost all of them were badly governed.[24]

Just as Plato's life experience led him to focus on better forms of government, it's possible that your life experience may highlight something that's wrong with our society. Perhaps there's a cause that's already close to your heart or some injustice in the world that you're already working to correct. If so, you can skip to the end of today's exercise and write down which cause you'll be working on this week. If nothing has come to mind—or if you'd like to explore a different cause from the one in which you're currently politically active—let's walk a bit in Plato's shoes to see what led him to embrace political reform as his main undertaking.

As a youth, Plato was eager to enter politics.[25] Unfortunately, he came of age at the time of the Thirty Tyrants. Plato initially hoped that they would rule justly, but those hopes were quickly dashed.[26] And we have seen why the democratic government that replaced them seemed little better. This suggests that two sources led Plato to take up political reform as his main cause.

- Personal frustration: Plato initially wanted to enter the public sphere, but his desires were thwarted by the political circumstances.

- Injustice: Everywhere he turned, Plato saw injustice being perpetuated by governments.

Plato's personal frustrations and the sources of injustice were both rooted in bad governance. This is plausibly what led to his interest in political reform, and ultimately his trip to Syracuse. These same two sources may be able to inspire you to find a cause you'd like to work on over the course of this week.

In the following pages, you'll find space to examine your thoughts about these two topics, along with questions to help spur your reflections. Give yourself five minutes (you may want to set a timer) to write down whatever comes to mind about your frustrations concerning the political sphere, as well as what you find unjust. Don't filter yourself when writing down your thoughts; just jot down whatever comes to mind. It doesn't matter whether the topics you contemplate are big or small, vague or specific.

Personal frustration

- *Are there specific laws, rules, or regulations at any level of government that have negatively affected you?*

- *Have you found it difficult to make your voice heard in the public sphere?*

- *Have you or anyone you're close to experienced difficulties that could have been made better by good public policy or law?*

- *Are there any current local or regional bills, laws, or ideas under consideration that you're in favor of and that would make your life better?*

- *Are there any political causes or parties you strongly align with based on your personal experience?*

_____

_____

_____

_____

_____

Injustice

- *Who is treated unfairly in your area, whether it be locally or nationally? How could they be treated more fairly?*

- *Are there abuses of power inside or outside the government that you think can be changed?*

- *What is the most pressing issue that would help the most people, either in your local community, nationally, or globally?*

- *Who are the most vulnerable people in your area, and how could their lives be made better?*

- *When was the last time you witnessed an act of injustice? What was it, and what could have made it right?*

_____

_____

_____

_____

_____

_____

After you've journaled, take another minute or two to see if there are any themes that particularly speak to you and that you'd be eager to work on for the rest of the week. If you're struggling, take more time to look for links between your own frustrations and injustice: for example, a law you're aware of that would make your life better but which could also help other vulnerable people. The confluence of injustice and personal frustration is plausibly why Plato decided to go to Syracuse; the combination of these two factors may help you choose a cause that's appropriate for you. And if nothing comes to mind, simply choose a cause that seems the most doable for you.

In the space that follows, write down the cause you'd like to work with in the coming week.

_____

_____

_____

_____

_____

_____

_____

_____

_____

_____

Don't worry about how you'll go about attempting to make a change within a political cause quite yet; that will be your task over the next two days.

Day 2: Educate yourself

Plato valued education highly, which he exemplified by educating himself, founding the Academy, and attempting to provide Dionysius with proper philosophical training, which he thought was a prerequisite to ruling well. Recall that Socrates chastised Alcibiades for wanting to jump into politics before being educated. The goal of today's exercise is to mitigate Alcibiades's and Dionysius's mistake by educating yourself on the basics of the political cause you chose yesterday.

Fortunately, you live in a time when you don't need a tutor who takes a weeklong journey by sea to educate you. Instead, you can teach yourself some of the basics through targeted internet research and reading.

Your sole task today is to set aside some time to learn more about your cause. Exactly what and how you'll do your research largely depends on the topic you chose, as well as how much you already know about it. However, we can provide some guidance to help you focus your efforts.

Our first suggestion is to restrict your research to the natural or easiest domain of your cause. Some causes—like world poverty—are by definition global in scale. Others—like political corruption—don't have a natural scale, since they can occur at the local, national, or even international level. In that case, we suggest choosing a domain that would be easiest to research and act upon. There's no need to research national politics if your concern is at the local level, and vice versa.

A second suggestion is to focus on answering key questions that you'd ideally have basic answers to by the end of your research.

- What are some of the specific problems pertaining to the cause you're researching? How exactly does it manifest itself?
  - » For example, "political corruption" is quite a broad term. How does political corruption occur in the region with which you are concerning yourself? In some countries, outright bribery isn't the norm, but "revolving door" job offers after a government official leaves office may be.
- Given the specifics you discovered previously, what are some proposed solutions?

» Continuing with the corruption example, term limits could be one possible solution. However, there's some research suggesting that term limits may be a mixed bag.[27] Try to gather a few proposed solutions along with basic pros and cons.

- Who are some of the players attempting to work on the proposed solutions or dedicated to your cause in general?

  » This is a critical step that will feed into the next exercise. Are there nonprofits advocating for solutions within your cause? Perhaps there are politicians who have proposed legislation addressing your issue (or perhaps *exacerbating* the issue) that you can find through a bill search at the local, regional, or national level. Are there local groups (donor pools, political clubs, activists, etc.) dedicated to your cause who you could reach out to or join to learn more and coordinate with? Create a short list of people who are already working on the issue and who you could possibly work with or donate to.

This exercise may be the most time-intensive of the bunch. Feel free to postpone it until you have enough time to give it your full attention. But keep in mind that your main goal this week is to get just enough information to take a single, simple political action; you don't need to become a policy expert to do that! If this seems overwhelming, try time-limiting your research: Give yourself an hour or two and stop when the time's up. Education's important, but it's not necessarily easy or quick.

Day 3: Choose who you'll work with (or against)

Plato withdrew from political life after Socrates's execution. However, when he saw the opportunity to change the situation in Syracuse in the form of a potentially teachable monarch, he leapt into action. One goal of yesterday's exercise was to uncover similar opportunities for change in the cause you selected. Today, you'll choose a target for your action.

Just like yesterday, the specifics largely depend on both the cause you chose as well as the information you uncovered. And just like yesterday, although we can't spell out particulars, we can still provide guidance to help you along. Your target will hopefully have been unveiled in yesterday's exercise when answering the third question regarding the main players in the space. Those players could have taken the form of potential allies or adversaries. An ally is someone who may be able to effect change in the direction you'd prefer to see, whereas an adversary is acting against your cause. The main player could also take one of several forms, such as a politician, a local or national organization, or a group of friends who may care about an issue similar to yourself.

From Plato's perspective, Dionysius fell into the category of potential ally and politician. However, your potential target may be adversarial, in which case you can choose to either act directly against them or work with groups that may oppose the target or their ideas. For example, if your research uncovered that your local representative was loosening anti-corruption laws, you can choose that politician as your target to attempt to directly influence their views. Alternatively, you can choose to support their opponents in an upcoming election, existing anti-corruption grassroots organizations in your area, or even reach out to a few like-minded friends to start your own anti-corruption group.

If your research hasn't uncovered clear potential allies or adversaries as your target for political action, we have a default suggestion: Choose your local or national political representative as your target for political action. Their raison d'être is to represent your voice in government, so expressing your informed views and preferences is a good place to start if you're looking to affect change.

In the space that follows, record who you've decided to work with—or against—regarding your cause.

_____

_____

_____

_____

_____

_____

_____

Day 4: Create an action plan

Plato's course of political action was likely clear to him because he had laid the proper foundations. His cause was well defined: political reform due to personal frustration coupled with a sense of injustice. He also understood political theory and practice through education. And he knew the main players in the political space, allowing him to discover an opportune target for political reform in the person of Dionysius.

Over the past three days, you've laid a similar groundwork to Plato, but to a milder extent. Still, we hope that your preparation has led you to a place where your path is apparent. If you've discovered a group you'd like to work with, your action step can be to join their next public meeting or become a paying member. If you have friends or acquaintances who are interested in your cause, reach out to them to plan a meeting and brainstorm some action steps. If you found an effective nonprofit working in the area you're interested in, donate to them or organize a donor pool to maximize your impact. The specifics of your action are highly dependent on your cause and what you've discovered about it along the way. The main requirement for your plan of action is that it's SMART: Specific, Measurable, Achievable, Relevant, and Timed.

- Specific: Your plan is clear enough to take immediate action.
- Measurable: It's crystal clear that you've performed the action.
- Achievable: The action can be easily performed.
- Relevant: Your action is directly related to the cause you chose.
- Timed: You lay out exactly when you'll take the action.

For example, if your plan is to "reduce corruption," it meets only the relevancy factor but fails in the others. However, if your plan is "to write to Senator X next Thursday requesting that they co-sponsor bill Y, which is related to anti-corruption," it meets all five SMART factors. Focus on the "achievable" portion: Your goal this week is not to solve the problem but to take a single, small, actionable step in the right direction.

If you've had trouble coming up with specifics, we suggest a default action of writing to your representative regarding your cause. Evidence suggests that reaching out to representatives matters.[28] One of us (Gregory) has had personal success in swaying political action by getting two state assembly members to cosponsor a bill, and one US representative to work toward freezing the assets of corrupt foreign oligarchs. Another one of us (Massimo) convinced his employer to send him to Washington, DC, to directly lobby senators and representatives for increased funding for higher education. And another of us (Meredith) worked with local students to advocate for more safety measures for pedestrians by reaching out to the Public Safety Department. When that didn't work, the students created educational videos to inform other young people about how to get around safely (after all, as Plato's case shows, not every attempt to influence the "powers that be" is successful!). This default suggestion also dovetails with Plato's actions: By reaching out to your representative concerning your cause, you are taking a small step toward trying to make a ruler into a philosopher.

In the space that follows, write out your action plan and check the SMART boxes to make sure it satisfies all five criteria. If it does not, rewrite your plan until it does.

My action plan:_____

_____

_____

_____

_____

_____

Is it:

- ☐ Specific? (clear enough to take immediate action.)
- ☐ Measurable? (You'll know when you performed the action and when you haven't.)
- ☐ Achievable? (It can be easily performed.)
- ☐ Relevant? (Your action is directly related to the cause you chose.)
- ☐ Timed? (You have scheduled when you'll take the action.)

Day 5: Act

Today's goal is simple: Put the SMART plan you laid out yesterday into action.

Of course, action may not lead to success. Plato's endeavors in Syracuse ultimately failed. But remember the theme of this section: It's not just about making the world better, it's building character. While it would be ideal if your actions succeeded, the results aren't ultimately up to you, as you learned in chapter 4. Even if your actions fail, you still did the best you could while providing yourself with ample opportunities to improve your character along the way. And regardless of the external outcomes, doing the best you can to make the world better has the side effect of making you better along the way, too—whether or not your action ultimately succeeds.

REFLECTION

Now that you've completed your action plan, take some time to reflect. Do you feel that you'd like to take further steps toward building a more just society? If so, what are some things you'd like to do down the road? Were you able to use any of the skills you've practiced in previous chapters along the way to help build your character or regulate your emotions while attempting to do some good? How did you feel about yourself afterward?

_____

_____

_____

_____

_____

_____

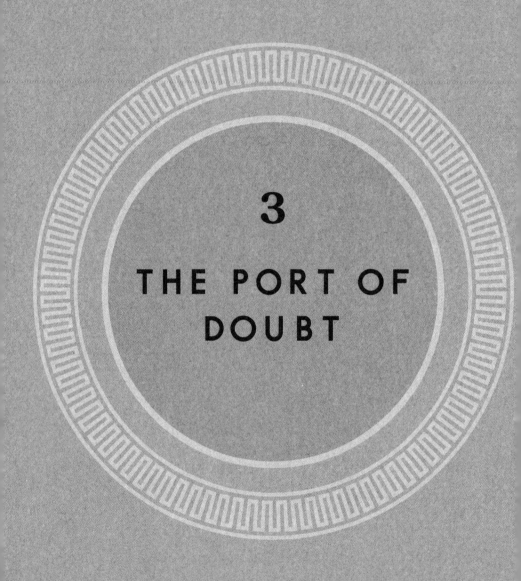

3
THE PORT OF DOUBT

T he final port in our journey is that of doubt, populated by four philosophies: "Socraticism" (chapter 7), Sophism (chapter 8), Academic Skepticism (chapter 9), and Pyrrhonism (chapter 10). Skepticism, which may be used as the umbrella term for these philosophies, has a long history that continues to this day.[1]

First we'll encounter Socrates, the most famous ancient philosopher, who was a crucial point of reference for many skeptics, as well as for many of the philosophers we encountered earlier. Nevertheless, the Sophists—especially Protagoras—who either came before Socrates or were his contemporaries, were not "skeptical" in the way he was. In fact, Plato wrote a number of famous dialogues—including one that takes the title from Protagoras himself—in which Socrates is shown locked in serious intellectual battle with one or another Sophist.

The next two philosophies, which are most often referred to as varieties of skepticism, are also quite different from each other. The Pyrrhonists thought that the goal of life is ataraxia, that is, tranquility of mind. And they were convinced that they had identified the path to it: *epoche*, or suspension of judgment.

The other skeptics, known as "Academic" because they technically belonged to the tradition of Plato's Academy (and, hence, of Socrates), agreed with many other Hellenistic schools that a good life is one of virtue. But they insisted that human beings can hardly achieve certainty on any subject matter because our senses and ability to reason are both fallible. Therefore, we have to content ourselves with tentative conclusions based on what appears most probable.

The result, in the cases of both Academic Skepticism and Pyrrhonism, is a very humbling philosophy of life, where people go around admitting that they don't know anything, or much of anything. Boy, could we use a bit more of that humility today!

Or could we? In good skeptical fashion, we can doubt even that humility and admitting ignorance can lead to a worthwhile life. While pleasure's payoff is immediate, and character building could bring peace of mind and make the world better off, it's not entirely clear that being skeptical has enough substance to be a full-fledged philosophy of life. Additionally, even if you desire peace of mind, it's not evident that skepticism is a better route to achieving that goal than, say, hedonistic Epicureanism or arete-oriented Stoicism.

As we start our journey to our next port of call, keep these doubts in mind. Perhaps you should be skeptical about skepticism. Or perhaps not!

Chapter 7

QUESTION EVERYTHING
WITH SOCRATES

Socrates was the first who brought down philosophy from the heavens, placed it in cities, introduced it into families, and obliged it to examine into life and morals, and good and evil.
—Cicero, *Tusculan Disputations*, Book 5

On the seventh day of the Delphic month—Apollo's birthday—the Athenian Chaerephon traveled to Delphi, the navel of the world, up in the misty hillsides of Mount Parnassus. He prepared to ask the famous Oracle a question.

Meanwhile, the Oracle, a priestess known as the Pythia, sipped water from a sacred spring. In the temple, she sat upon a bronze tripod, chewing laurel leaves from Apollo's holy tree. The Oracle inhaled the intoxicating gasses emanating from the earth below—including methane and ethylene—and entered an ecstatic state, channeling the god Apollo.[1] Chaerephon was then allowed to ask his question. Would he inquire about the nature of the cosmos, or about his own future success? Nothing of the sort. He asked, "Is anyone wiser than Socrates?"

The answer from the Pythia was clear: "No one." The Athenian smiled broadly—he practically worshiped his childhood friend. He hurried off toward Athens to share what the Oracle had told him.[2]

At the time, Socrates was about forty years old. Born in 469 BCE, he came from a middle-class Athenian family, his father a stonemason and his mother a midwife. Tough and impervious to the weather, he had fought with bravery in Athens's war against Sparta. He wasn't good-looking; he had a snub nose, and his eyes bulged out of his head and pointed sideways, making him the butt of jokes about his appearance (including unflattering comparisons to crabs and pigs). Nevertheless, he had married twice and fathered children.[3]

After his military days, Socrates did not follow a standard Athenian career path as a politician, merchant, or military officer. Instead, he became a street philosopher who pestered influential citizens and young people alike with probing questions. The philosophical "gadfly" often caught people out in logical inconsistencies or hypocrisy. Yet he kept asking, trying to find the answers to big questions—what is wisdom, courage, piety, justice?

That's why he was both shocked and a bit amused when Chaerephon approached with his story about the Oracle. "My friend, you astonish me!" Socrates said, rubbing his belly—which was feeling a bit empty. (Without a steady source of income, Socrates relied on friends for meals.)

"Have you been so impetuous as to ask the Oracle about *me*? And how could the god Apollo—who never lies—think that I am wise? I know for certain that I am not!" Socrates shook his head, but the conversation spurred him to begin a new quest: He set out to discover whether other Athenians were wiser than he was.

Socrates first visited a politician who people often called wise and asked him a few questions. When the answers he received didn't quite measure up, he provoked the politician's ire. Socrates went to talk to his students the next day, explaining, "I barely escaped without a beating. There's no wisdom to be found in that corner."

He went on, "I reflected: I am wiser than that man. Because in all likelihood, neither of us knows anything, but he thought he did, when he did not—whereas I did not know, and I knew that I didn't!"[4]

As he continued his investigation, he found this to be true everywhere. Later, he thought back to the famous inscription at the Oracle at Delphi: "Know thyself." Socrates explained what it meant in a conversation with his student Euthydemus: "Those who know themselves learn their own powers and limitations," he said. "They do what they understand, and so they can get what they want. They don't do what they don't understand. . . . They have conversations like this, where we try to figure out what's good and what's bad—testing each other."[5]

He went on to describe the opposite of knowing oneself: "Those without self-knowledge are deceiving themselves about their own powers and don't really understand other people or human affairs. They don't know what they want, what they're doing, and who they're dealing with. They miss the good and stumble into the bad."[6]

Socrates spent the rest of his life questioning everything. He sought to understand the limits of his knowledge and to expand on his understanding of the good. (It's worth mentioning that in a world of so many unknowns, Socrates benefited from a secret weapon: He claimed to have a divine inner voice, a "daimonion," that told him what to avoid doing. Think of it as a personified version of his conscience.[7])

Socrates's goal was to help his fellow Athenians experience these realizations, too—to see that what they thought was true was undermined by inconsistencies. He would begin a discussion by acknowledging his own ignorance, and as the conversation went on, it was gradually revealed just how little his interlocutors really knew.

According to Xenophon, Socrates said that "men become supremely good and happy and skilled in discussion," which he defined as "common deliberation or sorting." This was a skill to be valued and nurtured, which, if practiced well, could lead to excellence and good leadership.[8] And that's exactly what Socrates wished to teach the Athenians.

Socrates became a fixture in Athens's Agora, the city's marketplace of goods and ideas, holding forth in question-and-answer sessions, with a crowd of well-groomed young men in tow. However, his relationship with his students and with the politicians of his day did not sit well with everyone. His uncomfortable questions and his moral instincts made him unpopular with many powerful men. In Plato's *Apology*, Socrates says that the Thirty Tyrants, when they ruled Athens, commanded him and others to arrest a man they wanted to execute. Socrates disagreed with the trumped-up charges, so rather than obeying, he simply went home.[9] He acted ethically, at the risk of his own life.

The bad blood that dominated Athenian politics after democracy was restored came back to bite Socrates, ultimately leading to his arrest. When the philosopher was charged in 399 BCE with corrupting the youth of Athens and with impiety (disbelieving in the city's gods and introducing new ones), he didn't try to wiggle his way out of it, or flatter the court. He spoke honestly, explaining that if he were released, he fully intended to continue pursuing his knowledge-seeking discussions rather than curtail his activities or flee. He even made the point that he was "given by God" to the Athenians: Rather than focusing on himself, he said he was busy tending to Athenians' concerns, "coming to each one of you individually like a father or an elder brother, exhorting you to regard virtue."[10]

Socrates died at the court's order that year—drinking poisonous hemlock, surrounded by friends. He was celebrated after his death, with Plato calling Socrates "the most upright man of that day."[11] Though he wrote no books, Socrates inspired the work of his students Plato and Xenophon, along with many others who wished to question society's received wisdom about what is good and right.

Philosophy by refutation

Socrates is so important in the history of western philosophy that all philosophers who came before him, from Thales of Miletus to Democritus, from Heraclitus to Pythagoras, are still referred to today as "pre-Socratics," even though the only thing they have in common is that they were active before or at the same time as the gadfly from Athens.[12] One of the distinctive features of Socrates's approach to philosophy is that he did not write anything down but spent all his time in conversation with his students or anyone else who might be interested. This way of doing philosophy is often referred to as the Socratic method, although it turns out that Socrates used a number of interrelated approaches in the pursuit of his love of wisdom. Let us take a closer look.

Perhaps the best-known method deployed by Socrates is the *elenchus*, a word that means refutation. What might typically happen is that Socrates would inquire about a particular topic, say, the nature of piety, as in the Platonic dialogue known as the *Euthyphro*. He begins by eliciting other people's opinions about the subject matter. He then proceeds to ask questions meant at probing an initial answer suggested by one of his interlocutors, eventually showing that such an answer leads to contradictions, or that it is not as clear and compelling as it might have appeared at first. In the end, the answer is refuted and another, better one is proposed instead. The process then resumes until a number of possibilities have been discarded and everyone has achieved, by means of the *elenchic* process, a better understanding of the matter at hand. After all, even just discarding bad ideas is a form of progress.

Socrates often begins the proceedings by posing a "What is . . . ?" question. For instance, "What is piety?" He is not looking for specific examples, such as, "Sacrificing to the gods is pious or impious." Rather, he is after a comprehensive account of the concept under examination, in this case, piety.

Consider what happens in the *Euthyphro*, one of the best of the Socratic dialogues written by Plato. Socrates is about to go to court because he has been summoned by the high magistrate to answer charges of impiety and corruption of the youth, raised against him by Meletus, Anytus, and Lycon. Approaching the courthouse, Socrates meets Euthyphro, a priest who is also going to court to denounce his own father for the crime of manslaughter he has committed against a worker.

Socrates engages Euthyphro by asking him on what grounds he is so sure of doing the right thing. After all, people generally think that going against one's father is impious and that the gods don't favor those who turn against their parents. To this, Euthyphro replies that it is his business to know what is and is not pious. That opens up the discussion on the nature of piety at the core of the dialogue, a topic Socrates remarks is particularly urgent for him, since he is about to face a possibly capital charge of impiety.

Over the ensuing conversation, Euthyphro proposes a whopping five definitions of piety, with Socrates also contributing his own idea, each of which is examined and refuted by Socrates, prompting the next one to be suggested in turn. The first definition is that piety is what Euthyphro is doing right now.[13] But Socrates points out that that's not a definition, it's just an example. It doesn't get to the heart of the matter.

The second proposed definition is that piety is what pleases the gods.[14] That's better, says Socrates, because it's an actual definition, not a mere example. However, he continues, such definition won't do, as the gods are known to disagree among themselves about what they find pleasing.

Euthyphro then makes a third attempt: What all the gods love is pious, and what they all hate is impious.[15] Here Socrates poses a crucial question in return, which has since become known as Euthyphro's dilemma: Is what is pious loved by the gods because it is pious? Or is something pious because it is loved by the gods? Euthyphro picks each answer in turn but in both cases runs into trouble.

If something is pious simply because it is beloved by the gods, that means that piety is arbitrary: The gods are capricious, and they can (and often do) change their minds about what they like and dislike.* However, if something is loved by the gods because it's pious, this means that the criterion for piety is actually independent of the gods themselves. They, too, have to bow to an external standard of judgment.† Euthyphro, as a priest, doesn't like either scenario.

Later on in the dialogue, it is Socrates who takes the initiative and proposes the fourth definition: Perhaps piety is an aspect of justice.[16] But then Socrates himself raises an objection to his own proposal: Piety may be part of justice, in the sense that pious actions are also, at the same time, just. But surely there are actions that are just and not pious, for instance, showing concern for other people. The question then becomes: what makes pious actions different from other just actions?

In responding, Euthyphro articulates the fifth definition: The essence of piety is to look after the gods.[17] This, too, is found wanting by Socrates: The notion of "looking after" the gods implies that they are in want of something, an idea that itself would strike the Greco-Romans (and we moderns as well) as impious, the result of hubris.

An exhausted Euthyphro then proposes the sixth and final definition: Piety is an art consisting of sacrifice and prayer. It is a kind of knowledge of how to have intercourse with the gods, how to properly ask for things from them (prayer) and how to properly do things for them (sacrifice).[18] Hold on, replies Socrates, this sounds very much like a type of commerce, a quid pro quo, if you will, which again comes perilously close to impiety. No, no, responds a disturbed Euthyphro, and immediately repairs to the safer notion that piety has to do with what the gods like.

* This goes also for the Abrahamic god, who in the Old Testament first creates humanity and then decides this was a bad idea and sends a worldwide flood to cleanse the world.

† Notice that Euthyphro's dilemma has vexed philosophers and theologians ever since. It essentially argues for the conclusion that even if gods exist, they either have nothing to do with piety and, arguably, morality (first horn) or else piety and morality are arbitrary (second horn).

But now we have come full circle, since this is none other than the second definition discussed previously. Socrates at this point accuses Euthyphro of continuously changing his mind: "And when you say this, can you wonder at your words not standing firm, but walking away?"[19] He then suggests that they simply will have to start all over again, at which point Euthyphro beats the hastiest retreat in the history of philosophy: "Another time, Socrates; for I am in a hurry, and must go now."[20]

It's important to grasp that Socrates's concern—in the *Euthyphro* as in other dialogues—is not just with the thesis advanced by his interlocutors but with the interlocutors themselves, that is, with their character. His worries are both epistemological (about whatever thesis is being discussed) and ethical (about the person advancing the thesis).

Socrates's ethical concerns are more fundamental than his epistemological ones: Ultimately, he wants to help other people become better human beings, and a major path to ethical improvement is to improve the clarity of our thinking, which in turn helps us in our quest for self-knowledge. When Socrates refutes Euthyphro's arguments, in a sense he refutes Euthyphro himself, attempting to show him that the problem isn't just with what he specifically thinks about piety, but with his whole way of thinking, which is not virtuous.

It may seem strange to think of good reasoning as a virtue, let alone one that brings about ethical self-improvement. And yet remember that "virtue" comes from the Greek arete, which simply means excellence (of any kind). Socrates's philosophy, like that of the Stoics who followed him (see chapter 4), is intellectualist: It is through clear thinking that we see the path to moral virtue, and it is through clear thinking that we keep ourselves on that path. The Stoics even went a step further and added understanding of the natural world (what we would today call science) to the list of virtues, on the grounds that if we live according to mistaken notions about the nature of the world and of ourselves then we are likely to mis-live.

The Socratic method

Socratic dialogues often end in something called *aporia*, usually translated as confusion. This may sound more than a bit strange: Why would Socrates want to confuse people, first showing them that they are wrong in what they think and then leaving them without an alternative answer? Because wisdom begins with realizing that we don't know as much as we think we know (that was the meaning of the Delphic Oracle's strange pronouncement about Socrates). Moreover, any good teacher knows that you don't just feed the correct answers to your students, you lead them there indirectly so they improve their thinking and find the answers on their own. As we shall see in a few chapters, this was a major impetus for the "skeptical" turn of Plato's Academy.

Here is one formal structure of the Socratic method, as expanded by Plato and as it is often presented in modern settings.

1. You pose a question, such as, "What is knowledge?"

2. Your interlocutor puts forth a first answer: "Knowledge is true belief."

3. You guide the discussion further by unpacking the other person's provisional answer and probing into possible unstated assumptions. For instance, "One can have true belief without actual knowledge just because they got lucky and guessed correctly."

4. Your interlocutor acknowledges that there is something problematic about the first definition they suggested and proposes a new, updated one: "Knowledge is justified true belief."

5. Steps 3 and 4 are repeated, with the aim of refining your understanding of the concept under investigation, in this case, knowledge.

6. Either you settle for a good-enough, provisional explanation, or you acknowledge that you do not yet have a sufficient understanding of the issue.

So far, we've seen Socrates primarily in the role of a refuter of arguments, but he plays at least two more roles in the dialogues: one as a constructor, carried out by way of his dialectical approach, and another as a philosophical "midwife." Let's start with the first role.

The word "dialectic" comes from the Greek *dialegesthai*, which means "to converse." When Socrates practices dialectics he engages in short back-and-forth conversations structured around questions and answers; this is very different from what the Sophists were doing, with their approach centered on long speeches to the audience.

The Roman orator Cicero will later on point out that these are not mutually exclusive approaches to philosophical discourse, and modern research in
pedagogy agrees. It all depends on your audience and immediate objectives.
Sophist-style lectures are powerful ways to convey a lot of information to a
large number of people, as is still done in many classrooms and conference
settings today. However, Socratic-style dialectics are more conducive to
active philosophizing in a small group of people, where participants are free
to pursue different lines of inquiry in a less structured and more interactive
fashion. This second approach is also still practiced in modern classrooms
and boardrooms, as well as in certain types of psychotherapy sessions, and is
in fact known as Socratic dialogue.

One way to see Socrates-the-refuter as a complement to Socrates-the-
constructor is to realize that the elenchus and dialectics are mutually
supporting approaches. First, we clear away fuzzy thinking by way of the
elenchus (refuting); next, this leads to aporia (confusion), which opens
the mind to possibilities not yet contemplated; finally, we may engage in
constructive dialogue in order to arrive at better overall understanding.

The third role Socrates plays in the dialogues is that of philosophical
"midwife." One instance is in the Theaetetus, where the topic is the definition of knowledge. Interestingly, Socrates himself tells the title character, the mathematician *Theaetetus*, that Socrates's mother, Phaenarete, was
a midwife. Her role was to facilitate the birth of other people's babies—
whom, of course, she did not herself conceive.

Analogously, explains Socrates, he is a midwife for philosophical ideas,
his role being to facilitate other people—who already have the necessary
knowledge, perhaps without realizing it—to "give birth" to their philosophical thoughts.

A famous example of Socrates's midwifery is found in another dialogue,
Meno, which explores whether virtue can be taught. Socrates guides one of
Meno's slaves to solve a mathematical puzzle that the boy couldn't possibly
have known how to solve. This is a perfect case of intellectual midwifery, as
Socrates patiently guides the boy to reason his way through the mathemat-
ical problem.

Ideally, this is the kind of approach we would like to practice in our own
modern educational system. It's well known that simply spoon-feeding

information to students and asking them to regurgitate such information at the time of an exam is highly inefficient pedagogically and fosters a passive attitude in the student (not to mention one that aims at "beating the test" rather than acquiring understanding). Guided inquiry, by contrast, steers students while allowing them to work through the problem or issue at hand. Students end up owning the answer because they actively pursued it, shaping and refining their understanding in the process.

The nature of knowledge

Importantly, the *Theaetetus* is the dialogue where the most commonly accepted definition of knowledge is proposed: justified true belief.[21] Let us say that I claim to know that the planet Saturn has a system of rings surrounding it. What does it mean for me to "know" this? Three conditions have to be met, according to Socrates/Plato. First and most basically, I ought to actually believe what I claim to know. It would be rather strange if I said I knew something that I did not believe. Second, also somewhat obviously, my belief has to be true (as far as I am able to ascertain): If I claim that Saturn has rings, then my claim is true just in case it turns out, factually speaking, that there are indeed rings around that planet.[22] However, for something to count as knowledge, according to the discussion in the *Theaetetus*, it isn't enough that it be true and that I believe it. After all, I could have gotten lucky and guessed that it's Saturn, and not, say, Jupiter, that has rings, without really knowing the thing. What would upgrade my lucky guess to the status of knowledge? The ability to justify my claim.

In other words, if I say that I know Saturn has rings, you would be within your rights to ask me, "And how, exactly, do you know it?" If I lamely answer, "Somebody told me," or even, "I read it in an astronomy book," this wouldn't really qualify as knowledge. Rather, it would be hearsay, something I repeated because I trusted the authority who told me, or the book where I read it.

In the specific case of Saturn's rings, actual knowledge may come from telescope-mediated observations that I conducted. As it happens, one of us (Massimo) has pointed a telescope in the direction of Saturn several times in his life and has, indeed, observed the rings. Or it could come from having seen photographs taken by telescope, or even by spacecraft, plus knowledge of how such photographs were taken and what they represent. Or there may be yet other ways to justify Massimo's true belief in Saturn's rings that an astronomer would be more qualified to articulate.

It is important to appreciate that if we accept this view of knowledge as justified true belief, it turns out we all know far less than we think. Upon investigation, it may be revealed that some of our beliefs are not true and that we are in no position to offer reasonable justification for many others. For instance, Massimo "knows" that quarks are fundamental subatomic particles. But that's only because he's read it in a physics textbook and it has been confirmed to him by physicists of his acquaintance. Massimo doesn't really "know" that in the strict sense of being able to provide a convincing justification for his statement.

Which brings us back to one of the fundamental Socratic attitudes: humility. Recall again that the Oracle at Delphi said that Socrates was the wisest man in Greece on the grounds that he knew that he didn't know much (if anything). Socrates then embarked on a (rather impious, to be frank) quest to show that the Oracle was wrong, only to confirm, over and over again, that his fellow Athenians did not have knowledge, only that they thought they did. Some of them admitted as much, thus learning their lesson in epistemic (and moral) humility. Others became upset and eventually convicted Socrates and served him hemlock.

Before we leave this discussion and turn to how to actually live a Socratic life, it is interesting to observe that sometimes Socrates's humility is a posture and shouldn't be taken as absolute. For instance, when he explains to Theaetetus that, just like an actual midwife, Socrates himself is "barren" of philosophical ideas, this is hard to take seriously. He very clearly guides the slave boy in directions that will help him figure out the mathematical puzzle, strongly suggesting that Socrates knows exactly where the answer to the puzzle lies. He is, therefore, not at all "barren."

Or consider again his conversation with the priest Euthyphro. Despite several protestations by Socrates that he wants to be enlightened by his interlocutor so that he will be in a better position to defend himself from the accusation of impiety, it is clear at several places in the dialogue that Socrates is making fun of Euthyphro. Here's an example.

> *EUTHYPHRO: The best of Euthyphro, and that which distinguishes*
> *him, Socrates, from other men, is his exact knowledge of all such*
> *matters. What should I be good for without it?*
> *SOCRATES: Rare friend! I think that I cannot do better than be*
> *your disciple.*[23]

In this exchange Euthyphro is vainly boasting of his own capacities, and even speaks of himself in the third person. Socrates's response can only be characterized as an example of philosophical sarcasm.

Live like Socrates

While sarcasm is one way to interpret Socrates's exchange with Euthyphro, there could have been another intention behind Socrates's words: He could have sensed Euthyphro's vanity and was feeding into it in order to get him to engage in dialectic. Socrates may have had cause, since he ran into Euthyphro while Socrates was waiting for his own indictment hearing. Given that Socrates was brought up on the charge of impiety, he sought Euthyphro's advice about how to counter the charge. It's still likely that Socrates was being disingenuous in his praise of Euthyphro; instead of trying to knock Euthyphro down, Socrates was attempting to butter him up through sly rhetoric to induce Euthyphro to join him in philosophical dialogue.

But Socrates likely didn't engage in this conversation just to pass the time, or even to get good advice from a supposed expert in piety. Instead, Socrates's main goal may have been to subtly dissuade Euthyphro from denouncing his father in court. Indeed, this is the effect the biographer Diogenes Laërtius tells us Socrates had on Euthyphro: Apparently, Euthyphro was ultimately diverted from speaking against his father at his manslaughter trial.[24] It also fits quite well with Socrates's character: Xenophon's *Memorabilia* is rife with stories of Socrates trying to help others. He wasn't interested in philosophical conversation for its own sake: He used it to others' benefit. Diogenes also mentioned that Socrates used philosophical discussion to encourage people, as in the case of Theaetetus, where their conversation about knowledge "sent him away . . . fired with a divine impulse." The fact that they never came to a firm conclusion about what knowledge is may have instilled in Theaetetus a passion for learning and exploration. In short, Socrates helped both Euthyphro and Theaetetus become better people—in the former's case, by dissuading him from betraying his familial bond, and in the latter's, by igniting his drive for discovery.

So, the "Socratic method" (which, as we mentioned previously, isn't really a single method) was not just a teaching technique (or fluid set of techniques), but was used for the purpose of making people better. However, if the goal was to help people become better human beings, it sounds as if Socrates should belong in the Port of Character, the one very closely linked with the concept of virtue. After all, to practice "virtue" (arete) literally means becoming a more excellent version of yourself.

While it's true that Socrates was very concerned with virtue, the reason he is included in the Port of Doubt is because he bridges the conceptual gap between virtue and doubt. Knowing how little you (and those around you) actually know brings you closer to wisdom, and thus closer to becoming a better person.

In order to live like Socrates, you not only have to master the main three Socratic roles (refuter, constructor, and midwife) using two of his main methods (the elenchus and dialectic), but you also have to be able to read your audience and be skilled at rhetoric, all while serving the common good and improving yourself. Those are quite large shoes to fill—if he wore shoes; as we have seen, he often went barefoot!

While it would be hard to live a completely Socratic life, there are several takeaways you can apply to your own life to live semi-Socraticly. Such a life can be boiled down to three Ds.

- **Doubt:** Don't be confident of your own supposed knowledge, and question the knowledge of the haughty or powerful.

- **Discuss:** Examine assertions and engage in short back-and-forth conversations involving questions and answers instead of long-winded arguments. You can do this with others, as Socrates normally did. But as you'll soon see, you can also apply this technique to your own beliefs.

  Also, while Socrates often engaged in irony or possibly sarcasm, his conversations always attempted to seek the truth. Thus, Socratic discussions are a cooperative endeavor meant to reach a better understanding; they're not a rhetorical technique to convince others of a predetermined conclusion. The dialectic focuses more on crafting good questions than finding answers.

- **Do good:** Don't try to emulate Socrates just to be a gadfly or because you enjoy philosophical discussion. Do it to benefit others and to reinforce your own moral character.

A modern life that puts the three Ds into practice reaches toward the Socratic. Now it's time to try it for yourself.

Day 1: Self-examination, part 1

Plato's version of Socrates mostly portrays him engaging in dialectic with other people. However, we see instances where he involves himself in some self-dialectic, too. We encountered one example earlier in which Socrates brings up his own definition of piety while conversing with Euthyphro, only to shoot it down (page 139). This demonstrates that it's feasible to apply the Socratic method to your own views.

The dialectical method requires quite a bit of practice and can be unwieldy to try all in one go, so today's main goal is to get through Step 2 (where your interlocutor puts forth an answer to your first question).

Recall the first step: You pose a question, such as, "What is knowledge?"

You can, of course, pose such a question about anything. However, some questions are likely to have more impact than others. Since knowledge is an important concept, asking what "knowledge" really means is a significant question. On the other hand, asking, "What is brunch?" probably won't be as impactful a question.

One of Socrates's major areas of inquiry was ethical terminology, such as "What is justice?" Understanding what justice is could have a big impact on your life (as you may have experienced when exploring the Port of Character). After all, how can you know you're living up to your values (like being just) when you don't fully understand what makes something just in the first place? For this reason, we suggest that you stick to asking a question about *moral* or *value-laden* terms. Questions such as "What does it mean to be caring?," "What is courage?," or "What makes something 'good'?" are all fair game.

However, not all questions may be meaningful to *you*. In order to come up with a question that actually matters to you, start with a value or ethical judgment you already hold. For example, it's likely that you hold a low opinion of someone if you think they're cruel. In that case, you think, "Person X is cruel." From here, you can ask yourself, "What is cruelty?"

In the space that follows, write down a judgment you hold about something or someone.

_____

_____

_____

_____

_____

Now, ask a question about your judgment in the form "What is [judgment]?"

_____

_____

_____

_____

_____

_____

Now we can move on to Step 2. Your interlocutor puts forth a first answer, "Knowledge is true belief."

Today, you'll be serving as your own interlocutor. Notice the form of the answer. It's not an example of something that you think you know (Paris is the capital of France, 2 + 2 = 4, and so on). A proper Socratic definition doesn't just provide a list of examples; instead, it puts forth the conditions for *anything* to count as "knowledge." Thus, the definition is asserting that everything that would count as knowledge has to be both believed and true. One can also say that every true belief counts as knowledge. In modern parlance, these are known as *necessary and sufficient conditions* for knowledge. This means that, according to this definition, every statement that is both believed and is true must be knowledge, and every claim of knowledge must be both believed and true.

You can think of necessary and sufficient conditions as a checklist. In order for something to count as knowledge, it has to meet *all* of the following conditions.

☐ It's a belief.

☐ It's true.

"The moon is made of green cheese" wouldn't count as knowledge under this definition, since it's not true. "George Washington had only one original tooth in his mouth when he died" is true, and may or may not count as knowledge depending on whether you believed it before you read it. The equation "2 + 2 = 4" is both true and you likely believe it, so it counts as knowledge according to the definition we are considering.

Now it's your turn to come up with a similar checklist of necessary and sufficient conditions for the question you just generated. Feel free to start anywhere, even if it's silly or obviously wrong. That's what Socrates did with Theaetetus to arrive at a definition of knowledge. He started by (uncharitably) interpreting Protagoras's claim that "What seems to a man, is to him" as "knowledge is belief." Socrates likely thought this was a silly assertion, but it gave a place to start. He was then able to improve it by thinking about how the assertion goes wrong, pointing out that we don't treat all opinions equally, and those we put more weight on tend to be the true ones. Thus, Socrates improves on the original, imperfect definition of knowledge. The new definition gets knocked down later, but it's still an improvement!

In the space that follows, rewrite your previous question, and provide a list of conditions that have to all be satisfied.

What is _____?

To count as _____, it must *always* satisfy *all* of the following conditions:

☐ _____

☐ _____

☐ _____

☐ _____

☐ _____

Day 2: Self-examination, part 2

Today's goal is to attempt to poke holes in your definition from yesterday and try to refine it. Since you're working with your own thoughts, we'll condense Steps 3 to 6 of the Socratic method (page 142) into a more simple version.

> Step 1: Poke holes in your necessary and sufficient conditions.
> Step 2: Revise your definition to account for any problems.

You can repeat these two steps until you arrive at a definition with no clear problems, or until you get sick of it and experience *aporia* (confusion), as many of Socrates's interlocutors did. There's no shame in the latter, so don't feel discouraged if you reach aporia; you'll have a chance to explore this feeling more tomorrow.

Here are some tips for executing Step 1.

- **Test your original claim using your list of necessary and sufficient conditions.** Returning to the example concerning cruelty, recall that the question was generated from holding the belief that person X is cruel. You can use that person as a test case and ask yourself if you've listed *everything* that makes you think person X is cruel. Do they check all the boxes from yesterday's list? If not, your list needs revision. If so, imagine you could wave a magic wand and remove all the characteristics you listed from the person. Would that make the person not cruel anymore? If not, you have more conditions to add to your list.

- **Come up with counterexamples.** Try your best to come up with examples where all the checkboxes from your definition are fulfilled but where you don't think the definition is met. This is what Socrates does with the definition of "knowledge" as true belief; he gives the example of a good lawyer who convinces a judge of a crime using rhetoric. The crime did occur (so it's true) and the judge now believes it occurred, but he doesn't have good *reason* to believe it occurs, and thus doesn't have *knowledge* of the crime.

- **Draw out the necessary implications of your definition and test those implications.** Socrates uses this technique to counter a definition of "courage" as "not running away from the enemy during battle" in his dialogue with Laches. Socrates points out that this definition necessarily implies that fighting on horseback is never brave, since that necessarily requires quick withdrawals as well as charging. On horseback, you don't simply stand in place!

Here is a table to guide you through testing your definition from yesterday.

What is _____?

List of necessary and sufficient conditions for _____	Test for your necessary and sufficient conditions	Did your definition survive the test? If not, why did it fail?
Original ☐ ☐ ☐ ☐ ☐		
Revision 1 (or original, if it survived first test) ☐ ☐ ☐ ☐ ☐		
Revision 2 (or original, if it survived second test) ☐ ☐ ☐ ☐ ☐		

Finally, when you're done testing your definition, write *why* you stopped in the space that follows. Did you stop because you're satisfied with your definition? Because you just got sick of it? Because the exercise was too hard? Something else? You'll be exploring your feelings around your reaction to this exercise tomorrow.

_____

_____

_____

_____

_____

_____

_____

_____

_____

_____

Day 3: Explore your reaction to the Socratic method

Now that you've given your brain quite a workout over the past two days, it's a good time to take a break and reflect on your experience with the Socratic method. We've provided the following space to write down your thoughts. You're welcome to write whatever comes to mind, but in case you'd like some prompts, here are a few specific questions to reflect on.

- How did you feel while going through the exercise? Engaged? Frustrated? Confused?

- After going through the exercise, do you feel more curious about your beliefs, like Theaetetus did, or frustrated and unwilling to engage further, like Euthyphro?

- If you gave up yesterday's exercise due to frustration or aporia, how does that affect your certainty about your original claim?

- If you came to an acceptable definition, how does that affect your certainty about the original claim?

- How do you think you can use this technique in the future, and how willing are you to do so?

_____

_____

_____

_____

_____

_____

Day 4: Dialectic and elenchus with a friend

Up until now, you've been applying the Socratic method to yourself. Now it's time to engage with someone else. Your goal for this exercise is to find a willing friend to engage in the Socratic method with you. We've reproduced the six-step process of the Socratic method here, but this time with space you can fill in as the discussion progresses to help guide the conversation and keep it on track.

1. You pose a question: _____

_____

2. Your friend puts forth a first answer:_____

_____

3. You guide the discussion further by unpacking your friend's provisional answer and by probing into possible unstated assumptions that you and your friend both disagree with. Write the assumption(s) here.

_____

_____

4. Your friend agrees that there is something problematic about the first definition put forth and proposes a new, updated one: _____

_____

_____

5. Steps 3 and 4 are repeated a number of times, with the aim of refining your understanding of the concept under investigation. Write the new versions of Steps 3 and 4 here.

New definition	Problems with new definition

6. After you go through a few rounds, why did you stop? Did you settle for a good-enough, provisional explanation? Or did you both acknowledge that you do not have a sufficient understanding of the issue yet and stopped due to aporia?

_____

_____

_____

Day 5: Attempting to engage in dialectic or elenchus with a stranger

---

Now that you've had some practice with a friend, it's time to try your hand at engaging in the Socratic method with someone who hasn't agreed to it and who would benefit by a bit more aporia in their lives, perhaps because they're overly haughty or due to their position of power. Remember that Socrates didn't just debate for the sake of it: He did so to do good! Today, you should attempt to do the same.

Social media can be a good place to try this, although you'll have to adapt your approach to its asynchronous nature. You can reply to a politician or someone who seems overly certain and attempt to use the six steps in order to engage in Socratic dialectic with them. You can try to keep the conversation Socratic by leaning more on questions than assertions. For example, if a politician claims they stand for justice, instead of saying, "No you don't, because you support policy X," you can say, "Policy X seems unjust to me, but perhaps I misunderstand you because you're the expert here: What do you mean by 'justice'?" This approach ends in a question, and also applies some light praise to try to get the person to engage—you'll be playing Socrates to their Euthyphro.

If social media isn't your cup of tea, you can try engaging with someone who isn't a stranger, but isn't aware of your attempt to enage them Socratically. You could do this at an in-person meetup or reading group, or perhaps with a family member.

Whether you try this offline or online, there is an excellent chance that people you attempt to engage with Socratically will not cooperate. This in itself is a good lesson to learn. In addition, trying to engage in conversation with strangers online and especially in person may not be a good fit for you right now. If it seems like too big an ask, either because you're uncomfortable or simply can't find a good opportunity, feel free to skip this exercise and try repeating one of the earlier ones.

REFLECTION

Now that you've tried the Socratic method, take some time to reflect on your experience. Did you find it more useful to engage in the method alone, with a willing friend, or with a stranger? If you did try to engage with a stranger, it likely didn't go as well as it did for Socrates in Plato's dialogues. What lessons can you take away from that in terms of what type of people are worth engaging with Socratically and under what circumstances? What aspects of Socrates's method do you think may be useful for you to use again in the future, and what do you think you'll leave behind?

_____

_____

_____

_____

_____

_____

_____

_____

_____

_____

_____

_____

You've now gotten a handle on the basics of the Socratic method, so it's time to explore a new skeptical method of one of Socrates' interlocutors: the Sophist Protagoras.

Chapter 8

PRACTICE RELATIVISM WITH PROTAGORAS

*Of all things the measure is man, of the things that are, how they
are, and of things that are not, how they are not.*

—Protagoras, in Diogenes Laërtius,
Lives of the Eminent Philosophers, 9.51

S andaled feet slapped the stone walkway under the colonnade as the
men walked with a sense of purpose that morning in 434 BCE. The
house surrounding them, one of the finest in Athens, was full of wealthy
young men who had come there to learn from a famous teacher: the Sophist
philosopher Protagoras of Abdera. He was at the head of the pack, leading
while walking and talking. His students followed, and parted for him as he
swept back and forth.[1]

Those students were seeking the kind of education that Sophists offered:
the ability to make a good argument and give a convincing speech about
almost any subject. This skill could advance their careers in politics, serving
them well at the popular assembly or law courts.[2] As a prerequisite, the students had to be affluent, because if not, they wouldn't have been able to afford
Protagoras's fees—which were notoriously high. Only those with time and
cash could attend Protagoras's traveling school as it made its way through
Greece.[3] Those included his host in Athens, Callias (son of the richest man
in Greece, Hipponicus[4]), along with his guests and the students who had

followed Protagoras from other cities. At the gathering, other Sophist teachers, including Hippias of Elis and Prodicus of Ceos, also held court, with young men paying close attention to their words.

Some Athenians stayed away from this Sophists' den. They perceived the Sophists' words as *deinos*, a Greek term meaning "clever" but also "frightening."[5] Their polished language was viewed as incredibly powerful, perhaps threateningly so. But they earned respect, too, from those in high places. The Athenian leader Pericles, a statesman at the height of his career, became an admirer of Protagoras and in 444 BCE asked him to write the constitution for the new Pan-Hellenic colony of Thurii in Southern Italy.[6]

Protagoras was born in Abdera, in Thrace, on the north coast of the Aegean Sea, around 490 BCE.[7] The details of his early life are a mystery, but a few stories offer clues. Some said he began by working as a porter and encountered the philosopher Democritus, also from Abdera. The story went that Democritus, known for his atomic theory, noticed a complex geometric knot that Protagoras had made for his bundle of wood, and decided that the young man was intelligent enough to learn philosophy. Others said his family hosted the Persian king Xerxes while he was in Greece, and that Xerxes arranged to have Protagoras educated by the Magi, Persian spiritual teachers.[8]

Protagoras's birth in Thrace made him a foreigner in Athens. His reputation and his accumulating wealth were always a little precarious when he set foot in the city that had a xenophobic bent, despite the warm welcome that the gathered young men gave him. But there was a good reason for his popularity: Protagoras could give these ambitious Athenians a chance at success. They lived in a highly litigious society where leaders often found themselves in court, and their democratic government was greatly influenced by public speeches. Being able to make a good argument for your side could lead to wealth and power in Athens—and a well-stated case could save your property or perhaps even your life.[9]

As Protagoras walked through the colonnade that day in 434 BCE, he spoke to his students as a group. "I'm pleased to see all of you here today— you who have decided to learn the art of the Sophist," he remarked. "We teachers of this art follow in the footsteps of great poets and prophets— Homer, Hesiod, even Orpheus. In the past, unfortunately, many famous thinkers have hidden their Sophism, fearing that other people would judge them and look down on their beautiful arguments.[10] But not me. I'm here to acknowledge myself as a Sophist and teacher of humankind. I have been working in this profession for many years, and I am happy to speak with all who wish to improve themselves." At this, one man whispered to his friend, "Yes, for a handsome fee," provoking a chuckle.

Protagoras was undeterred. "And, if you learn from me, on the very first day, you will return home a better man than you came, and better on the second day than on the first, and better every day than you were on the day before," Protagoras added with a slight smile. He directed a serious look at those who had been laughing, his full beard quivering slightly as he nodded in their direction. "With my teaching, you'll become formidable leaders. You'll build Athens into a stronger polis than the world has ever seen."

In Protagoras's school, his students spoke of many topics, including politics, virtue, and war. Protagoras was always willing to see both sides of any argument. He helped his students see that, too, and learn to make their own case. Protagoras's idea that "man is the measure of all things" gained him renown as a thinker who privileged a human-centered interpretation of the world, and who focused on human skill and progress.[11]

His questioning of what most people took for granted, however, may have been a bridge too far for the leaders of Athens. After Protagoras penned the controversial lines in his now-lost book *On the Gods* asserting he was "not able to know" if the gods existed or not, the Athenian assembly banished him from the city and country, according to some commentators. The Athenian officials sent a herald to gather up Protagoras's books from all those who owned them in Athens, and took the volumes to the marketplace—where they publicly burned them.[12]

Protagoras wrote many books that are now lost. In addition to *On the Gods*, he wrote *Truth*, *Antilogiae* (On Contradiction), *On Ambition*, *On Incorrect Human Actions*, *On Those in Hades*, *On Sciences*, *On Virtues*, and more. He lived to be at least seventy years old, possibly as old as ninety. Some say he died on a shipwreck fleeing a trial in Athens, or on a journey to Sicily,[13] but others say he died peacefully, with his reputation completely intact.[14]

Plato's antipathy

Plato profoundly disliked the Sophists. Even today the word carries deeply negative connotations because of Plato's treatment of Sophistry in his dialogues. A dictionary definition says that a sophist is "a person who reasons with clever but fallacious arguments."

There were two reasons for Plato's dislike and for the lifelong campaign he mounted against the Sophists. First, Plato was attempting to draw a distinction between the sort of philosophy he was practicing at the Academy (see page 142) and what the Sophists were teaching,[15] an early example of competition between intellectuals, if you will. According to Plato, the Sophists were not doing real philosophy, but rather, selling their techniques to the highest bidder in order to teach rhetorical skills aimed at personal advantage—what we nowadays in fact call sophistry (or, with a bit of a more positive spin, lawyering).

Second, Plato indirectly blamed the mistaken association between Socrates and the Sophists for the unjust trial and death of his mentor. You see, the playwright Aristophanes had written a play, *Clouds*, in which he made fun of the Sophists, depicting them as teaching that moral values are relative, that the gods don't exist, and that anyone who applies himself can win an argument by cunning rather than by reason. And Aristophanes's sophist character was named Socrates.

But the Sophistic movement was more complex and interesting than Plato's slanted caricature. To begin with, it was a movement, not a school. The Sophists were independent itinerant teachers who did not necessarily share a core set of doctrines, though some of their ideas were similar. That is why we focus here primarily on Protagoras of Abdera (490–420 BCE), arguably the first Sophist, not as a representative of a group of thinkers, but as his own man.

Understanding each other

Protagoras's philosophy hinged on three main concerns[16]: 1) the study of the meaning of words (*orthoepeia*, in Greek, meaning right speech); 2) the notion that man is the measure of all things; and 3) agnosticism about the gods and general skepticism of religion. Let's examine each in turn.

Orthoepeia is crucial for understanding what other people mean and for explaining ourselves to others. Even today people don't necessarily appreciate this point. One often hears the phrase "That's just semantics" used in a dismissive fashion, as if semantics—that is, the meaning of words—were not crucial to all of human discourse. Much misunderstanding and even aggravation that takes place during conversations, especially on difficult or delicate matters, results from the fact that people talk past each other because they are using the same words with different meanings.

But what is the broader purpose of learning orthoepeia? In Plato's *Protagoras*, a dialogue prominently featuring our Sophist, the title character claims that he is in the business of teaching "the proper management of one's own affairs, how best to run one's household, and the management of public affairs, how to make the most effective contribution to the affairs of the city by word and action." Moreover, he promises to "make men into good citizens."[17] Interestingly, this is how one could also describe Socrates's aim in wandering the streets of Athens and talking to the young people he found there. In a sense, what Protagoras wished to achieve was pretty much what *every* Hellenistic school attempted—to make people good—though of course each one went about it in its own distinctive way.

It's telling that Protagoras[18] says good citizenship consists of the exercise of self-restraint and the practice of justice. He further claims that these attitudes come naturally to humans because we are social animals. In order to do well as a species, we need to preserve the social order and work cooperatively with fellow human beings. This is not far from the take that the Stoics—not usually associated with the Sophist movement—articulated by way of their well-known concept of telos, or "living according to nature" (see page 6).

Moral relativism?

Protagoras is perhaps most famous for his alleged relativism, especially in matters of ethics. He notoriously said that "Of all things the measure is man, of the things that are, how they are, and of things that are not, how they are not."[19] In other words, everything can be measured by human standards. But what, exactly, did he mean by that?

A classic example of the principle concerns people's perception of things such as temperature. Jen says that it's cold, while Beth claims that it's hot. A thermometer can certainly establish the objective truth about *temperature*, but it won't settle the issue of whether Jen or Beth (or both!) are justified in feeling what they are feeling. After all, the same temperature can feel hot to someone and cold to someone else, depending on their individual physiologies, or even whether they are sick or healthy.

The notion that men (or women—or more broadly, human beings) are the measure of all things, therefore, doesn't need to be taken as a universal statement about the nature of the world. Rather, we can understand it simply as an observation about the fact that when it comes to human matters, our subjective perceptions determine our values and priorities, thus driving our actions.

If human beings truly are the measure of things in this way, then it follows that human law itself (*nomos*, meaning custom) is not universal and unchangeable, but evolves over time and can be further changed as the result of ongoing discussions among people. Here we find ourselves considering a sharp contrast concerning the origin and nature of laws and customs. Are they arbitrary and always in flux, or do they result from objective facts about the world and human nature (*phusis*)? According to many Sophists, the answer is both!

A number of Sophists thought that human laws are arbitrary and often harmful because they tell us to reject the only true dictate of Nature: to take care of ourselves first and foremost. This model was proposed by Glaucon, a distant relative of Plato, in the second book of Plato's magnum opus, *Republic*. Glaucon challenges Socrates and suggests that human beings are fundamentally selfish, adding that the true meaning of justice is to be able to do as one wishes. Any law that gets in the way of that is therefore unequivocally unjust.*

But we have seen that Protagoras rejects this sort of "ethical egoism" on the very Stoic-sounding basis that human beings are *naturally* cooperative because we depend on each other in order to survive and thrive. Nomos and phusis, therefore, are connected, according to Protagoras, but in the sense

---

* This is essentially the philosophy of modern Objectivists like Ayn Rand.

that human law attempts to mirror and implement the true natural law. These contrasting interpretations of human nature as fundamentally selfish or cooperative is one major reason we cannot talk of a coherent School of Sophistry but rather of a loosely connected group of individual thinkers.

Despite Protagoras's disagreement with other Sophists, he proved to be highly controversial. His sentiment that "whatever things seem to each city to be fine and just are so for that city, so long as it maintains them"[20] again caused him to be misunderstood as a moral relativist, and if one is a relativist about law then the step is short to become a relativist about adultery, impiety, theft, and murder. This notwithstanding, the fact is that even Plato clearly stated that Protagoras was nothing if not an upright citizen and a courteous and generous person.

Then again, Protagoras was allegedly the first one to say that on any given matter there are two theses, which can be made to be equally compelling,[21] the same approach that we will find in both the Academic Skeptics (chapter 9) and the Pyrrhonists (chapter 10). And yet, Protagoras also defended his own position as an expert on certain topics, a claim that would appear to be in tension with the notion that there are always two or more equally compelling lines of argument at play in any controversy.

Protagoras squared this particular circle by proposing that no "appearance" (what things seem like) is truer than any other appearance, but nevertheless some such appearances are better for specific pragmatic purposes.[22] For instance, Protagoras himself was hired as an expert to draw up the constitution of the Athenian colony of Thurii (near modern Sibari, in southern Italy) around 444 BCE.[23] He likely did not argue that one constitution is "truer" than another one, but simply that the one he wrote was best, given the specific needs of the city of Thurii.

Gods and religion

On the subject of god, Protagoras was agnostic. "Concerning the gods," he said, "I have no means of knowing whether they exist or not or of what sort they may be. Many things prevent knowledge, including the obscurity of the subject and the brevity of human life."[24] This is as clear and as reasonable a statement of agnosticism as one gets. Protagoras was not the first to doubt the existence of the gods. The pre-Socratic Xenophanes noticed that people make their gods in their own image and had speculated that if cattle and horses had gods they would look like cattle and horses![25] Another pre-Socratic, Anaxagoras, stated that the sun is a molten rock ("larger than the Peloponnesus"), implying that he did not believe the star to be a god.[26]

Moreover, Democritus, a near-contemporary of Protagoras and the originator of the doctrine of Atomism that was later taken on by the Epicureans (chapter 2), said that religion arose when primitive people became frightened by natural events like celestial and atmospheric phenomena.[27] And Critias, a relative of Plato, wrote in a play called *Sisyphus* that humans invented laws in order to regulate their lives. However, since people were still behaving anti-socially too often, someone had the brilliant idea to invent the gods as further help toward restraining human behavior.[28]

Protagoras's clear and cogent statement about the gods, however, must have hit a nerve, because according to some sources it led to the burning of his books and to his prosecution. As a result, he had to leave Athens to—rather ironically—avoid an end similar to that of Socrates. He allegedly drowned while escaping by sea. Or maybe not, as Plato claims that Protagoras, throughout his lifetime, maintained a reputation as an upstanding citizen.[29] Even so, the mere existence of the alternative account signifies that Protagoras's thinking about gods was considered highly controversial by some ancient authors.

The other Sophists

Protagoras was not the only Sophist, of course, though he was likely the first one to use that term, and was certainly one of the most influential. Other members of the loosely defined movement include Gorgias of Leontini, Hippias of Elis, Prodicus of Ceos, and Euenus of Paros.

Gorgias taught rhetoric, which he saw as analogous to martial arts: Although you could use the skill for good or for bad, you, not your master, are responsible for such a choice. This may sound like an excuse to deflect the sort of criticism raised by Socrates and Plato, but it makes sense. Today we still teach all sorts of skills—science, math, writing—with the assumption that people will use them for good, so the martial arts analogy is apt.

Hippias was famous for competing in eristic (debate) contests at the Olympic Games and winning prizes! Just imagine a society in which the quintessential athletic contest, the Olympics, were open to philosophers and debaters, who could win laurels just like runners and wrestlers. This tradition, incidentally, continued into Roman times. The *Ludi Capitolini* (Capitoline Games) were instituted in 387 BCE in honor of Jupiter Capitolinus (the Capitoline is one of Rome's famous seven hills) in order to commemorate an important victory against the Gauls by the semi-legendary statesman and general Marcus Furius Camillus. The games started on the fifteenth of October and lasted sixteen days. The emperor Domitian (51–96 CE) revived the practice and made it similar to the Olympic Games: The competition was held every four years and rewarded poets, comedians, historians, musicians, and orators, in addition to athletes.

The last Sophist we are going to mention briefly is Prodicus, whose performances were so expensive that Socrates says he attended a one-drachma lecture by him but couldn't afford the full course, which cost fifty drachmas.[30] At the time, one drachma was the daily income of a skilled craftsman. It is thus fair to say that the major Sophists were celebrities of the time, much sought after and well paid. Hippias, for instance, boasted of having made the incredible sum of fifteen thousand drachmas, that is, thirty years' wages for a skilled craftsman, in a single visit to Sicily![31] The Sophists were also employed by various poleis, often by their own cities as diplomats and occasionally, as we saw in Protagoras, to draft the local constitution.

Live like Protagoras

While the Sophists' practices were diverse, a common thread binding them was public lecturing and engagement that promised to improve their clients' lives. At first blush, this makes it sound like a modern Sophist would be akin to today's self-help gurus. However, a key aspect of the Sophists' approach, which sets them apart from the self-help common in today's society, is that they were engaged in politics as well as in crafting the next generation of politically engaged citizens. Of course, the Sophists' political tutelage could be uncharitably interpreted as a money grab in order to cater to the narcissistic needs of political climbers. However, a more charitable interpretation is that the Sophists aimed to improve their polis by training people in how to better serve their society.

According to this more moderate interpretation of the Sophists' project, a modern Sophist would help craft better citizens by teaching them how to make wise political decisions. However, some went beyond that. Recall from the beginning of this chapter that Protagoras considered himself a "teacher of humankind" who was "happy to speak with all who wish to improve themselves." This makes it sound as if Protagoras' three main philosophical concerns (orthoepeia, or right speech; man being the measure of all things; theological agnosticism) could constitute the backbone of a philosophy of life.

The exercises over the next few days will guide you in applying Protagoras's ideas to your own life to help you see if this is true for you. After all, you're the measure of all things!

Day 1: Explore obstacles to knowledge

Skepticism about the gods was a key feature of Protagoras's worldview. What's particularly interesting about Protagoras's approach wasn't his theological skepticism per se, but the reasons he gave for it: "Many things prevent knowledge, including the obscurity of the subject and the brevity of human life."

These reasons are interesting because they can be applicable to domains beyond theology. For example, people studying highly technical subjects have to spend years—or even decades—of their lives mastering, testing, and expanding scientific theories. Science has become so specialized that a solid-state physicist would have a difficult time commenting knowledgeably on the details of cosmology. This type of specialization goes far beyond science into how modern economies function. No single person could learn and implement all there is to know in order to build a modern automobile: too much technical expertise is needed—more than can be learned and applied by a single person in a single lifetime! As Protagoras says, our lives are so short and some matters so obscure that there's reason to hold your opinions lightly, except in the few domains in which you hold expertise.

The fact that life's short and knowledge is obscure suggests that it's reasonable to be skeptical of most things, not just the gods. But Protagoras may have had additional reasons in mind that further justified his skepticism, since he explicitly mentions that the two reasons he gave in support of his agnosticism were two of "many."

Today's exercise will help you get a firmer grasp of the general foundations of skepticism by expanding Protagoras's list of reasons for being skeptical. Use the space that follows to work through what obstacles prevent you from gaining knowledge. Also, write a brief justification explaining how attaining knowledge is prevented, starting with Protagoras's two reasons.

What prevents attaining knowledge?	Why does it prevent attaining knowledge?
The obscurity of certain subjects	
The brevity of life	

Day 2: Explore both sides of a person

Now that you have a better sense of *why* you should be more doubtful, today's exercise will teach you *how* to be more doubtful. While you may have many beliefs that can be brought into question, today we'll focus specifically on your respect or contempt for a particular person.

First, think of a specific person about whom you have strong positive or negative feelings and write their name in the space that follows. On a scale of 1 to 10, rate how strongly you like or dislike this person, with 1 being the deepest contempt and 10 being the strongest respect and write the score next to their name.

_____

Next, write a paragraph defending your view. If you strongly admire the person, try to praise them as much as possible. If you strongly despise the person, write a paragraph condemning them.

_____

_____

_____

_____

_____

Now comes the hard part. Protagoras taught his students to "praise and blame the same man."[32] Based on the surviving evidence, we can't tell with certainty what his motivation was for doing this. However, it's clear that this is a special case of his more well-attested view that both sides of an argument can be made with somewhat equal strength. It's also quite possible that this technique ties in with his take on orthoepeia, which was mentioned earlier in this chapter and which you'll explore more in the next exercises.[33]

The technique of simultaneous praise and blame may have been taken up by future skeptics for the purpose of either attempting to assess the strongest versions of both sides of an argument to get a better idea of what's "correct" (see chapter 9, especially in the vignette of Carneades and Day 5's exercise), or as an exercise to help instill doubt (see chapter 10, especially the exercises for Days 2 and 4). Marcus Aurelius may have also used a similar technique to help cull his annoyance when he thought about people's perceived wrongdoing.[34]

For your next step, you'll see if Protagoras's technique can yield similar fruits. In the space that follows, write a paragraph condemning the person you started out praising, or praising the person who you started out despising. Do the best you can to defend the view of the person that is the opposite of what you started out with.

_____

_____

_____

_____

_____

Finally, on a scale of 1 to 10, rate how strongly you like or dislike this person after this exercise, with 1 being the deepest contempt and 10 being the strongest respect. Did your view change at all? If not, why don't you think it did? If so, why do you think your view changed? Write your new rating, along with your answers to these questions, here.

_____

_____

_____

_____

_____

_____

Day 3: Explore many sides of an event

Protagoras didn't just apply his method to impressions of people but to events as well. We're told of one such application when he sat down with Pericles for an entire day to determine what was "responsible" for the death of an athlete who was accidently killed by a javelin.[35] They analyzed whether it was the javelin, the man who threw the javelin, or the competition's referees who were responsible for the athlete's death, according to "the most correct reasoning."

A cynical take on why they had this protracted conversation is that Protagoras saw this as an excellent opportunity to rack up billable hours with the wealthy Athenian politician. But a more charitable interpretation from some scholars suggests that this is an example of how Protagoras put his skepticism to practical use.[36] While the facts of the matter are clear, who or what was "responsible" for the athlete's death varies depending on one's perspective and goals. To say who's responsible requires "most correct reasoning," or correct speech: orthoepeia.

For example, imagine that a dog is let loose and bites someone, causing moderate injury. What (or who) caused the injury? From a doctor's perspective, the most useful way to frame this question is that the dog caused the injury, since this suggests how to medically treat the wound. From the victim's perspective, the irresponsible owner is what led to the injury, since the owner had a duty to control their dog in public. This approach is a good fit for taking the owner to court. In short, what "cause" means depends on perspective.

Protagoras's flavor of relativism doesn't allow for infinite flexibility. For Protagoras, nomos (custom) and phusis (human nature) are connected. He likely thought that "correct" reasoning led to a clear answer, or at least narrowed down the number of "correct" answers. However, the answer is relative to each person, their perspective, and their goals. For example, it wouldn't be "right speech" for the doctor to say that the cause of the injury was irresponsible dog ownership, because that is not helpful from a medical perspective. The doctor's goal is to treat the injury properly, not to determine moral or legal culpability. In short, the "correct" thing to say depends on who you are and what your goals are. Orthoepeia is not as much about objective truth as it is about subjective fit.

With all this in mind, it's time to turn back to the example involving the javelin. For today's exercise, try to "correctly fit" a person's perspective to each of the three possible culprits for the athlete's death: the javelin, the man who threw the javelin, and the referees. From whose perspective would each of these causes be *orthoepic*, or correctly spoken? We'll give our own answers in the paragraph that follows, but don't peek until you've tried answering for yourself!

What's responsible?	From whose perspective would this be "correctly reasoned" to be responsible? Why?
The javelin	
The man who threw the javelin	
The referees	

While there are many possible answers, here are a few to consider. If one were a coroner, "correct reasoning" would make the javelin the cause of death, since that's the object that led to the athlete's injury and ultimate demise. The organizers of the athletic event may hold the referees responsible, since part of their job is to make sure the field is clear and to keep the athletes safe; training or replacing the referees would likely lead to fewer injuries at the next event. However, the referees may have a different take, and hold the javelin thrower culpable, since he had a responsibility not to put fellow athletes at risk before throwing the javelin. From Pericles's perspective, he may see both the referees and the thrower as blameworthy, since this is most likely to serve his goal of preventing similar accidents in future events: Punishing both publicly may set an example for future competitors and referees to be more careful in the future.

Day 4: Explore cultural relativism

Protagoras's brand of relativism extends beyond individual perspectives and can apply to cultures as well. He says as much in a quote you encountered earlier in this chapter: "Whatever things seem to each city to be fine and just are so for that city, so long as it maintains them."

Again, note that Protagoras's relativism does not allow for infinite flexibility. If something does *not* "maintain" a polis (city), it is not correct to say (orthoepeic) that those things are actually fine or just, even if people believe they are! For example, it's likely that the Spartans thought that their subjugation of a group of people called the Helots "maintained" their city, and thus it was a just thing to do, however abhorrent this treatment may be from a more compassionate viewpoint.* The number of Helot revolts the Spartans had to quell leaves this claim open to question, even from a Protagorean perspective. Was the subjugation of the Helots really serving the Spartans, given how much effort and blood they had to put into maintaining that subjugation?

Nevertheless, there may be clearer examples of behaviors that certain cultures or subcultures engage in that "maintains" them by helping them survive and flourish. Your exercise today is to come up with some examples.

In the space that follows, write down a list of practices that a culture (for example, a nation or a people) or a subculture (a specific subgroup within a culture: say, political conservatives or punk rockers) engages in that they think is "fine" or "just" and which may "maintain" them. You don't have to agree with the practices or find them "fine" or "just" yourself—in fact, it may be useful if you try to list certain practices you aren't particularly fond of. These practices only have to serve the (sub)culture well.

(Sub)culture	Action or practice they consider "fine" or "just"	How does this clearly "maintain" the (sub) culture?

* While Protagorean relativism doesn't leave room for infinite flexibility, it is still quite a distance from the Port of Character from which we set sail in the last section. From a virtue ethics perspective, treating people with intentional cruelty to serve your own ends is a mark of poor character any way you slice it.

Day 5: Putting it all together

By now, we hope you have a better sense of Protagorean skepticism, relativism, and orthoepeia. Today, your goal is to bring these concepts together using the example of Plato and Protagoras. As you learned earlier in this chapter, Plato didn't have a particularly positive view of the Sophists, including Protagoras, for several key reasons. However, perhaps you've taken a bit more kindly to Protagoras at this point. Or maybe not.

Is your view of Protagoras favorable or unfavorable?

_____

_____

_____

_____

_____

Now that you've written down your view of Protagoras, you'll make him proud by defending the opposite view. If you like Protagoras, you'll be attacking him. If you don't, you'll be defending him. If you're neutral, flip a coin and pick a side at random.

First, take a few moments to review your reasons to doubt from Day 1's exercises and apply them to your current view of Protagoras in the space that follows.

_____

_____

_____

_____

_____

Assuming you've loosened your view a bit, write a paragraph in praise of Protagoras if you aren't much of a fan, or one condemning him if you're fond of his approach.

_____

_____

_____

_____

_____

_____

_____

At this point, your biases may have been reduced a bit more as you've considered the other side. Now for the final step: Given who you are and your goals in practicing a life philosophy, consider whether it's orthoepic (correct to say) that a Protagorean approach to a life philosophy is "useful" to you or not. When attempting to answer this question, clearly state what you want out of a philosophy of life, and try to determine whether Protagoras's version of Sophism would help serve your goal.

_____

_____

_____

_____

_____

_____

_____

To quickly review, here are the steps to take if in the future you'd like to approach a question the way Protagoras did.

1. Instill doubt by reviewing reasons for doubting and/or arguing from both sides.

2. Consider different options and perspectives.

3. Choose the most fitting answer to the question from the standpoint you chiefly care about, which better serves the end(s) of that perspective.

REFLECTION

Now that you've had a taste of Protagorean relativism, do you miss the moral compass that the philosophies from the Port of Character provided? Do you think the Protagorean approach is enough of a foundation for a philosophy of life? Do you think a more relativistic perspective would make you more tolerant over time? Are some aspects of Protagoras's form of Sophism more appealing to you than others?

_____

_____

_____

_____

_____

_____

_____

_____

_____

Chapter 9

EMBRACE UNCERTAINTY
WITH CARNEADES

We should not be too confident in our belief of anything.

—Cicero, *Tusculan Disputations*, 1.32

The sun beat down on the crowd gathered that afternoon in 155 BCE in Rome's Forum. They eagerly awaited the appearance of the Greek philosopher Carneades, the head of the Academy founded by Plato, who had traveled from Athens as part of a delegation of three philosophers sent to argue their city's case against a burdensome fine before the Roman Senate. When not engaged in that business, they gave public lectures.

Many of the educated youth of Rome were drawn to the novelty of hearing a Greek thinker deliver a speech.[1] The Romans had just begun to discover how entertaining these Greek philosophers could be, with their intelligent arguments that unfolded in unexpected directions.

And Carneades, nearly sixty years old, had the reputation of being the best orator of the bunch. Judging from the public lecture he had given the day before to a Roman crowd hanging on his every word, this talk would be worth hearing. Some Roman senators, including the influential traditionalist Cato the Elder, were there, too.[2] At the front of the audience, a large group of young, well-dressed men gathered around as the philosopher adjusted his cloak and prepared to address the audience with a piercing look.

"Justice," the philosopher began in Greek, speaking before the crowd of hundreds[3] in an exceptionally loud voice, "is *not* natural."[4] Several people in the audience whispered to each other their surprise. This was the exact opposite of the point that Carneades had defended in his public lecture just a day earlier.[5]

"If it were natural, it would be the same to all people. But no. Justice and injustice are very different in different nations and cities." Carneades paused to look at his audience, and went on. "In Egypt, a bull is worshiped as a god and other animals are held sacred. In Greece and Rome, shrines are filled with statues of gods in human form, which the invading Persians thought was evil. The Persian king Xerxes had all Athenian temples burned because he said it was sacrilegious to keep the gods—whose home is the entire universe—confined within walls," Carneades explained. "What's more, the Gauls and Carthaginians believe that human sacrifice is pious and pleasing to the gods!"

Noise rose from the crowd as some called out, "Yes!" and "That's right!"

Carneades took a deep breath and continued. "Justice is not only different in different places—it also changes in thousands of ways in a single city, even over a few years' time. For example, a woman's right to inherit property and money has been limited since the passage of the Voconian law[6] in Rome. That law advantages men, and is full of injustice to women. Why should a woman not have money or property of her own?" The audience murmured to each other. Was this really an attack on how justice was administered here in Rome?

"If God had provided laws for us, then all would obey the same laws, and the same people would not have different laws at different times. In fact, laws are imposed upon us by governments, enforced by fear of punishment, not by a God-given, natural sense of justice. There is no such thing as natural justice, and therefore, people are not just by nature."

The audience stirred uneasily. Hadn't the very same Greek philosopher spoken on the same steps the day before, giving a persuasive case *in favor of* justice? Which argument was true?

Carneades wasn't done yet. "After all, just look at Rome. She has won her empire by injustice both to gods and to people. A policy of justice would make her again what she was in the old days, a miserable, poor village." Some in the crowd now grumbled more loudly. They were incensed at this attack on their city. Cato's face had turned sour. Still, Carneades continued.

"What is usually called justice is really mutual self-restraint, which is a result of weakness. Rulers rule for their own advantage, not in the interest of the governed. And in the end, it's not wise to be just. Wisdom urges us to rule over as many subjects as possible, to enjoy pleasures, to become rich, to be the masters of others; justice, on the other hand, instructs us to be fair to people, to consider the interests of the whole human race, to give everyone his or her due, and not to touch sacred or public property, or that which belongs to others. What, then, is the result if you obey wisdom? Wealth, power, riches, public office, military commands, and royal authority, whether we are speaking of individuals or of nations. And justice? Poverty, powerlessness, subservience, obscurity."

As he finished speaking, some in the crowd applauded the philosopher's eloquence, but others booed, shifted on their feet, and even yelled back. "Carneades, you go too far!" cried a young man, a protégé of Cato, who feared that Rome was already overly influenced by the Greeks.[7] "Just yesterday, you said that true law is right reason, and is in agreement with nature! You spoke of one eternal law for all nations and times, and that God was its author and judge. Do you not recall those arguments? And now, you speak against justice and slander the government of Rome!"

"Of course I recall. And this is not slander," Carneades said, unafraid to confront his heckler. "I know it may be uncomfortable to realize that you may not know as much as you thought. I am showing you both sides, so you may consider the evidence for each position, and decide how persuasive it is. This is the only way you can begin to see what is probably true, my friend. In fact, I invite you to do your own research! You'll find a lot to inform you about justice here in Rome, and in Rome's provinces," he said, as if speaking to one of his own students. "After all, my fellow philosophers and I have come here to the Senate to talk about justice toward Athens, so I hope we can all see that there's more than one side to this story."[8]

Others gave their support. Another man called out, "May we all speak with such a tongue as Carneades!" Many of the young people present vowed to study philosophy more deeply after this display. The crowd wandered away, but this speech left an indelible impression on them, and on the history of Academic Skepticism.

Carneades was a natural orator and teacher. He was gifted with a powerful voice, and a mind to go with it. The philosopher was born in 214 BCE in Cyrene, the Greek-speaking city on the Mediterranean coast of North Africa (modern Libya) that also gave birth to Aristippus and the Cyrenaics (see chapter 1). He left home to study philosophy in Athens, the center of Hellenistic Greek learning.[9]

Carneades was a student at Plato's Academy and also studied with Diogenes of Babylon, the Stoic scholarch (leader) and a pupil of the influential Stoic logician Chrysippus. Stoic thinking influenced Carneades, and eventually drove him to argue against some of its tenets. He told his students that "had there been no Chrysippus, I would not have existed." (This was a parody of the famous verse about Chrysippus's huge influence on Stoicism: "Had there been no Chrysippus, there would have been no Stoa."[10])

A diligent young man focused on ethical philosophy, Carneades sometimes let his hair and nails grow long as he studied with intense concentration. He became known as a remarkable public speaker—so much so that other teachers would end classes early to free their students to attend his lectures. Carneades's thinking was shaped by the Academic Skeptic tradition, like that of an earlier leader of the Academy, Arcesilaus.[11]

Carneades became scholarch of the Academy before 155 BCE, when he was called upon to make his journey as an ambassador from Athens to Rome, alongside Critolaus of Phaselis, a Peripatetic, and Diogenes of Babylon, a Stoic. The issue at hand stemmed from a fine imposed on Athens after the city's soldiers sacked a town allied with Rome. The three Greek philosophers arrived in the capital of the Roman Empire in an official diplomatic capacity; the Athenians knew the rhetorical powers that they could bring to bear in arguing against the fine. Ultimately, the three were successful in their mission before the Senate, which lowered their fine substantially, to one fifth of the original five hundred talents. (In fact, in the end, Athens did not pay at all.[12])

Though Carneades and his colleagues sparked a new interest in philosophy among the Romans, they were soon chased from the city at the insistence of Cato the Elder, who feared their influence on young Romans. As the Greek biographer, historian, and philosopher Plutarch put it, Cato saw young Roman men "quitting all their pleasures and pastimes as they ran mad . . . after philosophy." Cato felt that the youth would "prefer the glory of speaking well before that of arms and doing well." He argued that the Greek philosophers could much too easily persuade people to do what they wished. So he pressed the Senate to have them cleared out of Rome.[13]

After Carneades returned to Athens, he continued to teach as the head of the Academy. He wrote nothing down, and lived into old age still teaching, and often saying, "Nature, which holds this frame together, will surely dissolve it."[14] He died in 129 BCE at the age of eighty-five.[15]

Later, his student Clitomachus, a philosopher from Carthage, succeeded him as scholarch of the Academy and continued to develop Carneades's ideas. In that way, Carneades influenced Skeptic thinkers throughout the rest of the Academy's history until the sack of Athens at the hands of the Roman general Sulla in 86 BCE. Carneades's arguments also influenced the philosopher and politician Marcus Tullius Cicero, Rome's most celebrated Skeptic thinker.[16]

A brief history of the Academy

Today, the word "academic" indicates a range of matters having to do with colleges and universities, from academic standards set for students to academic journals where faculty publish their technical papers. Sometimes the word is even used in a derogatory fashion, to indicate irrelevance, as in "that's just academic."

The Academy, on the other hand, was the school founded by Plato around 383 to 387 BCE (see chapter 6), located beside a grove of olive trees sacred to Athena, less than a mile northwest of Athens proper. The place was named after a mythical Greek hero, Akademos, who was said to have saved Athens from a war with Sparta (only temporarily, as it turned out).[17] As a place of philosophical learning and research, the Academy underwent a number of transformations during its more than nine hundred years of existence, until it was shut down by the Christian emperor Justinian in the year 529 CE.

After Plato died, in 347 BCE, the Academy was taken over by his nephew Speusippus, who inaugurated the period that scholars refer to as the "Old Academy." Speusippus, Xenocrates, Polemon, Crates, and other scholarchs (directors) of the school during this period continued the work of Plato using his approach. There was no established set of doctrines to be accepted, but rather, a constant open dialogue between teachers and students and among the teachers themselves. The Old Academy pursued research and teaching in all the areas of philosophy first explored by Plato, including metaphysics, epistemology, political philosophy, and ethics.

The Old Academy was followed by a phase referred to as the "New Academy," which is when the skeptic turn that concerns us here took place. The initiator of the new approach was Arcesilaus of Pitane, who became scholarch around 266 BCE. He was followed by a number of others, chief among whom we find Carneades of Cyrene (who took over the school in 155 BCE), and Philo of Larissa (scholarch beginning in 110 BCE).[18]

The skeptical phase of the Academy ended in 90 BCE, when Antiochus of Ascalon became scholarch, rejected skepticism, and began the project of forging a syncretic approach that melded Platonism, Aristotelianism, and Stoicism. This is when the period known as "Middle Platonism" began; it ended with Plutarch of Chaeronea (46–119 CE), one of the most important philosophers of the early modern era.

Finally, the contribution of Plotinus of Lycopolis (204–270 CE) marked the advent of what became known as Neoplatonism (chapter 13), a hybrid religious-philosophical approach that influenced Judaism, Christianity, and Islam throughout the Middle Ages.

The debate with the Stoics

Let us return to the skeptical period between Arcesilaus and Antiochus. Skepticism—both the Academic kind we are examining in this chapter and the Pyrrhonian version we will turn to in the next one—is more strongly established on epistemology (how we know things) than on metaphysics (how things are). Which makes sense, since in order to make claims about how the world works (metaphysics) we need to have a decent understanding of the evidence for such claims (epistemology). All of the other philosophies we have examined so far—such as the Stoics and the Epicureans—also have something to say about epistemology, but at the same time they rely heavily on their own versions of metaphysics. Skepticism sets itself apart because it either makes metaphysics strongly dependent on epistemology (Academic Skepticism) or goes so far as to refuse to even entertain the possibility of a metaphysics (Pyrrhonism).

The New Academicians thought that there are two—and only two— sources of knowledge: our senses and reason. In this, the skeptical approach was no different from the Stoic one, with one crucial caveat: While the Stoics thought that absolute, infallible knowledge is possible, at least for the sage (their ideal human being), the Skeptics rejected that notion, pointing out that both reason and the senses are known to be fallible, and there is no way for us to tell for sure when they do fail and when they don't. There is, according to the Skeptics, no mark or criterion that separates true from false "impressions" (such as our initial judgments concerning a perception or an idea).

The debate between Skeptics and Stoics is summarized in one of the Roman philosopher Marcus Tullius Cicero's books, aptly titled *Academica*, which is also one of our main sources for the philosophy of the Skeptical Academy. It is there that Cicero gives us this memorable capsule of the Stoic position, attributed to the founder of the sect, Zeno of Citium.

> *Zeno professed to illustrate [the Stoic theory] by a piece of action; for when he stretched out his fingers, and showed the palm of his hand, "perception," said he, "is a thing like this." Then, when he had a little closed his fingers, "assent is like this." Afterwards, when he had completely closed his hand, and held forth his fist, that, he said, was comprehension. From which simile he also gave that state a name which it had not before, and called it katalepsis. But when he brought his left hand against his right, and with it took a firm and tight hold of his fist, knowledge, he said, was of that character; and that was what none but a wise man possessed.*[19]

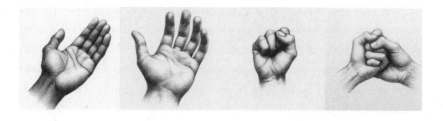

Zeno is saying that there are degrees of understanding. The least reliable of these is simple perception, as when I'm seeing what appears to be a person on the other side of the street. We then move to assent, meaning a judgment about whether a given perception is true or not: I am indeed perceiving a person, and it is my brother! Even better is when we have "comprehension," which the Stoics referred to as a *kataleptic* impression—that is, an impression that is undeniable, such as going out during the day and instantly knowing that it is, in fact, day, and that there cannot be any mistake about it. Finally, we have knowledge, which is reserved to the sage because it requires infallible reasoning based on one's perceptions. The sage is somehow (which is never quite made clear) capable of discerning what separates apparent from real kataleptic impressions, and that's why she can arrive at actual knowledge.

Baloney, reply the Skeptics (we are paraphrasing here). There is no mark, no criterion of truth, and therefore not even the sage can arrive at sure knowledge. Their argument was that every conceivable true impression can be matched by an impression that looks the same but is not true. As a result, even apparently kataleptic impressions can be false.

For instance, I may *think* that it is my brother on the other side of the street, but it turns out to be his doppelgänger, whose existence was not known to me. It may *look* to me as if it is surely day right now, but in fact I stumbled on the set of a movie that is using very powerful lights to make it seem that way. Or perhaps I'm simply hallucinating because I have a fever, or I have ingested bad food. The point is that there is no absolute, reliable way to tell.

The probability criterion

What then? Can we never know anything to be true? Enter Carneades's concept of the *pithanon*, a term that means something like persuasiveness or likelihood, and that Cicero translated into Latin—with a pure stroke of genius—as *probabilis*, from which we get the modern word probability.[20]

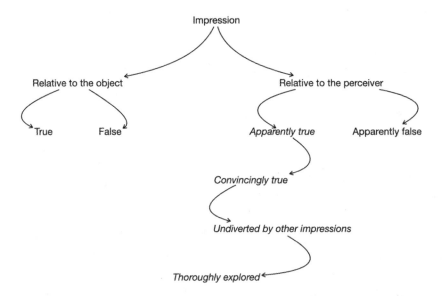

Here's how it works. The starting point is, once more, any given impression. Consider the impression (again, our preliminary, precognitive judgment) that vaccines are efficacious against strains of the COVID-19 virus. Objectively, this notion is either true or false. Period. (See the left side of the preceding diagram, "relative to the object"). But, alas, we do not have access to an objective, god's-eye view of the world. We have only our subjective beliefs to go by. The question, then, is whether we should believe that COVID-19 vaccines are effective, on the basis of what we know about the issue. (See the right side of the diagram, "relative to the perceiver.")

At first glance, the notion may seem to us either "apparently true" or "apparently false," following the terminology in the figure. Let's assume for the sake of argument that we go for apparently true. This means that, upon reflection, whatever we understand about vaccines and viruses makes us lean slightly more toward accepting rather than rejecting the notion under consideration. Just to fix our ideas, let's say that we think there is a bit more than a 50-50 chance that vaccines are effective against COVID-19.

That may not be enough to prompt us to get up from the couch and make an appointment with the doctor to get vaccinated. So, Carneades would say, we need to investigate the matter a bit more. We then talk to our doctor on the phone and read a bit about the topic in reliable mainstream media. As a result, our belief has changed a little; it has become stronger, moving from merely "apparently true" to "convincingly true." If we want to (roughly) quantify our new belief, let's say that it has moved from just above 50 percent to a relatively solid 70 to 80 percent.

This may be enough to motivate us to make the appointment and get vaccinated. But then we hear on social media about a controversy concerning vaccines, and especially those recently developed to combat COVID-19. Some of your own friends and relatives are telling you scary stories about COVID-19 vaccines, or even about vaccines in general.

So now you take the time to do a bit more systematic research on the topic. But you are not a virologist or epidemiologist—heck, you are not even a biologist! What to do? You talk to a friend who *is* an expert on the subject. He assures you that he has looked into the available scientific literature pretty thoroughly and that there is not only very solid evidence that COVID-19 vaccines work, but in fact everything we know about viruses and vaccines is in alignment with that conclusion. To use Carneades's terminology, the impression has now reached a higher subjective level of reliability, because it is "undiverted," meaning that it is not contradicted by any known fact to date. If you were to bet on it, your confidence has now risen to over 90 percent, more than good enough to get yourself vaccinated.

Your biologist friend, however, may be even more confident than you, and rightly so, on the basis of his in-depth understanding of the technical literature. He knows that the issue has been, as Carneades puts it, "thoroughly explored." Lots of independent labs have carried out controlled experiments and confirmed that, on the whole, COVID-19 vaccines are both effective and safe. That's why your friend has already had himself and his whole family vaccinated. You could say that his level of confidence is over 99 percent.

A most useful equation

We mentioned that Cicero translated Carneades's Greek term pithanon as probabilis. Indeed, there is a modern approach that very much resembles Carneades's concept of increasing degrees of confidence in our assessment of impressions, a concept that we have been sneaking into the previous description when we started attaching approximate numbers to the four levels of Carneades's analysis.

The approach in question is known as Bayesianism,[21] which stems from a short paper by the English mathematician Thomas Bayes published posthumously in 1763. The paper introduces a method to update one's assessment of the probability of a given event (or notion) on the basis of new information (data, arguments). In simplified fashion, Bayes's relation looks like this.

$$P(T \mid E) \sim P(E \mid T) * P(T)$$

Where Ps are probabilities, T is a given theory (say, that COVID-19 vaccines are effective), and E is the evidence pertinent to that theory. The symbol ~ means "is proportional to." There is a slightly more complicated version of the equation, featuring a denominator by which the right side is divided, which turns "is proportional to" into "is exactly equal to." But we don't need to complicate our lives too much for the present purposes.

What does this equation mean, and what does it have to do with Carneades, who lived two millennia before Bayes? If read out loud, the Bayesian relation would be: The probability of a theory given the available evidence (also known as the posterior probability) is proportional to the probability of observing said evidence if the theory were true (also known as the likelihood), multiplied by the a priori (based on background information) probability of the theory being true (also known as the prior probability). That is: posterior ~ likelihood * prior.

The way this works in practice is this: We usually have preliminary information about any given impression. For instance, we have basic knowledge
of viruses and vaccines. That background information is quantified as the
"prior" in a Bayesian framework. Let's say, for instance, that the current
prior for vaccines working, as a general prophylactic tool, is 80 percent,
analogous to Carneades's "convincingly true."

Now we look at the new evidence specifically concerning COVID-19
vaccines and it seems to go in the direction of the conclusion that they do,
in fact, work. That is, their likelihood is high. This means that our posterior
probability, obtained by combining the prior and the likelihood, will be
higher than the prior itself, say, 95 percent. Our assessment of the notion
that vaccines are effective has moved from "convincingly true" to "undiverted" territory. Had the likelihood, by contrast, been lower, the posteri-
or probability may actually have gone down when compared to the prior
probability, and we would have lost a bit of confidence in the effectiveness
of vaccines. Graphically, it looks something like this.

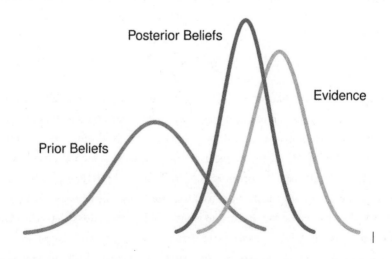

You can see that evidence "drags" posterior probabilities (or beliefs) higher (or lower) than the prior probabilities (or beliefs), as it should. That is, it
stands to reason that evidence and argument change our assessment of the
persuasiveness (pithanon) of a particular notion, just as Carneades suggested.

We want to make clear that we are not suggesting that Carneades somehow anticipated Bayesianism. The two frameworks are significantly different, and the first one is qualitative, while the second one is quantitative. Nonetheless, there are enough satisfying parallels to think that a modern Skeptic in the Academic tradition could use Carneades's approach as an approximate tool, or the Bayesian approach as a precise, quantitative one.

But is it a philosophy, or an attitude?

Now that we know a bit about Academic Skepticism, we can begin to wonder whether it is actually a philosophy of life, analogous to the ones we've studied so far, or if it should be characterized as a philosophical attitude informing one's philosophy of life. Cicero, who was inspired by the teaching of Carneades and was a student of Philo of Larissa, certainly thought of it in terms of a philosophy for life, as is clear if one reads some of his major treatises, especially *On the Ends of Good and Evil*, *On Duties*, and *Tusculan Disputations*.[22]

Then again, Cicero's specific philosophy as it emerges from these and other books was essentially a version of Stoicism. *Tusculan Disputations* and *Stoic Paradoxes* are explicitly and thoroughly informed by Stoic philosophy, and in *On Duties* he acknowledges a strong influence from the Stoic teacher Panaetius. More generally, Cicero saw little difference among what he considered the three major philosophies of his time: Platonism, Aristotelianism, and Stoicism, and indeed actively attempted to reconcile them with each other in the kind of syncretism that was pursued by another of his teachers, Antiochus of Ascalon.

Cicero could be critical of the Stoics when he thought it necessary. In *On Divination*, he rejects the Stoic credence in the possibility of reading the future by looking at the entrails of animals or the flight of birds, mounting what modern scholars think is the first sustained attack on pseudoscience.[23] It is this ability to critically discern what is and is not worth accepting in any set of ideas that separates the skeptical attitude from what the Pyrrhonists famously labeled "dogmatisms."*

---

* However, as we shall see in the next chapter, from the Pyrrhonist perspective, even the Academic Skeptics were "dogmatic," meaning that they asserted opinions that were, according to the Pyrrhonists, unwarranted.

As Cicero explains:

> As other schools maintain that some things are certain, others
> uncertain, we, differing with them, say that some things are
> probable, others improbable. . . . Our New Academy allows us
> wide liberty, so that it is within my right to defend any theory
> that presents itself to me as most probable.[24]

Philosophy, after all, is not a religion, and it ought not to be constrained by the acceptance of rigid teachings. Since ultimate truth constantly eludes humankind, our best and most honest course of action is to provisionally assent to what is probable and leave open for the future the possibility of changing our minds.

Live like Carneades

Whether Academic Skepticism is a full-fledged philosophy of life or an attitude one takes toward the world is open to debate (just as Carneades would want it!). Regardless of which side of the argument you fall on, being an Academic Skeptic in today's world requires some amount of intentional training in order to improve at it. And just like the other philosophies of life we've covered so far, training oneself in Academic Skepticism aims toward a particular goal, which Cicero sums up nicely in the quote that started off this chapter: We should not be too confident in our belief of anything. Instead of aiming for certainty, the world would be better off if people held their beliefs more loosely and acted on the basis of pithanon over *katalepsis*—probability over certainty.

Carneades went about practicing this in two ways: by "spreading the gospel" of uncertainty through his persuasive two-sided argumentation and by weakening his own grip on firm beliefs through his habit of measuring the persuasiveness of impressions.

A modern Academic Skeptic practice would involve both mastering Skeptic epistemology and aiming one's rhetorical skills to instill doubt, not to persuade others of a specific thesis. The next five exercises will be mostly focused on loosening your own beliefs through digging a bit deeper into how to apply Skeptic epistemology, but you'll also get a taste of Skeptic rhetoric at the end.

Day 1: Practice recognizing the four types of impressions

Let's start off with a pop quiz to help you get more familiar with sorting impressions into Carneades's categories. Recall that Carneades classified our impressions about things according to four levels, listed in increasing order of pithanon (probability).

1. Apparently true: a belief that is supported with very weak evidence.

   - These beliefs are fuzzy and could very well be wrong.

   - Examples are hearing a rumor from an unreliable but occasionally correct source, and seeing someone from a distance who looks like your friend but could be someone else.

2. Convincingly true: a belief that seems clear at first blush.

   - For example, getting wet while outdoors from droplets in the sky is a convincing impression of rain.

3. Undiverted: a belief that is supported by multiple lines of evidence.

   - For instance, if you're sweating in the blazing sun in Memphis, Tennessee, and your calendar says it's August 2, you have an undiverted impression that it's a summer's day, since the temperature, the sun in the sky, and the calendar all align in support of the impression.

4. Thoroughly explored: a belief that is supported by multiple lines of evidence after intentional, careful, thorough exploration.

   - Someone holding a PhD in evolutionary biology would have a thoroughly explored belief in the theory of natural selection.

The following are a couple of major points to keep in mind about these four levels of impressions.

The levels are about the *justification* for an impression. They're not about how strongly you *feel* about a belief, but about how well you're *justified* in holding the belief. You may feel quite strongly about some belief, but your feeling may be miscalibrated if it doesn't align with how much evidence you have to support that belief. Living like Carneades means practicing aligning your feelings with the pithanon of each impression!

These levels are *relative to the perceiver*. Because Carneades's levels are not about the *truth* of any given belief but about how well supported the belief appears to be, different people can have access to weaker or stronger evidence, or even reasonably evaluate differently the very same evidence. A schoolchild who is told for the first time that Washington, DC, is the capital of the United States is less justified in believing this than an active US senator!

Keep these points in mind while you list the following impressions in their appropriate categories. We will share the answers in the following.

Impression	Perceiver	Apparent, convincing, undiverted, or thoroughly explored?
There's beer in the fridge	Someone who vaguely recalls that there may be a couple of beers left in their fridge, but isn't quite sure	
There's beer in the fridge	Someone who—at this very moment—is looking at two bottles of beer in their fridge, and just reached out and grabbed one	
The charge of an electron is 1.602×10^{-19} C	A physics student* using this value in a calculation after looking it up in a reliable book	
The charge of an electron is 1.602×10^{-19} C	A physics student who measured this value with acceptable error in a physics lab experiment	
The idea that factory-farmed meat is ethically wrong	Someone who was disgusted after visiting a slaughterhouse for the first time	

* This was before the fundamental charge was strictly defined in 2019.

Here are our answers.

1. This is a pretty good example of an apparent impression. The person who is thinking that there may be beer in the fridge is relying on a fuzzy memory and has no corroborating evidence beyond that.

2. This is an undiverted impression. The person has visual and tactile evidence that there's beer in the fridge, since they're both seeing and touching the bottle. They get bonus epistemic points after they open the bottle and take a sip, since they'll also be tasting the beer! If the person only saw the beer in the fridge but didn't touch or taste it, then it would be a convincing impression, since they have a clear visual impression of the beer. The fact that other senses are coming into play that don't contradict what their eyes tell them is what makes this an undiverted impression. Notice that the same impression can be ranked differently depending on how much information the person has!

3. Given that the student is relying on an indirect report from a reliable source, we take this to be a convincing impression. However, it's arguable that this could be an apparent impression, since typos can occur.

4. The fact that the student is running a serious experiment to measure the charge of the electron puts this impression in either the undiverted or the thoroughly explored category. It could be considered undiverted in that the experiment provides a set of consistent impressions that don't contradict the value the student found. On the other hand, assuming the student is running a well-controlled experiment, this could fairly be considered a case of a thoroughly explored impression. We lean toward the former, since a thoroughly explored impression likely involves integrating a single finding into a wider body of knowledge beyond that which a single experiment could provide. Again, notice that the same impression can have different levels of justification depending on who has the impression; justification is relative to the perceiver.

5. This is a tough one whose answer depends on how well the person has thought deeply about ethics. If the person has philosophical training in ethics, perhaps their impression that factory-farmed meat is wrong could be considered strong or undiverted. On the other hand, if the person just equated being disgusted by something

with it being ethically wrong, then it's an apparent impression, and perhaps even an apparently false one. After all, you can't literally see wrongness in the world the way you can see color: You have to infer it. And if the person makes an unreflective leap from "I'm disgusted" to "That's wrong!" then the belief isn't well founded at all, no matter how strongly the person feels about it.

You may have noticed that there's room for doubt in some of our answers. If you feel uncomfortable with not having clear-cut answers to these questions, take as an apparent impression that leaving some room for doubt may be beneficial for you: Becoming more comfortable with uncertainty is a key benefit of this philosophy!

Day 2: Categorize some of your own impressions

Now that you have a better (but, we hope, still tentative; don't be too certain of anything!) handle on Carneades's categories, you're better prepared to apply them to some of your own impressions. Set down five of your impressions here, categorize them, and write out your justifications.

Your impressions can range from mundane sense impressions ("There is a book in front of me now") to deeply held beliefs (insert your own political or religious views here). We suggest that you try to gather a variety of impressions, and that you come up with at least one impression for each of Carneades's four categories.

Impression	Apparent, convincing, undiverted, or thoroughly explored?	Justification

Before you move on, did you notice whether any of your strongly held impressions were less justified than you initially thought? If so, chalk that up as an impression that doing some work to adopt an Academic Skeptical stance may be of particular benefit to you. You'll be exploring this idea a bit more in the next exercise.

Day 3: A qualitative lesson in Bayesianism

Today's theme continues the focus on justification and knowledge, but we'll be turning away from the methods of the Academic Skeptics to explore some key takeaways of Bayesianism, which is in line with Academic Skepticism and would make for a powerful tool in an aspiring Academic's mental tool kit.

While the most powerful applications of Bayesian thought require doing some math, there are also a handful of lessons that one can take away from the Bayesian approach that don't require much math at all. Today's exercises will focus on helping you internalize one of these qualitative takeaways: that belief comes in degrees.

One major lesson from both Bayesianism and Academic Skepticism is that belief isn't a binary (on/off; either/or) phenomenon; you can (and should) believe things more or less strongly. And if you're thinking well, the strength of your beliefs should be proportionate to the evidence available to you.

For today's exercise, do a quick check of the impressions you listed yesterday and see if the Carnedean category to which you assigned each belief matches how strongly you believe the impression. In the following table, write your impressions and rankings from yesterday. In the final column, write how strongly you believe the impression.

Impression	Apparent, convincing, undiverted, or thoroughly explored?	How strongly do you hold this belief on a scale of 1 (not at all strongly) to 5 (extremely strongly)?

Does your strength of belief tend to match the level of evidence you have for the belief? If not, the next lesson may be of some help.

Day 4: The Bayesian strength of evidence

Just like your degree of belief, evidence can also be strong or weak. Although evidence should always nudge your prior belief, strong evidence should move it more than weak evidence. This raises the question: What makes a piece of evidence strong? A particular form of Bayes's theorem that uses odds instead of probabilities* helps answer this question. It can be written as follows.

$$O(H \mid E) = O(H) * [p(E \mid H) / p(E \mid \text{not-}H)]$$

Here, H stands for your hypothesis about the world. E is a piece of evidence you're considering. O(x) is the odds of something happening. The pipe ("|") means "given that . . ." or "assuming it's true that . . ." So $O(H \mid E)$ is the odds of your hypothesis being true given the evidence. O(H) is the prior odds of your hypothesis being true before seeing the evidence. Finally, the mess of symbols on the right is known as the likelihood ratio, and can

---

* The first form of Bayes's theorem we mentioned in this chapter involved probabilities. Odds are related to a probability, "p," by the equation: odds = p / (1 − p). So if the probability of something is 1/3, or 0.33, then the odds are: 0.33 / (1 − 0.33) = 0.33 / 0.67, or 1:2 odds. This can be interpreted as the event being twice as likely not to happen as to happen.

be read as the probability of your evidence actually occurring if you assume your hypothesis is true (p(E|H)) divided by the probability of that same piece of evidence occurring assuming your hypothesis is *false*: [p(E|not-H)].

That's a mouthful! The important thing to keep in mind for this lesson lies in that last piece: the likelihood ratio, which ultimately determines the strength of your evidence. Note that if the likelihood ratio is big (as an example, for the hypothesis that there's beer in the fridge, given you're literally at the fridge looking at the beer, it's highly unlikely you'd see the beer if it weren't there!), your posterior odds will be big, since you're multiplying your prior beliefs by a big number.

Big posterior odds given the evidence = prior odds
of the hypothesis * **a big number**

On the other hand, if the likelihood ratio is small (for example, your cold clears up a week after you take a homeopathic remedy; since most colds clear up after a week,[25] this is very poor evidence that the remedy did anything!), your prior beliefs should only be nudged a little.

Smaller posterior odds given the evidence = prior odds
of the hypothesis * **a smaller number**

Thus, the likelihood ratio is what determines how strong your evidence is. The bigger the likelihood ratio, the stronger the evidence. And what makes for a large likelihood ratio is that the evidence you're considering is much more likely to occur if your hypothesis were true than if it were false. In other words, the more strongly your hypothesis predicts the evidence ahead of time, the stronger the evidence will be in favor of the hypothesis if and when you actually see it!

This has been a whirlwind tour of some pretty deep epistemic principles, and it's okay if you didn't take it all in. The main thing we'd like you to take away from this lesson is that to properly assess the strength of evidence, you have to take into account how well the hypothesis predicts the piece of evidence, as well as how surprising the piece of evidence would be if your hypothesis were false.

To take a simple example, suppose you notice someone smirking in the audience while you're giving a presentation. The hypothesis that they think you said something foolish would predict that they'd smirk. On its own, this seems to be evidence that they think you're an imbecile. But there are many other reasons why that person may be smirking. Perhaps they were daydreaming and thought of a joke. Perhaps they just saw a funny meme on their phone. Perhaps they're genuinely impressed with your presentation! These are just a few examples of alternative hypotheses that would also account for their smirking. Thus, their smirk counts as very weak evidence that they think you're foolish, since many alternative hypotheses also can explain their smirk.

This powerful idea has an important corollary that is essential for a modern Skeptic to grasp: **There is only one way a hypothesis can be true, but there are many ways it can be false.** Thus, if you don't consider all the ways you could be wrong, then you may very well fall into confirmation bias and overconfidence when assessing evidence.

Thinking of alternative hypotheses that can explain a piece of evidence is a very helpful qualitative takeaway from Bayesianism for a practicing modern Academic Skeptic, since it moves you toward the key goal of Skepticism: not being overconfident in your beliefs about any specific hypothesis.

To get a better handle on what makes evidence stronger, try coming up with a strong and a weak piece of evidence for one of your beliefs that you previously examined. To assess the strength of the piece of evidence, you need to take into account how likely it would be to see the evidence if your belief were true *and* how likely that same piece of evidence would be if it were false. Write the strong and weak evidence for one of your beliefs along with your reasoning here.

———————————————————————————————

———————————————————————————————

———————————————————————————————

———————————————————————————————

———————————————————————————————

Day 5: Argue from both sides

The final exercise of this section will pivot away from Bayesianism and back to classic Academic Skepticism. Recall from the opening vignette that Carneades created quite the kerfuffle in Rome when he argued one day for justice and another day against it to try to help his audience assess the totality of evidence and to prevent them from closing their minds. Today, you'll attempt to apply this technique to your own beliefs, while also getting a chance to review the philosophies you've covered so far over the course of this book.

First, take a moment to reflect on all the philosophies we've discussed up to this point, from Aristippus's Cyrenaicism to Protagoras's form of Sophism. By now, you may have discovered that you like some of these approaches better than others.

Next, choose one of your most favorite or least favorite philosophies among those you've encountered so far. In the space that follows, write the name of the philosophy, and on a scale of 1 to 10, rate how confident you are that at least some aspects of that philosophy are a very good—or a very poor—fit for you in crafting the kind of life you'd like to live.

_____

_____

_____

_____

_____

_____

_____

_____

_____

Next, write two short essays: one in defense of the philosophy as a good fit for you, and one to argue that the philosophy is a poor fit . . . whether it's your favorite or least favorite!

We suggest that you spend a limited, set amount of time on each essay. About ten minutes per essay should be enough, but feel free to take more or less time.

In defense of _____ [insert philosophy here]:

_____

_____

_____

_____

_____

_____

_____

_____

_____

_____

_____

_____

_____

_____

Against _____ [insert philosophy here]:

_____

_____

_____

_____

_____

_____

_____

_____

_____

_____

_____

_____

_____

_____

_____

_____

_____

_____

_____

_____

Finally, take a few moments to rate how confident you are that the philosophy is a good or poor fit for you on a scale of 1 to 10. If the technique did its job, then your confidence may be a bit lower. If not, then that may be evidence that Academic Skepticism—or at least arguing both sides—isn't a good fit for you!

REFLECTION

Take some time to review your hard work over the past few days. At this point, are you missing the ethical components from the philosophies of the Port of Character, or the emphasis on pleasure of the first two philosophies we covered in the Port of Pleasure? Or are you finding the focus on doubt and epistemology to be a better fit for you? Which of the techniques that we covered—Carneades's four categories, basic Bayesianism, and arguing both sides—did you find the most useful? Did any of these techniques help instill doubt? If so, how did it feel and do you think more doubt in your life would be beneficial in any way?

_____

_____

_____

_____

_____

_____

_____

_____

_____

_____

Chapter 10

SUSPEND JUDGMENT WITH PYRRHO

The chief good is the suspension of the judgment, which tranquility of mind follows like its shadow.

—Pyrrho, in *Diogenes Laërtius*, 9.107

The ship was thrashed by wind and waves. Lightning and thunder crashed above, and sheets of rain pummeled the deck. The wooden vessel creaked as it swayed up and down on the choppy waters of the Mediterranean, and people on board threw their arms up to the sky in fear, yelling out to the gods for protection.

A man seated on deck, the Greek philosopher Pyrrho of Elis, suddenly stood up to address his fellow passengers. "See there, that little pig?" he called out to the others as he pointed at the animal, his voice calm despite the weather.

The passengers turned to look at a young pig rooting around for scraps of food on deck. "He goes on eating, no matter the conditions, with no sense of concern or suffering," Pyrrho said. "This is the kind of freedom from worry that we should cultivate through philosophy, if we don't want to be disturbed by the things that happen to us. We should all take that pig's example, and act that way, too."[1]

"But Pyrrho, this storm will kill us all! Of course we're worried!" a passenger cried out.

"We have no way of knowing what's to come," Pyrrho said. "In fact, we cannot really judge what's happening right now. Is it a terrible storm? Or is it just a gust of air and a spot of water, about to stop momentarily? Is this ship safe or in danger? Let us keep our passions in check, since we can never be certain!"

He gestured around at the rain pouring down. "All this? Our senses do not tell us the truth about reality," Pyrrho added. "Why waste these moments thinking about it?"

He sat back down, suddenly motionless, his face impassive and his brow unwrinkled as the rain washed over his hair and beard. The passengers on deck looked at each other. Who was this Pyrrho, and how could he remain so calm? Pyrrho wandered off, talking to himself as he often did, while the winds finally began to die down.

One man turned to the others. "You know, Pyrrho began as a painter," the man explained. "But he took up philosophy as a young man. He accompanied Alexander the Great on his campaign in India, along with his teacher Anaxarchus of Abdera."[2] The others looked at him with interest.

A woman nearby chimed in. "That Anaxarchus, he was quite a character, too," she said. "He was close to Alexander, and they called him 'Eudaimonicus'—'Sir Happy.' Anaxarchus wasn't even bothered when the tyrant of Cyprus had him thrown in a sack and beaten with iron pestles. When the tyrant was going to cut out his tongue, they say he bit off his own tongue and spit it out. Can you imagine?"[3]

The man spoke up again. "Incredible. And now, here Pyrrho is, tranquil in this awful weather. I wonder what really happened in India that transformed him from an unknown painter into this man who acts like he's made of stone."

Pyrrho sat peacefully on a ledge on the deck, lost in thought—just as he had often been since his fateful journey to Asia with the Macedonian king.

Pyrrho had been born in Elis, a city in the western Peloponnese on the Ionian Sea, around 360 BCE. He began as a painter, depicting torch runners in the gymnasium in his hometown, but then decided to travel with the philosopher Anaxarchus, a follower of the atomist Democritus.[4] He joined Alexander's retinue during the campaign in India.

After voyaging through central Asia, they stopped in Gandhara, in northwest India, where they spent more than two years. Along the way, Pyrrho met philosophers and religious practitioners from across the region, including a group from India that the Greeks called gymnosophists, or naked sages, as well as the Persian Magi, or wise men.[5]

Some of these sages removed their clothing without a care for the weather, allowing the physical elements to challenge them. Pyrrho noticed that they remained motionless for long periods and could endure pain without complaint, and they spoke their mind. When a philosopher from India openly criticized Anaxarchus for catering to the king, Pyrrho started thinking about withdrawing from court altogether.[6] Over time, Pyrrho learned more from the Indian thinkers. The reason for the sages' imperturbability, he discovered, was their suspension of judgment about the world, and their letting go of the need for certainty. It occurred to Pyrrho that things are not beautiful or ugly, just or unjust. They simply are. And people mostly act out of habit and custom, not actual knowledge of good or evil based on objective morality.[7]

The young Pyrrho began cultivating indifference and a lack of attachment to the world around him, including a concerted effort not to trust his senses. It was a physically treacherous way to live, even after he returned home to Greece. Legend has it that he'd almost gone off the side of cliffs, and that he'd nearly failed to step aside for oncoming wagons. Pyrrho was fortunate to have friends who often helped him to avoid truly dangerous situations.

For the rest of his days, Pyrrho never seemed to worry that he would be judged for doing what was "beneath" him. He lived in Elis with his sister Philista, a midwife, and helped out around the house, cleaning and dusting, and selling young birds and piglets at the market.[8]

Pyrrho realized that he did not follow his own precepts perfectly. He vigorously defended Philista against those who criticized her, becoming irate. He said that it was acceptable to show emotion on behalf of a woman like her.[9] Another example came when he was around vicious dogs—he usually paid little notice until one of them attacked him directly, and then he ran away. That was an exception to his undisturbed demeanor: "It's hard to move beyond our human nature entirely," Pyrrho said, when questioned about it. "But we should struggle against adversity, if not by deeds, then at least by words!"[10] A tough test of his untroubled calm, or ataraxia, came when he had to undergo surgery for a wound he sustained. As the physician worked on him with his tools, cauterized his flesh, and used antiseptic ointments to treat him, Pyrrho didn't even change the expression on his face.[11]

Despite never writing a word of philosophy, Pyrrho's pursuit of the suspension of judgment won him followers and admiration. He was granted the rights of citizenship by Athens and made a high priest by his fellow citizens in Elis, who built a statue in his honor in the marketplace. He lived until around 270 BCE, dying at about ninety years old.[12]

Some of Pyrrho's students sought to emulate his tranquility as they lived; others worked to spread his thinking. They included, most prominently, Timon of Phlius, who wrote a book of "lampoons" making fun of Greek philosophers, and Nausiphanes of Teos, a follower of the philosopher Democritus, who was later a teacher of Epicurus.[13] Pyrrho also taught Arcesilaus, who later brought his ideas to Plato's Academy.[14] Later generations of philosophers, including the commentator Sextus Empiricus, built on Pyrrho's approach. A Greek with Roman citizenship, Sextus authored *Outlines of Pyrrhonism*.[15] Far beyond ancient times, Pyrrho's ideas served as an influence (and often a foil) for skeptics such as the seventeenth-century philosopher René Descartes and the eighteenth-century thinker David Hume. Recent scholarship has richly explored the link between Pyrrho's thinking and the philosophies and wisdom traditions he encountered in India, including those of the early Buddhists.[16]

The mysterious Pyrrho

Pyrrhonism is the second major school of Ancient Skepticism. Although, since Pyrrho of Elis actually lived between 365 and 265 BCE—that is, before the "skeptical turn" of Plato's Academy—Pyrrhonism may be the first school, chronologically speaking. Pyrrho died (as far as we can tell; the exact year is uncertain) at the time that Arcesilaus took over the Academy and shifted its emphasis toward skepticism.

But the history of Pyrrhonism is a bit more complex than that. To begin with, we don't know much about Pyrrho himself, and he did not leave any written documentation of his thought. His student, Timon of Phlius, did, but unfortunately Timon's own writings are lost to the sands of time. So, all we have is indirect evidence through the writings of later commentators, some of whom were hostile to the skeptic tradition.

As we have seen, Pyrrho is presented as the protagonist of a number of sensational anecdotes by Diogenes Laërtius in his *Lives of the Eminent Philosophers*. For instance:

> He led a life consistent with this doctrine, going out of his way for nothing, taking no precaution, but facing all risks as they came, whether carts, precipices, dogs or what not, and, generally, leaving nothing to the arbitrament of the senses; but he was kept out of harm's way by his friends who . . . used to follow close after him.[17]

This is hardly credible, especially because Pyrrho is alleged to have lived to the ripe old age of eighty-five, possibly even ninety-five, which is extremely unlikely if he really was *that* careless with his life. Laërtius continues: "But Aenesidemus says that it was only his philosophy that was based upon suspension of judgment, and that he did not lack foresight in his everyday acts."[18]

In other words, Pyrrho navigated everyday life in the same way that most people do and reserved his skepticism for a higher level of philosophical discussion. Nevertheless, his student Timon depicts him as having arrived at a godlike calm thanks to his philosophical practice. Whether this is true or just adulation by a student is impossible to tell.

Be that as it may, Pyrrho achieved a remarkable reputation during his lifetime. We are told that his native city, Elis, in the western Peloponnese (Greece), passed a law according to which all philosophers should be exempt from taxation.[19] We wouldn't mind if New York (where Greg and Massimo live) and California (where Meredith resides) followed suit!

Diogenes Laërtius also recounts the fascinating story about Pyrrho's going to India with Alexander the Great, under the guidance of his teacher, a mysterious figure known as Anaxarchus*: "[He traveled] everywhere so that he even forgathered with the Indian Gymnosophists and with the Magi. This led him to adopt a most noble philosophy . . . taking the form of agnosticism and suspension of judgment."[20]

---

* We know very little of Anaxarchus, but apparently he was an atomist like Democritus, shared philosophical commonalities with both the Cynics (chapter 5) and the Cyrenaics (chapter 1), and may in fact have been the actual originator of what we think of today as Pyrrhonism, specifically that we should be agnostic about the nature of things and that we should cultivate suspension of judgment in order to achieve mental tranquility.

The Magi were Persian priests of the Zoroastrian religion, well known to the Greek world, but we know much less about the Gymnosophists. Diogenes Laërtius says that Pyrrho's philosophy was developed as a result of his contact with a group of Eastern philosophers, the only well-established direct link between an Eastern and Western philosophical tradition.[21]

To get a better idea of Pyrrho's approach to the life worth living, consider three fundamental questions we are told he considered[22]: "(i) How are things by nature? (ii) What attitude should we adopt toward them? (iii) What will be the outcome for those who have this attitude?" Here are his answers.

> Pyrrho declared that (*i*) things are equally indifferent, unmeasurable, and inarbitrable. For this reason (*ii*) neither our sensations nor our opinions tell us truths or falsehoods. Therefore, for this reason we should not put our trust in them one bit, but we should be unopinionated, uncommitted, and unwavering, saying concerning each individual thing that it no more is than is not, or it both is and is not, or it neither is nor is not. (*iii*) The outcome for those who actually adopt this attitude, says Timon, will be first speechlessness, and then freedom from disturbance.

According to Pyrrho, then, (i) we cannot know how things actually are, and therefore (ii) it makes no sense to formulate opinions about them, and even less to become so attached to such opinions that we get upset if someone challenges them. Moreover, (iii) if we manage to shed such unnecessary and unfounded opinions we will achieve serenity of mind, or what he calls freedom from disturbance (ataraxia, in Greek).

Be reasonable

This is pretty much what we know about Pyrrho himself. But the history of Pyrrhonism continued with twists and turns. As we saw in the last chapter, the first scholarch of the Skeptical Academy was Arcesilaus of Pitane (315–241 BCE), who is said to have espoused a form of skepticism not very different from that of Pyrrho himself, thus inextricably linking the two versions of ancient skepticism.

This is not surprising, as Arcesilaus crossed paths with Timon (325–235 BCE), who was Pyrrho's only student. Arcesilaus is reported to have practiced the time-honored skeptical approach of arguing both sides of a given question, with the intent of generating aporia (confusion; see pages 141–42) in his listeners.[23] Moreover, Arcesilaus also claimed—in perfect Pyrrhonian fashion—that the only rational option is to suspend judgment.[24]

However, Arcesilaus did propose a criterion for deciding when and how to act while adopting a skeptic attitude: *to eulogon*, the reasonable, which may have helped Pyrrho navigate everyday occurrences without risking his life. It is not clear what "reasonable" means in this context, but if Arcesilaus meant something like commonsensical, then perhaps this, too, was inspired by Pyrrho. That criterion is distinct from what later Academic Skeptics, like Carneades, proposed and which we have already discussed in chapter 9: *to pithanon*, what is persuasive, or probable.

Regardless of the initial similarities, Academic Skepticism and Pyrrhonism diverged after Arcesilaus. The first revival of Pyrrho's approach is attributed to Aenesidemus (first century BCE). He wrote the now lost *Pyrrhonian Discourses* (*Pyrrhoneia*). Again, the vicissitudes of the two types of skepticism are intertwined, as Aenesidemus was actually a member of the Skeptical Academy under Philo of Larissa (who, you may recall, was one of Cicero's teachers).

Aenesidemus used to summarize the Pyrrhonian creed as "we determine nothing," meaning that the only thing a Pyrrhonist would feel comfortable asserting is—as the modern scholar Harald Thorsrud puts it—that "some property belongs to some object relative to some observer or relative to some set of circumstances."[25] What did he mean, exactly? For instance, a true Pyrrhonist would never say "this table is round," but rather, something along the lines of "this object that is used as a table appears to me now to be of circular shape." Talk about qualifying one's statements!

The ten modes

The most important reason to mention Aenesidemus is that he contributed a famous technique to the Pyrrhonist arsenal, the so-called ten modes. These are ways to remind ourselves that there is always room for doubt about any categorical assertion. Here are the modes.

i)   Different animal species perceive the world differently.

ii)   Different people perceive the same things differently.

iii) The same person perceives the same thing differently, depending on the exact circumstances.

iv)   Sensorial perception varies with physical changes in the environment.

v)   Sensorial perception varies depending on how things relate to each other.

vi)   We perceive objects only through air and other media, not directly.

vii) Objects change color, size, temperature, and so forth depending on the circumstances.

viii) All perceptions interact with each other (they are not independent of one another).

ix)   The impact of our perceptions on us becomes less strong with repetition, as we get used to a given stimulus.

x)   People are brought up with different beliefs, under different customs and laws.

The point of this list is that it provides us with ample evidence that the way we perceive and understand the world is relative to a number of external factors, including biological and cultural. As a result, how can anyone convincingly affirm any alleged truth about any particular fact or idea?

Five more modes

The next big name in Pyrrhonism is that of Sextus Empiricus, who lived in the second or third century CE. Again, we don't know much about him (this seems to be a trend with the skeptics!), except that he was a doctor. He wrote *Against the Professors* (in other words, those who profess, who claim to be in possession of some truth) and *Outlines of Pyrrhonism*.

Sextus distinguishes three fundamental philosophical positions: dogmatists (who think they have discovered some truth), negative dogmatists (who think that truth cannot be discovered), and skeptics. He positions the Academic Skeptics in the second group (a bit unfairly), though it is not at all clear that they claimed that truth is impossible in principle, as distinct from the more modest claim that nobody has yet convincingly shown to be in possession of any truth.

We find in Sextus the description of the same skeptical path we have encountered before: We notice disagreements among people on subject matter X or Y → this troubles us → we discover that different accounts about X or Y seem to be equally convincing (equipollence) → consequently we suspend judgment → and therefore we achieve mental tranquility.

Skeptical tranquility is Zen-like (remember the connection with the Eastern traditions!). It comes indirectly, by giving up the assumption that the truth is necessary. It should be noted that this doesn't mean giving up the search for truth, or declaring that it cannot be reached, or that it doesn't exist. The truth may be "out there,"* as the saying goes, but we haven't found it yet.

Sextus also tells of five more "modes," introduced by a first-century skeptic named Agrippa. (Yes, you guessed it: We don't know much else about him either!) These are particularly worth considering, as three of the modes are still used today in cutting-edge debates in logic and epistemology. They are as follows.

i)   Disagreement: People, including philosophers, disagree on all sorts of issues.

ii)   Relativity: Things appear differently to us when their relations to each other change, or when the conditions change.

iii) Infinite regress: Whenever we are given an explanation for a certain notion we can always ask for an explanation of the explanation, and so on, ad infinitum.

iv)   Assumption: One way to stop an infinite regress is to assume a particular starting point as unquestioned, but that means we have no further explanation to provide in defense of whatever starting point we chose.

v)   Circularity: Another way to stop an infinite regress is to engage in circular reasoning, where, at some point, some of the things to be explained take on the role of things that provide explanations.

---

* The truth is out there" is the famous tagline of the long-running television series *The X-Files* (1993 to 2003, with an extra season from 2016 to 2018).

Note that the first two of Agrippa's modes are essentially a (very condensed) summary of the ten modes of Aenesidemus. But the big whopper is represented by the last three, which are often referred to as Agrippa's trilemma, or Münchhausen trilemma.* Their importance lies in the fact that together they exhaust the logical space of possibilities for justifying knowledge: *Every* time we want to give grounds for a claim to knowledge, according to the trilemma, we end in an infinite regress, or in having to make an arbitrary assumption, or in circular reasoning. It may not have been Agrippa's intention, but three of his modes taken together come pretty close to constituting an airtight argument that human knowledge is, in fact, impossible. Of course, this is not something a Pyrrhonist would want to say, because that would put him straight into the category of negative dogmatists, and to be a dogmatist of *any* kind is not acceptable for a follower of Pyrrho.

The criteria for action

Let us assume that we deploy the ten modes of Aenesidemus, or the five modes of Agrippa, and that we practice suspension of judgment in pursuit of ataraxia (tranquility). How then, are we to live our life, exactly? This is a question that Pyrrhonists have always been asked by their critics. Remember the incredible adventures of Pyrrho-the-careless told by Diogenes Laërtius: Without their friends watching out for them, how could Pyrrhonists conduct their lives? Another way to put it is: How can we live without positive beliefs?

The answer lies in what is sometimes referred to as the fourfold observances: Pyrrhonists live by following Nature (using their Nature-given perceptions and abilities to think); by being alert to their feelings (which tell them when they are hungry or thirsty); by following established laws and customs (without claiming that they are "true," "just," and the like); and by heeding expert advice whenever available (to learn to play a musical instrument, or to write, for example).

---

* The term Münchhausen trilemma is a reference to the imaginary character of Baron von Münchhausen, who was once stuck with his horse in a mire and was able to get himself out of the potentially fatal predicament by pulling his own hair. The idea is that it would take something like a miracle to avoid the consequences of the trilemma.

Is this really different from the other skeptics, the Academics? Comparisons between the two schools have been made since antiquity.[26] By this point, the divergence between the two approaches ought to be clear, despite the reciprocal influences we have pointed out, and are perhaps best summarized in the contrast between Arcesilaus's *to eulogon*, if we interpret it to mean to follow common reason, and Carneades's *to pithanon*, interpreted as to follow what appears probable upon investigation. In the first case, one ends up living according to commonsense, in the second, by inquiring into everything, believable or not. The Pyrrhonist will eschew scientific speculation and metaphysics; the Academic will embrace them, but on a probabilistic basis only, without the certainty of a dogmatist. However, both approaches put the questioning of human knowledge at the center of their conception of a good human life—and that is what makes a skeptic.

Live like Pyrrho

A modern Pyrrhonist's practice is focused on the goal of ataraxia. All that a Pyrrhonist—both ancient and modern—does is in service of this goal. The Pyrrhonist engages in questioning—not to get to the truth of the matter, but to achieve mental tranquility.

Pyrrhonism is one of the few Greco-Roman schools—alongside Stoicism and Epicureanism[27]—that is practiced today by people like Douglas C. Bates, whose ideas we'll touch on briefly in Day 5.[28]

Day 1: Explore Pyrrho's "three fundamental questions" for yourself

---

Pyrrho's philosophy was spurred on by his asking himself three fundamental questions about the way the world is and our relationship toward it.

- How are things by nature?
- What attitude should we adopt toward them?
- What will be the outcome for those who have this attitude?

Over the course of this book, you've studied and applied philosophies of life that other people created, perhaps by considering questions similar to Pyrrho's. They provide a good jumping-off point for you to craft your own philosophy of life.

Today's exercise is simple: Answer Pyrrho's three fundamental questions to the best of your ability. Try to be as succinct as possible, but take your time in considering your answers. Before you proceed, perhaps one more example of how one could answer these questions would be helpful. A Buddhist may give the following answers.

- Things are by nature not-self, unsatisfactory, and impermanent.
- We should take an attitude of nonattachment toward them.
- The outcome will be liberation from suffering.

Now it's your turn. Write your answers in the space that follows. Next to each one, rate how confident you are about it on a scale of 1 (not at all confident) to 10 (completely confident).

How are things by nature? _____

_____

What attitude should we adopt toward them?_____

_____

What will be the outcome for those who have this attitude? _____

_____

Day 2: Apply the first two modes

Today, you'll be stepping into the shoes of a Pyrrhonian skeptic and do what Pyrrhonians did in ancient times: attack a philosophy. More specifically, your own. Attack each of the answers to your own questions from yesterday using one of the first two of Agrippa's modes. Recall that the first two modes are as follows.

i)   Disagreement: People, including philosophers, disagree on all sorts of issues.

ii) Relativity: Things appear differently to us when their relations to each other change, or when the conditions change.

As an example, here are some ways a Pyrrhonian may attack the Buddhist's answers to Pyrrho's three fundamental questions.

- Things are by nature not-self, unsatisfactory, and impermanent.

  » Mode ii: Could these claims of nature change under different circumstances? This seems like a necessary consequence if you believe the third one—impermanence. But if the impermanence of things is itself subject to change, then wouldn't some things be permanent?

- We should take an attitude of nonattachment toward them.

  » Mode i: Some disagree. For instance, the philosopher E. M. Cioran stated: "My faculty for disappointment surpasses understanding. It is what lets me comprehend Buddha, but also what keeps me from following him."[29] Given such disagreement, why should one believe the Buddhist over Cioran?

- The outcome will be liberation from suffering.

  » Mode i and/or Mode ii: Quite the opposite. Some people in some circumstances have followed Buddhist or Buddhist-inspired meditation instructions and have suffered adverse mental health effects.[30] Given that people suffer on this supposed road to liberation, why should we expect liberation in the future when such practices *increase* the suffering of many?

Rewrite your responses to your answers to Pyrrho's three fundamental questions in the space that follows. Then, attempt to rebut them using the first or second Agrippean modes. After you write out each rebuttal, re-rate your confidence in your initial answers to the three questions from yesterday. Did your confidence in your answers change at all?

How are things by nature?

  » Your answer from Day 1: _____

_____

» Your refutation using one of the first two modes of Agrippa:

_____

» Your new confidence in your answer from Day 1: _____

_____

What attitude should we adopt toward them?

» Your answer from Day 1: _____

_____

» Your refutation using one of the first two modes of Agrippa:

_____

» Your new confidence in your answer from Day 1: _____

_____

What will be the outcome for those who have this attitude?

» Your answer from Day 1: _____

_____

» Your refutation using one of the first two modes of Agrippa:

_____

» Your new confidence in your answer from Day 1: _____

_____

Day 3: Attempt to avoid Agrippa's trilemma

Applying the first two of Agrippa's modes is the first of two steps in the process of how a Pyrrhonist tries to impose equipollence on their philosophical adversaries (and how practicing Pyrrhonists can help purge their own minds of dogma). The goal of this first step of the process is to bring up the possibility of doubt. The second is to point out that any responses to assuage the doubt that was raised in the first step must fall into one of the three horns of Agrippa's trilemma.

iii) Infinite regress: Whenever a justification is given, the Pyrrhonist can ask what the justification for the *new* claim is . . . forever. To cut off the infinite regress, the opponent must either engage in either Mode iv or Mode v, as follows.

iv) Assumption: Simply stop at a foundation without justification.

v) Circularity: Use claims earlier in the argument to justify later claims.

Your exercise today will be to attempt to justify your answer to one of Pyrrho's three fundamental questions while not getting trapped in Agrippa's trilemma—or admitting that you have. To narrow your task, we suggest focusing on defending just one of your three answers.

The process for defending your view is simple: State a reason why you believe your assertion. Then, briefly play the role of the Pyrrhonian and ask yourself what justifies the claim. This can be in the form of one of the following questions. Alternatively, you can come up with your own.

- Why do I believe this claim?
- What makes this claim justified?
- What evidence supports this claim?
- How do I know this is true?

Next, answer the question. Then, ask a question about the new claim. Keep on repeating this (possibly infinite!) process until one of four things happens.

- You reach a clear assumption you can't justify: Mode iv.
- You have to appeal to an earlier claim to justify a later one: Mode v.
- You get sick of the process (similar to the aporia Socrates's interlocutors experienced as we mentioned in chapter 7).
- You successfully ground your belief without growing frustrated or falling into Modes iv or v.

As an example, let's say our theoretical Buddhist attempts to defend their answer to Pyrrho's second question.

> A1: *We should take an attitude of nonattachment to things that are not-self, unsatisfactory, and impermanent.*
>
> Q1: *Why do I believe this claim?*
>
> A2: *Because it leads to the end of suffering.*
>
> Q2: *How do I know this is true?*
>
> A3: *Because the early sutras contain several examples of this happening for people who practiced Buddhism.*
>
> Q3: *And why should I believe what's in the sutras?*
>
> A4: *Because I've experienced a reduction in suffering while practicing myself.*
>
> Q4: *And why assume I'll completely end suffering if I keep practicing?*
>
> A5: *Well, if a little practice goes a little way, it makes sense that a lot of practice could go all the way!*
>
> Q5: *Why do I believe that?*
>
> A6: *It just makes sense.**

Now it's your turn to try this method with one of your answers to Pyrrho's questions from Day 1. At the end of the exercise, rate your confidence in your answer on a scale from 1 (not at all confident) to 10 (completely confident).

_____

_____

_____

_____

_____

_____

_____

* Mode iv, assumption

Day 4: Be skeptical of your daily thoughts

Recall that the ultimate goal of Pyrrhonism is mental tranquility. Gaining tranquility involves constantly monitoring your thoughts for signs of dogmatic belief and trying to bring yourself to a state of equipollence. Agrippa's five modes are a powerful way to do this. However, they're also unwieldy to use in your day-to-day life, especially without practice.

Fortunately, there are several shorter methods for practicing Pyrrhonists to work with their own dogmas, although these methods may not be sufficient to tackle strongly entrenched beliefs.[31]

Today's practice involves going about your day and noticing whenever something is bothering you. If the bothersome thought is simple, try one of the shorter modern Pyrrhonian methods presented here. On the other hand, if the thought has a strong emotional valence, make a quick note of the thought, and toward the end of the day, in the space that follows, try to use Agrippa's full-fledged methods that you've been practicing over the past few days.

If the thought doesn't pack a strong punch or you can try to instill some equipollence, if you think you're able to, by quickly arguing against the premises behind the thought by asking yourself the following.

- How do I know this is true?
- Would everyone have the same reaction I'm predicting?
- In what similar circumstances have my expectations been wrong in the past?

Another possible shortcut is to change your wording. If your emotionally charged thought involves stating that something is or is not the case, you can reword your thought to emphasize that it's an appearance, not a necessary fact. For example, if you believe a medical procedure *is* going to be painful, reword your thought to state that "It appears that it may be painful," or "It's possible that it could be painful. Or maybe it won't."[32]

In summary, here's your Pyrrhonian mission for today.

- Go about your day as you normally would.

- Note any disturbing thoughts that come up, which (according to the Pyrrhonists) is an indication that you are holding on to a belief.

- Depending on the strength of the belief, do one of the following.
  - » Try to quickly change your wording, or question the belief underlying the disturbing feeling.
  - » Quickly make a note of the feeling and the circumstances, then try applying Agrippa's five modes later on in the day using the space that follows.

Here's some room to argue against your disturbing thoughts.

Write the disturbing thought.

_____

_____

_____

_____

_____

_____

Argue against it.

_____

_____

_____

_____

_____

Day 5: Ponder the criteria for action

Pyrrhonian practice doesn't just involve disputation, but also provides four criteria by which to act.

1. Natural senses and perceptions

2. Feelings

3. Established laws and customs

4. Heeding of expert advice

Trying to live according to these four criteria may not make for an engaging practice for the day, since we suspect that most people already live according to these criteria to a large degree! Doug Bates, a modern Pyrrhonist, seems to agree: "In observing a Pyrrhonist, the typical person would see someone who looks pretty much like any ordinary person. The only clues that the person was a Pyrrhonist would likely be their skepticism regarding various controversies of their day."[33]

What makes a Pyrrhonist's life different lies primarily in what they do with their minds while acting. By attempting to consciously live according to the four criteria of action, the Pyrrhonist "remov[es] attention away from . . . speculative issues," resulting in "a drastic reduction in what one needs to . . . worry about,"[34] according to Bates. In short, the main purpose of the criteria for action isn't to act appropriately or correctly but to help attain mental tranquility by removing worrying about non-evident matters.

Your final exercise for this week is to assess this claim. Do you think that living more simply by just living according to the four criteria for action will lead to mental tranquility? On the one hand, it could lead to a lot less worrying. On the other hand, several philosophers you've studied over the course of this book may disagree, as in Mode i: disagreement. In the space that follows, write your thoughts about the fruits (or lack thereof) of living according to the criteria of action.

_____

_____

_____

REFLECTION

You've now completed the main tour of ancient Greco-Roman philosophies of life and, in a sense, you've come full circle. We started out with a philosophy many people in modern society live by to some degree—Cyrenaicism—and we've ended with a philosophy that can also lead to a conventional life, at least when seen from the outside. What are your thoughts about the power of Agrippa's modes in instilling *epoché*? Do you think this actually leads to mental tranquility, or is there more to tranquility than loosening one's grip on dogmatic beliefs? Did you experience any glimpses of tranquility while practicing this week? Are the four criteria of action enough to craft a worthwhile life when combined with Pyrrhonism's cognitive methods?

_____

_____

_____

_____

_____

_____

_____

_____

_____

_____

_____

4

HERE BE DRAGONS

The last leg of our journey into Hellenistic philosophy sets off into strange, uncharted waters. Supposedly,[1] ancient maps labeled that sort of territory with *hic sunt dracones* to indicate that unknown perils could lurk there. While the philosophies we cover in this section may not be that dangerous, they are still somewhat strange and little-explored as philosophies of life, as they are perhaps a bit more difficult to practice in modern times. Still, they are historically important. And who knows, maybe you will read one of the following chapters and make Pythagoras go viral again.

The three schools of thought presented here are Pythagoreanism (chapter 11), Megarianism (chapter 12), and Neoplatonism (chapter 13). As we shall see, Pythagoras was incredibly famous in the ancient world, but not for the theorem you might be thinking of. Stilpo and the Megarians are virtually unknown to modern readers, yet there was a time in Greece when everyone wanted a piece of Stilpo. As for the Neoplatonists, they had the dubious honor of being the last pagan bastion against the tide of Christianity, and one of their members, Hypatia of Alexandria, may have paid the ultimate price for it.

Both the Pythagoreans and the Neoplatonists leaned toward what we would today call mysticism, though in very different ways and for contrasting philosophical reasons. People even thought that Pythagoras had a divine nature and went around sporting a golden thigh (thought to be a sign of godliness). And the Neoplatonist Plotinus's soul was supposedly so great that magic spells meant to hurt him bounced off him and harmed the spellcaster instead[2]; moreover, his protective spirit was said to be a full-blown god.[3] Stilpo was one of the foremost logicians of the ancient world and managed to influence the most successful school of all time: the Stoics. Maybe this isn't as flashy as having golden limbs or reflecting magic spells, but we find it pretty impressive!

Since Pythagoreanism was arguably the first philosophy of life articulated by the Greco-Romans and Neoplatonism was the last one, this port spans the entire arc not just of Hellenism but of antiquity as a whole: from the sixth century BCE to the sixth century CE.[4] This is an incredible period of well over a millennium, a time that saw the invention of philosophy and the establishment of a new tradition of writing things down for posterity. Its influence on Christianity and on Western thought more broadly is hard to overestimate. Perhaps these strange, less explored philosophies may make a difference in your own life as well.

Chapter 11

PYTHAGORAS THE MYSTIC

We should behave toward one another so that we avoid making enemies of our friends while also making friends of our enemies.

—Pythagoras, in Diogenes Laërtius,
Lives of the Eminent Philosophers, 8.23

In the center of the crowded marketplace, a young dog snatched a piece of low-hanging fish from a vendor's table. "Hey, stop that, you miserable creature!" the fish seller cried out. Picking up a long wooden spoon, he began thrashing the animal, hitting it around the head and shoulders. The dog's painful whine at being beaten echoed to all who passed by. Pythagoras just happened to be walking past with a few of his friends. As soon as he heard the dog's yelp, his hand flew to his heart.

"You there, don't hit that pup!" Pythagoras yelled to the man with the spoon, who looked up, surprised. "That dog possesses the soul of a dear friend of mine, a friend not long dead—I recognized him by the sound of his crying voice! He has suffered enough!"[1]

Around him in the marketplace, people laughed at the ridiculous assertion. A man's soul, inside a dog? And recognizable by a whine, at that? But the philosopher was quite serious, and a few others in the crowd nodded in agreement. They had heard about the idea that Pythagoras taught his students: Souls are immortal, and they are transmitted from person to person—or from person to animal—after death.

Pythagoras's soul, some said, had once inhabited Aethalides, celebrated in Greek lore as a son of the god Hermes and as a hero who had participated in the journey of the Argonauts to find the Golden Fleece. Pythagoras also traced his soul to another famous man: Euphorbus. He was a Trojan warrior who had been responsible for the death of Achilles's companion Patroclus; he was killed by Menelaus in revenge. Less illustriously, some said that Pythagoras's soul had been a fisherman from Delos just before its latest incarnation.[2]

After tossing a coin to the fish seller and comforting the dog, Pythagoras and his friends walked back to the site of their community in Croton, a Greek colony on the east coast of southern Italy. There, the Pythagoreans formed a group of three hundred members who practiced communal living and shared property.[3] The group emphasized that "friendship is equality"[4] and included women as well as men who committed to living by the practices Pythagoras taught. Some of those practices were unusual—for example, they were forbidden to pick up crumbs from the table.[5] Other practices included vegetarianism and minimizing sexual relations, especially during warmer months. Pythagoras advised that having sex would make you weak and less healthy.[6]

Much of the Pythagoreans' way of life, however, was shrouded in secrecy. Followers practiced long periods of silence (potentially five years!).[7] Pythagoras wrote no philosophical texts himself. It seems that many of his teachings were passed down by word of mouth in this close-knit community.

In Pythagoras's youth, he left the Greek island of Samos, where he had been born in 570 BCE, the son of a jewel engraver, to study with various teachers of philosophy and religion. He learned from the work of the natural philosophers Thales and Anaximenes, but his search to understand life's mysteries took him far beyond Greece, to Egypt. According to the Greek writer Iamblichus, he spent twenty-two years there studying with priests whose knowledge spanned the religious, the mathematical, and the astronomical. He likely visited Babylon, and he might have gone further afield (some said he studied with the mythical Hyperboreans, ancient people from the far north).[8] Known as the "long-haired Samian,"[9] a nickname bestowed upon him when he was young, Pythagoras earned respect from a range of wise teachers.

He returned to Samos in about 530 BCE, when he was around forty years old, to pursue philosophy there. When confronted with the tyranny of the local ruler Polycrates, he decided to escape, and sailed to Croton. In his fifties, he began teaching in earnest, after synthesizing all he'd absorbed from his wide-reaching studies.[10]

To some, he was more than just a regular man. Legends sprang up among his followers about Pythagoras's divine attributes. Some believed he was the son of Apollo and that his father had received a prophecy about his birth from the Pythian Oracle in Delphi—hence his given name, Pythagoras.[11] Others swore that he had a golden thigh (a sign of godliness) and could communicate with natural phenomena, such as rivers, using words.[12]

In Croton, Pythagoras became a popular figure and was invited to give talks to the locals (open to men, women, and children).[13] He was said to have traveled to Greek cities in southern Italy and Sicily to encourage "a love of liberty" and to oppose slavery.[14] He and his followers exerted significant political influence, which may have ultimately contributed to his downfall. Accounts of his death indicate that local leaders became enraged with Pythagoras and his community, and he left in fear of his life. Some say he died violently after an attack by political enemies, while others suggest it was after being cut off under siege without food. The limited information we have points to his death taking place around 495 to 490 BCE in Metapontum, in southern Italy.[15]

Don't know much about Pythagoras . . .

We don't know much more about Pythagoras's life and philosophy, though that hasn't stopped people from calling themselves Pythagoreans and attributing to him all sorts of fundamental philosophical ideas, including those that were actually originated by Plato, Aristotle, and others. Indeed, over the centuries, people went so far as forging a number of treatises in the name of either Pythagoras or one of his early pupils in order to increase his fame and support whatever version of "Pythagoreanism" they wished to peddle.

There were good reasons that Pythagoras was so famous in antiquity. However, these reasons have little, if anything, to do with his still-popular image as geometer and mathematician. For instance, he very likely did not discover the celebrated theorem that bears his name, and he probably did not provide proof of it either.[16] Pythagoras's early fame was instead related to four things: his reputation for expertise on the fate of the soul after death, his knowledge of proper religious rituals for the care of the soul, his renown as a wonder-worker, and his founding of a sect that was characterized by a strict and rather unusual way of life.

That said, Pythagoras did value numbers and their relationship to the cosmos, although that aspect of the original Pythagoreanism was most likely developed by his immediate followers, particularly Philolaus (probably from Croton, 470–385 BCE) and Archytas of Tarentum (around 435/410 to 360/350 BCE). These two sides of Pythagoreanism were sufficiently distinct conceptually (and possibly materially) that later traditions referred to people practicing Pythagoreanism as a philosophy of life as *acusmatici*, from the Greek word *acusmata*, meaning "things heard," because they tried to conform their lives to a number of sayings attributed to Pythagoras. The second group was referred to as *mathematici*, a term that is rather self-explanatory. Of course, nothing would stop an acousmatic from being a mathematician, and vice versa.

Just as historians of philosophy face a "Socratic question" (because Socrates didn't write anything and we must rely on secondary sources to reconstruct his philosophy), we have a "Pythagorean question," for the same reason. Except that it's even worse with Pythagoras. Concerning Socrates, we have multiple accounts by contemporaries, chiefly Plato and Xenophon. For Pythagoras, the first fragments available to us date to 150 years after his death. By the end of the first century BCE, there were already a number of forgeries of his works in circulation, and by the third century of the common era, he had become a legend, a man to whom all that is good and interesting in philosophy was attributed, regardless of well-known historical documents attesting to the contrary.

All of this notwithstanding, scholars have been able to piece together a reasonable account of Pythagoras's life and philosophy, as well as of the multifarious evolutions of later Pythagoreanism and Neopythagoreanism, by using a judicious combination of early sources, chiefly Plato and Aristotle, and later ones, including the second-century commentator Diogenes Laërtius and the Neoplatonists Porphyry (234–305 CE) and Iamblichus (245–325 CE).

To give you a taste of the difficulty of the task, here is an example of how people have tried to glorify Pythagoras: Many in antiquity attributed to him the very invention of the word philosophy, accompanied by the notion that a philosopher is someone who does not have knowledge and yet hovers between ignorance and knowledge. Sound familiar? That's pretty much a description of Socrates, and the corresponding conception of philosophy is very obviously Platonic, not Pythagorean.

Let's take a look, then, at what we think we know of the original Pythagorean philosophy,[17] beginning with Pythagoras's conception of the soul.

Taking care of your soul

By all accounts, Pythagoras believed in metempsychosis, the doctrine of the reincarnation of the soul, as we have seen in the episode of the puppy/ recently deceased friend. Because of Pythagoras's attested use of the word *psychê* to refer to the soul, the incident tells us something fascinating about Pythagorean metaphysics. Psychê is an aspect of the soul shared by animals and humans, but not present in plants, which means that Pythagoras did *not* think we could reincarnate as plants. Moreover, psychê does not include *nous*, that is, intellect, so—unlike in Plato—it isn't the rational soul that transmigrates but the part that is defined by such emotions as pleasure and pain. Curiously, this anticipates one of the most compelling modern arguments in favor of animal welfare, the one articulated by the eighteenth-century Utilitarian philosopher Jeremy Bentham: "The question is not, Can they reason? nor, Can they talk? but, Can they suffer?"[18]

Incidentally, a story about Pythagoras that is often told is that he prohibited the consumption of beans on the grounds that one of our ancestors might be reincarnated as one such plant. This story is highly unlikely to be true. It is far more probable that, if Pythagoras indeed prohibited his students to eat beans, it referred specifically to fava beans, common in the Mediterranean area, and known to be lethal for some. Nowadays we recognize a medical condition, known as favism,[19] which affects about four hundred million people worldwide and causes thirty-three thousand annual deaths. It results from a genetic defect in the enzyme Glucose-6-Phosphate Dehydrogenase (G6PD). Certain foods, including fava beans, may trigger the effects of G6PD deficiency, which results in the destruction of red blood cells. Pythagoras, it appears, was a good observer of nature, and was onto something here.

Dicaearchus of Messana (370/350–323 BCE) was a student of Aristotle who wrote about Pythagoras in one of his books, *On Lives*. Dicaearchus tells us that Pythagoras believed that "after certain periods of time the things that have happened once happen again and nothing is absolutely new."[20] This looks like a formulation of the doctrine of eternal recurrence, which is often attributed to another pre-Socratic philosopher, Heraclitus of Ephesus, who was a major influence on the Stoics. Heraclitus and Pythagoras were roughly contemporaries, though it isn't known whether one got the idea from the other, or if they both articulated it independently. Such are the mysteries of the history of philosophy.

Miracle worker

The ancient tradition also alleges that Pythagoras performed miracles. According to the Neoplatonist Iamblichus (see chapter 13),[21] the Pythagoreans said that "of rational beings, one sort is divine, one is human, and another such as Pythagoras." It's not bad to be in one's own category, between the human and the divine!

Miracles attributed to Pythagoras include killing a serpent by biting it (!) as well as being seen at the same time in two places: the cities of Croton (modern Calabria, southern Italy) and Metapontum (modern Basilicata, southern Italy).[22] These Christlike stories about a philosopher were not unique in the Greek world. The pre-Socratic thinker Empedocles (494–434 BCE), for instance, was said to be able to teach his students how to control the winds, and even how to bring back the dead. Empedocles apparently took himself seriously enough that he died by jumping into the Etna volcano in Sicily, to make sure people believed in his divine nature.[23] However, not everyone was as enthralled with the "divine" Pythagoras. His contemporary Heraclitus referred to him as "the chief of charlatans"[24] and characterized his alleged wisdom as "fraudulent art."[25]

Divine or not, Pythagoras was credited with being an expert in religious rites, which played a very important role in Ancient Greek life. This makes sense, since he was also recognized as an expert on the afterlife: If one knows about the fate of the soul, presumably one also knows how to take care of it. Although Pythagoreanism was not a religion, members of the sect thought that religious rites were important, which is why they taught and respected them. For instance, they made sure to pour libations to the gods in specific manners, they entered temples barefoot before sacrifices, and they did not wear images of the gods on their rings.

The Pythagorean way of life

Arguably the most important aspect of Pythagorean philosophy, and the one that most concerns us here, is Pythagoreanism as a way of life, which does appear to go back to the founder of the school (not being an addition by one or more of his later pupils). As we have seen, members of the school were bound by certain practices, one of the most important of which was silence. There were also a number of doctrines that Pythagoreans were not to discuss in public, including the divine nature of Pythagoras himself. Practitioners also followed more or less arbitrary precepts, such as to avoid public roads while traveling, or to put on the right shoe first.

Several sources say that Pythagoreans were vegetarians, which makes sense in light of their beliefs in metempsychosis. Indeed, another Neoplatonist, Porphyry (chapter 13)[26] quotes the philosopher and mathematician Eudoxus (fourth century BCE), who was a student of Plato, as saying that Pythagoras "not only abstained from animal food but would also not come near butchers and hunters." However, Aristotle[27] says that when Pythagoras was asked what is most just, he replied, "to sacrifice [animals]." This need not be in contradiction to the practice of vegetarianism because of the importance of sacrificial rites in Greek religion, and because animals destined to be sacrificed were assumed not to have been chosen by the gods as vehicles for reincarnation.

One important value for Pythagoreans was friendship. Iamblichus[28] reports a likely mythological story of two friends, Damon and Phintias, who lived in Syracuse, in Sicily. The story was originally told by Aristoxenus, an

Aristotelian philosopher of the fourth century BCE. Dionysius II, tyrant of Syracuse, was envious of the friendship between Damon and Phintias, and decided to test it by falsely accusing the latter of treason and condemning him to death. Phintias accepted the injustice but asked for a reprieve in order to settle his affairs, at which point Damon volunteered to take Phintias's place, as a guarantee that the latter would actually show up for his execution. Phintias remained true to his friend and returned in time to be executed! Dionysius was properly impressed and asked to join the partnership between Damon and Phintias. He was rejected, and we are not told how he took it.

Pythagoreanism was open to women, which was also unusual for the times. Pythagoras, anticipating the Stoics, believed that women should be taught philosophy, on the (to us) very obvious ground that they are rational creatures. Iamblichus, in his *On the Pythagorean Way of Life*, compiled a catalog of known Pythagoreans, which includes seventeen women, identified by name. One of them was Theano, who lived in the sixth century BCE. She was famous enough that several books, which have not survived, were forged and then attributed to her posthumously. One fragment attributed to Theano, from her work *On Piety*, survives in a collection by Stobaeus,[29] and concerns the Pythagorean understanding of the cosmic role of numbers.

> *I have learned that many of the Greeks suppose Pythagoras said that everything came to be from number. This statement, however, poses a difficulty—how something that does not even exist is thought to beget things. But he did not say that things came to be from number, but according to number. For in number is the primary ordering, by virtue of whose presence, in the realm of things that can be counted, too, something takes its place as first, something as second, and the rest follow in order.*

Another famous Pythagorean woman was Timycha, who was a fierce member of the sect. Iamblichus[30] says that when the tyrant Dionysius (the same fellow as before) wanted her to divulge the school's secrets, she bit off her tongue to preempt the possibility that she would yield under torture.

There is one more important aspect of Pythagorean practical philosophy to consider: The Pythagoreans were very involved in politics, which caused them significant trouble (see the following). We have reports of many members of the sect becoming prominent politicians in various cities throughout Magna Graecia (the Greek-speaking areas of southern Italy), so much so that they generated enough envy to trigger bloody coups against them. This happened multiple times, both during Pythagoras's own lifetime and later on, during the middle of the fifth century BCE. According to the Greek historian Polybius (200–118 BCE), "the leading citizens of each city were destroyed,"[31] meaning that there were so many Pythagoreans in high office, and so many of them were slaughtered, that this left several cities without leadership. Practical philosophy can be a dangerous business!

Can we live like Pythagoreans today?

While there's a lack of reliable material concerning the details of Pythagoras's life and Pythagorean practices, it's clear that Pythagoreanism can accurately be called a way of life. However, it's a philosophy of life that isn't well suited for modern practice, in our view.

To be fair, doubts could also be raised about other philosophies of life we covered earlier in this book. For example, in chapter 9, we considered whether Academic Skepticism is better viewed as an attitude than as a full-fledged philosophy. And it's unlikely that Plato taught a single, dogmatic, practicable philosophy of life at the Academy. Instead, the Academy during Plato's time seemed more focused on gathering like-minded folks together to discuss and debate theoretical matters, akin to a modern research university or think tank.[32] This is one of the reasons that in chapter 6 we focused on Plato's political adventures in Syracuse instead of encouraging you to adopt a modern form of full-fledged Platonism. So why do we think that Pythagoreanism in particular isn't practicable in today's world?

In part, it has to do with the lack of reliable sources that flesh out the basis for Pythagorean practices. There's a dearth of well-founded material concerning Pythagoras, his beliefs, and his followers' way of life. We have a decent amount of information concerning some of their practices, but many of them seem quite arbitrary, such as never picking up crumbs from a table and putting your right shoe on first. It's possible that these practices have solid foundations in Pythagorean theory, but it's nearly impossible to see it based on the available evidence. Of course, there were other admirable aspects of the Pythagorean way of life that don't require as much justification, such as the emphasis on friendship and attempts to become politically involved. However, we've already explored these aspects in chapter 2 (Epicurus was big on friendship!) and chapter 6 (which focused on Plato's political involvement), respectively.

A second reason for thinking that Pythagoreanism isn't practicable in today's world is that those aspects of the Pythagorean life that have clear justification rely on mystical metaphysics as their basis. The clearest example of this is Pythagoras's justification for abhorring animal cruelty, which was based on metempsychosis, or reincarnation of the soul. Of course, if you believe in reincarnation, you could modify this idea and make it into a practice to help you be more compassionate. One way to do this would be to actively imagine a deceased loved one's soul inhabiting the bodies of people you find difficult: If you imagine difficult people as being those you care about, this could naturally generate more sympathy for them. However, this kind of practice would be challenging for people who find reincarnation implausible.

Another metaphysical belief that could be hard to swallow is Pythagoras's concepts about numbers and their relationship to the cosmos. Just as with reincarnation, some people believe in the power of numerology, such as Kabbalists and practitioners of feng shui. However, unlike reincarnation, there may be lessons from Pythagoras's interest in numbers from which both mystical and scientifically minded readers can learn something. These lessons come from the (probably fabricated)[33] story of Pythagoras's hammers.[34] According to the first-century Neopythagorean Nicomachus,[35] Pythagoras was deep in thought, pondering how to devise an instrument to measure musical pitches exactly. Inspiration struck when he walked by a blacksmith's shop and noted that most of the sounds of four hammers striking anvils harmonized with each other, while one particular pair of hammers didn't. He recognized the harmonious sounds as being the octave, fourth, and fifth of the musical scale. Rushing into the shop, he discovered through some experimentation that the notes the hammers produced were generated only from the weight of the hammers. He then raced back home to reproduce these tones by hanging weights from strings. The weights' ratios were similar to the hammers he heard earlier. This ultimately led him to invent an instrument called the monochord, which was so important to Pythagoras that his dying wish was that his students study music with it![36]

Pythagoras's excitement could plausibly be traced to his belief that numbers had corporeal substance: By noticing and replicating patterns produced by ratios, he may have thought that he was able to peer into the fabric of reality itself.[37] However, you needn't believe such things yourself in order to take away some lessons from the story: Being curious about the natural order of things around you, paying careful attention, and testing the implications[38] of your ideas and worldview can pay both spiritual and practical dividends.

REFLECTION

Since the philosophies presented in this final section of the book are a bit different from the others, we'll take a different approach in guiding you through their practical implications. Instead of leading you through five days' worth of exercises, we'll prompt you to explore some aspects of each philosophy that we think may be practical. You're welcome to use one or more—or none!—of the prompts in your exploration. The goal is to provide you space to discover those aspects of the philosophy you think could be useful or to justify why the philosophy doesn't resonate with you.

- Recall the story of Pythagoras and the abused dog that started this chapter off. Pythagoras intervened because of a metaphysical belief: that the dog had the soul of a recently deceased friend. Describe at least one metaphysical belief you hold and how it determines some of your ethical beliefs. Some metaphysical beliefs that could influence your ethics include the existence or nonexistence of God and whether objective morality exists.

- Recall that the Pythagoreans put a heavy emphasis on a specific notion of friendship: "friendship is equality." This was exemplified by the story of Damon and Phintias—who apparently valued each other's lives as much as they valued their own—and evidenced by the fact that all property was communal. If you agree with this notion of friendship, explain why. If you don't, spell out your notion of friendship.

- The Pythagoreans were heavily persecuted for their political involvement. Under what circumstances would you find it acceptable to be persecuted for political activism? Where would you draw a line and avoid politics if it meant being persecuted?

_____

_____

_____

_____

_____

_____

_____

Finally, in the space that follows, make a list of Pythagorean ideas, practices, or activities that you may find useful in your own life.

_____

_____

_____

_____

_____

_____

_____

_____

Chapter 12

STILPO THE MEGARIAN

For Stilpo, after his country was captured and his children and his wife lost, as he emerged from the general desolation alone and yet happy, spoke as follows to Demetrius, called Sacker of Cities because of the destruction he brought upon them, in answer to the question whether he had lost anything: "I have all my goods with me!"

—Seneca, Letters, 9.18

T he bearded men gathered around the old philosopher, forming a circle. This time, they weren't there to debate him—a frequent pursuit that the older man quite enjoyed—but to learn from him. Stilpo the Megarian had managed to steal these Greek philosophy students away from other famous philosophical schools and now counted them as his own.

Stilpo surveyed the group one by one. "It was a wise choice to give up my youthful devotion to wine and voluptuous living and to devote myself to philosophy instead—where I've found far finer friends!"[1] Stilpo said. He turned his head in the direction of the sole woman seated among them: Nicarete, a former courtesan and a philosophy student in her own right, who lived with Stilpo as his companion.

She nodded and flashed a smile. "Yes, very fortunate indeed. Who knows where that dissolute living might have landed you," she said. The men laughed.

"Well, Nicarete, have no fear." Stilpo waved his hand about his home's inner courtyard and said, "You know that none of this really belongs to me. I make my way through life with just one thing I work to preserve: my mind, and the virtues that emanate from it."[2]

Stilpo the Megarian was not just any teacher. He was the man who had inspired all of Greece to "Megarize"—to speak in his philosophical style—after he left behind his libertine youth, as well as his training as a Cynic.[3]

As Stilpo developed his own philosophy, he gained students from around Athens. He attracted several who had left the Lyceum (the school founded by Aristotle) to join him, including Metrodorus, Timagoras, Clitarchus, Simmias, and another Aristotle, this one from Cyrene. He also counted Paeonius, a defector from the Dialecticians, among his followers.[4] He apparently taught the philosopher Pyrrho of Elis (chapter 10) as well.[5]

His biggest coup, perhaps, was persuading Zeno of Citium—later the founder of Stoicism—to leave Crates the Cynic (the husband of Hipparchia; see chapter 5) to become his pupil. Zeno studied under Stilpo for ten years. He even taunted his former master, Crates, saying that rather than trying to drag him away from Stilpo by his cloak, Crates would do better to try to grab Zeno in the same way the eloquent Stilpo had done. Zeno said, "Crates, the clever way to seize a philosopher is by his ears. So persuade me and drag me away by them. For if you use violence, my body will be with you, but my mind with Stilpo."[6]

Born in West Attica sometime between 380 and 360 BCE, Stilpo didn't operate by the book. He didn't mind when critics told him that people, especially the working men of Athens who liked to come out to see him speak, found him to be a "strange beast." To those critics, Stilpo simply replied, "They come to see me not as a beast, but as a genuine man."[7]

Stilpo was true to himself, unafraid to say things that seemed outrageous, yet he managed to gain others' respect along the way. He often won over those who debated him, and some became his keen admirers. Those included not just his students, but also a Greek orator, Alcimus, and a natural philosopher, Phrasidemus the Peripatetic, according to the ancient biographer Diogenes Laërtius. At times, Stilpo seemed to cast doubt on the holiness of the gods, but managed to get away with it.[8]

Though nine dialogues were attributed to him, only a few very short fragments of Stilpo's written work have survived.[9] He lived to be an old man and died around 280 BCE.

One, two, three schools?

Modern scholars are divided on whether there was a single Megarian school or more than one.[10] Regardless, they were some of the most influential and yet mysterious philosophical sects of the Hellenistic period. The Megarians are associated with Euclid (435–365 BCE) and Stilpo (360–280 BCE), both hailing from Megara. A second school, the Dialecticians, is often linked to Diodorus Cronus, who died around 284 BCE. Yet another possible school, the Eristics, is said to have been started by Eubulides of Miletus, and flourished in the fourth century BCE.

The Megarians were known for focusing on ethics, the Dialecticians on practical logic, and the Eristics on logical puzzles and paradoxes. The historical record is scarce, so much so that we don't have basic biographical details of some of the major players. For the purposes of our discussion here, we will treat the Megarians-Dialecticians-Eristics trio as one school, possibly characterized by three phases, or preoccupied with different but overlapping subjects, depending on which particular philosopher we consider at any given time.

Euclid of Megara (not to be confused with Euclid of Alexandria, the Greek mathematician known for his work on geometry) was one of Socrates's close associates, and Plato tells us that he was present at Socrates's death, in 399 BCE. After that unfortunate episode in the history of philosophy, Euclid moved back to Megara, where he welcomed and sheltered Socrates's former students, including Plato.

Stilpo may or may not have been Euclid's student (most likely not, if their reported dates of birth and death are correct). He was known for his integrity and patience, not to mention his formidable skills at debating other philosophers. When Megara was sacked and Stilpo lost everything, his reputation was such that Demetrius, who had conquered the city, offered Stilpo compensation for damages incurred. Stilpo replied that he had everything that was truly good with him, meaning his virtue,[11] a response that would have befitted both a Cynic (chapter 5) and a Stoic (chapter 4).

Diodorus was also a fascinating character, celebrated for his dialectical skills. He had five daughters: Argia, Artemesia, Menexene, Pantaclea, and Theognis. Remarkably for the time, Diodorus taught philosophy to all of them, and they all became well-known dialecticians in their own right.

We know little of Eubulides, except that he was a contemporary of Aristotle and that he wrote several critical treatises against Peripateticism. He has the distinction of having taught logic to the great Athenian orator Demosthenes, as well as having been the teacher of Apollonius Cronus, who in turn taught Diodorus Cronus (who, it is said, inherited his last name from his master). Eubulides is credited with the invention of a number of well-known logical paradoxes, including the Liar and the Sorites (which we'll cover later in this chapter).

Regardless of how many schools and major figures there were, the Megarians are historically crucial, since they influenced major successive schools, especially Stoicism. Zeno the Stoic was apparently taught by both Stilpo and Diodorus Cronus. Since Stilpo himself was strongly influenced by the Cynics (and possibly taught by the legendary Diogenes of Sinope), this goes a long way toward explaining why it is reasonable to think of Stoicism, at least early on, as a syncretic school merging influences from the Cynics, the Megarians, and, if they existed as a separate entity, the Dialecticians.

The only real thing is the Good

What did Megarian-Dialectician-Eristics philosophy actually consist of? Let's begin with their epistemology (theory of knowledge) and resulting metaphysics (understanding of the world), before moving on to logic and paradoxes.

In a sense, Euclid united Socrates's search for knowledge with the earlier so-called Eleatic (named after the pre-Socratics Parmenides and Zeno, both from Elea) emphasis on reason. According to the Megarians, we have two types of perception: sensual and rational. The first allows us to grasp the constantly changing world of phenomena, while the second one gives us access to the world of unchanging and universal truths.

These philosophers, like Plato, also thought that universal truths are real, while changing phenomena are a reflection of the true reality and are therefore of inferior quality, so to speak. They argued that matter, of which ordinary phenomena appear to be made, does not exist. That's because its constituents are infinitely divisible (thus rejecting Democritus's concept of "atoms," which was the basis of Epicurean metaphysics), and this means that, in a sense, matter is a passing phenomenon, not a fundamental constituent of reality. This may sound very strange, and yet some modern physicists and philosophers have argued that there are, at the bottom, no "things," that is, no objects, only relations between points in space, a notion referred to as structural realism.[12] While it is a stretch to think of the Megarians as structural realists, it is no more of a stretch than referring to the Atomists and Epicureans as forerunners of the modern view of matter. Indeed, if anything, the Megarians got closer to contemporary understanding!

If everyday phenomena and even matter itself is not truly real, then what is? According to the Megarians, one thing and one thing only—and we call that thing by a variety of names: the Good, Reason, God. This sounds very Platonic, but even more, it is very Parmenidean: It was the pre-Socratic Parmenides who first described two views of reality: the way of *Aletheia* (truth) and the way of *Doxa* (opinion). *Aletheia* describes a timeless world consisting of a single unchanging universal, while *doxa* refers to the changing world of phenomena. Indeed, Zeno of Elea formulated his famous paradoxes (such as Achilles and the tortoise) precisely in order to defend Parmenides's apparently indefensible notion that time is an illusion.[13] And it was Parmenides's views that later influenced Plato.

Paradoxes, paradoxes!

Speaking of Zeno of Elea, the Megarians and their associates deployed an approach first pioneered by the Eleatics whenever they wanted to argue against an opponent. Instead of doing what is standard in logic, that is, attacking the premises of an argument to maintain that the conclusions do not follow, they attacked the conclusions, attempting to show that they were absurd. This approach, known to us as *reductio ad absurdum* (literally, reduction to absurdity) is still used in philosophy and rhetoric today.

One famous example of Megarian-inspired reasoning is the Sorites paradox, from the Greek word *sōrós*, meaning "heap." It is attributed to either

Euclid or Eubulides, and it goes like this.

> *Premise 1: 1,000,000 grains of sand is a heap of sand.*
> *Premise 2: A heap of sand minus one grain is still a heap.*
> *Sequential steps: If 1,000,000 grains is a heap, then 999,999 grains*
> *is a heap.*
> *So, 999,999 grains is a heap.*
> *If 999,999 grains is a heap, then 999,998 grains is a heap.*
> *So, 999,998 grains is a heap.*
> *If . . . so . . .*
> *Conclusion: So, 1 grain is a heap.*

The conclusion is, obviously, absurd. And yet the premises seem as solid as they come. The paradox is meant to highlight that there is something missing either in our conception of heaps, or in the sequential steps, or in both. It shows that some concepts, such as that of a heap, do not admit of clear-cut definitions but are instead based on an underlying reality that can best be described as a continuum. Paradoxes like this eventually prompted logicians to go beyond classical, Aristotelian logic and adopt such alternatives as many-valued or fuzzy logics.

The Stoic logician Chrysippus responded to the Sorites paradox by saying that at some unspecified point it becomes clear that the "heap" is no longer such, and that it behooves us to halt the sequence safely before that point is reached. Some modern scholars have suggested that this indicates that Chrysippus was aware of what is nowadays called the problem of higher-order vagueness.[14] Either that, or Chrysippus was making fun of Eubulides.

The Master Argument

One major piece of philosophical work for which the Megarians were famous, and through which they influenced other schools, especially the Stoics, was the so-called Master Argument, attributed to Diodorus Cronus. It says that of the following three propositions, only two (at most) can be true.[15]

i) **Past truths are necessary.** If something happened in the past, it was bound to happen.

ii) **Nothing impossible follows from something possible.** Just because it is possible to fly, it doesn't follow that human beings can fly.

iii) **Something is possible which neither is nor will be true.** It is possible that I'd be in Rome tomorrow, but it turns out I won't.

Modern logicians are uncertain about whether the three propositions are truly partially incompatible with each other; unfortunately, Diodorus's proof for this has not survived. But assuming it is the case that all three of them cannot be true at the same time, the ancients disagreed (for very important practical reasons) about which of the three propositions had to be abandoned.

Diodorus himself argued for the rejection of iii, which means that what is possible is limited to what either is or will be true at some point in the future. The second head of the Stoa, Cleanthes of Assos, rather strangely preferred to reject i, making past truths contingent rather than necessary. Finally, the third head of the Stoa, Chrysippus of Soli, rejected ii.

Chrysippus's move is interesting because it means that he retains the necessity of the past (unlike Cleanthes), as well as the notion that there are things which are possible but do not happen (unlike Diodorus). This amounts to introducing a distinction between two types of necessity: metaphysical (all things are fated and predetermined by antecedent causes) and logical (some things are logically possible but do not happen).

Why is this important? Because it is at the core of the Stoic argument for what nowadays is called compatibilism[16] between the apparently contradictory notions of determinism and free will. Chrysippus's idea was that we are part and parcel of a cosmic web of cause-and-effect relations, and that when we make a decision, it is "ours" in the very real sense that it is generated by our internal decision-making machinery (our nervous system, especially the executive function of the brain, in modern parlance). Even though our decisions are determined by cause and effect, we are still responsible for making them, since they originate in us. The Megarian perspective attributed to Diodorus, that there is no distinction between what is possible and what must happen, would seem to eliminate the compatibilist notion of free will, and therefore would do away with ethical responsibility.

Can we live like Megarians today?

Although the Megarians were a loose movement, it's possible to view it as a way of life. After all, Stilpo was renowned for his resilience and integrity, and he seemed to have used philosophy to overcome his overindulgence in wine and sex. Furthermore, the Megarians concerned themselves with the nature of the good. Finally, Euclid of Megara was closely associated with Socrates, and many of Socrates's students went on to found their own practical philosophies, so it would be strange for Euclid to be the odd one out. Nonetheless, we're not confident that becoming a modern Megarian is viable for a few reasons.

The first reason is that we have very little evidence about who the Megarians were, what they believed, and—most important—how they lived their philosophy (if they did at all). The historical record is scarce, so we can't guide you in the particulars of the Megarian way of life. For example, it's quite possible that the Megarian notion of the unity of the good (see page 243) and the nonexistence of anything that's not good[17] may have had some practical implications for how the Megarians lived. However, for lack of evidence, we're not clear on what these implications would be.

Although our ancient sources tell us that Stilpo reaped the fruits of philosophical practice, these fruits may have very well arisen from the same soil as Cynicism. Recall that Stilpo possibly trained as a Cynic, and thus his famous resilience and self-control may be due more to his exposure to Cynicism than to Megarianism proper. And even if it were not, much of Megarian philosophy is represented by Stoicism (chapter 4). So any unique aspects of a possible Megarian ethical practice are either lost to time or incorporated in other philosophies we've already explored.

Some aspects of Megarian practice are still available to us in the form of their logic, epistemology, and paradoxes. But, in our view, these aren't enough on which to found a modern practice. One could possibly say the same thing about the Academic Skeptics, but we have one notable example in Cicero—an Academic Skeptic who largely (but not completely) took up Stoic ethics as a way of life while modifying it to suit Academic epistemology. It's possible that Stilpo did a similar thing with Cynicism, but if so, we don't know anything about it. Plus, we have a more fleshed-out example in the form of Stoicism. (Recall that Stoicism's founder—Zeno of Citium—studied with both Stilpo and Diodorus Cronus.) Logic is an important part of Stoic philosophy, but its connection to Stoic ethics is much more apparent than the theoretical connection between Megarian epistemology and ethics.

Finally, it's possible that large swaths of what we're calling Megarians—in particular, the so-called Dialecticians and Eristics—didn't really use philosophy in a practical way. Ancient practitioners of this philosophy seem more renowned for their skills in debate (after all, "eristic" means something like "strife-makers") than for seeking to improve their own character, at least in the literature that still survives today.

REFLECTION

Now it's your turn to chart these unnavigated waters to see if there are any particular ideas that resonate with you. As with the last chapter, we'll provide a list of prompts that can provide some guidance, but you're welcome to write about other ways you think Megarian philosophy may—or may not—be useful to you. Remember: The goal is simply to explore ideas that you can glean from this philosophy!

- When Stilpo chose to replace his "youthful devotion to wine and voluptuous living" with philosophy, he made "far finer friends and companions." Do you think you would benefit from replacing some hobbies or activities with others in a similar way? If so, lay out a plan.

- Recall that the Megarians held that matter doesn't really exist; only the Good/Reason/God does. And this can be understood only by rational, not sensual, perception. Do you believe that ethical truths can be derived from reason alone? Or do we need "sensual perception" to discover facts about the world that can't be obtained solely through rational analysis? Defend your answer, focusing on how you think we can know what's good and what's not.

- If you think it isn't worth investing time in paradoxes like the Master Argument and the Sorites paradox, defend your view. But if you think there's something useful to be gained from studying such paradoxes, what is it?

_____

_____

_____

_____

_____

_____

_____

Use the space that follows to catalog any specific ideas from the Megarians that you found interesting or useful.

_____

_____

_____

_____

_____

_____

_____

_____

Chapter 13

HYPATIA THE NEOPLATONIST

Because she was skilled and articulate in her speech and wise and politically virtuous in her actions, the city seemingly loved her and particularly prostrated itself before her and the governors always greeted her first when they came into the city.

—Damascius, *The Life of Isidore*, 43E,
cited in Edward J. Watts's *Hypatia: The Life and Legend of an Ancient Philosopher*

I t was evening, and Hypatia's students had left for the day. Clothed in a tribon—a coarse, simple philosopher's cloak—Hypatia sat in her study, intent on her work, her long hair swept up in a bun. She made calculations with an astrolabe, a delicate metal tool designed to estimate the positions of stars and planets. Her head bent, Hypatia dipped her reed pen in ink and purposefully wrote figures that nearly filled the papyrus scroll in front of her.

It had been a long day for the philosopher, beginning in the morning with numerous citizens of Alexandria gathered outside her door to ask for guidance on their disputes and difficulties. She then gave a public lecture on Plato and Aristotle, and finally, in the late afternoon, held a private seminar on astronomy.[1] Hypatia was a singular figure in this Roman city of five hundred thousand people[2] situated at the edge of Egypt—the rare woman who ran her own school of philosophy, published books on mathematics, spoke publicly about complex ideas, and whose guidance was valued by her fellow Alexandrians.

Suddenly, a servant came running into her study. "My lady, Governor Orestes is here to see you!"

"Show him in," she replied, setting down her pen.

"Hypatia, I have come again for your advice," said the Roman prefect as he entered with his two armed guards. He sat across from Hypatia and looked earnestly in her direction. The conflict in the city had reached a boiling point, as Orestes was acutely aware. Angry factions of Christians, Jews, and pagans threatened and even murdered each other in the streets. The Christian Patriarch of Alexandria, Cyril, sought to take advantage of that anger as a way to gain more power. Orestes, also a Christian, stood against him, and he relied on Hypatia as a pagan ally.

"Alexandria is in chaos. Your wisdom is sorely needed to help restore it to order," Orestes pleaded. It wasn't the first time that Orestes had visited Hypatia. She was accustomed to consulting with Alexandria's leadership, whether they were Christian, Jewish, or pagan. She was open to all who sought wisdom, from leaders to students to everyday Alexandrians.[3]

Now that she was in her sixties, all of her students were Christians— the dominant religious group in Alexandria. It hadn't always been that way. When Hypatia was born, in 355 CE in Alexandria, the majority of the city had been pagans—like Hypatia and her family—who worshiped a combination of Greek, Roman, and Egyptian deities. Her father, Theon, a mathematician and philosopher, had been one of the last members of the celebrated Museum, a place of worship for the cult of the Muses. The Museum had been host to numerous researchers in literature, philosophy, and science, and was home to the renowned Alexandrian Royal Library, which in its prime held nearly five hundred thousand papyrus rolls. In that atmosphere, Hypatia collaborated with her father on mathematical books, including a thirteen-book commentary on Ptolemy's *Almagest*.[4]

As Hypatia grew in wisdom and in years, both the Museum and the Royal Library were destroyed in a civil war (both were gone by the mid-third-century).[5] Then another of Alexandria's pagan places of worship and study, the

Serapeum, also the site of a major library, was destroyed by a Christian mob in 392 CE with the tacit complicity of Roman leaders.

But Hypatia carried on. Her style of Neoplatonism did not explicitly go against the Christian thinking of her day. Her approach was in keeping with the Neoplatonist Plotinus's method of seeking "the One"—a divine force at the center of the universe—through contemplation and purification. This spiritual and intellectual practice stood in contrast to the rituals and animal sacrifices central to other forms of Neoplatonism, which may well have offended Christians. Her teachings began with mathematics, which was of intellectual interest to people of all religious backgrounds; she made the case that math was the first rung of advanced study, followed by the more advanced field of philosophy. And along with her Plato-inspired ideals, she felt that a philosopher had a duty to help her or his city and its leaders live by philosophical principles whenever possible.[6] That approach informed her desire to assist her visitor Orestes.

"Orestes, I'll do my best to make progress toward harmony," Hypatia said. "We can convene the city's key leaders and ask them to put aside their petty power struggles to contemplate what is truly valuable—a higher form of justice."

"I fear it may be too late for that," said the Roman leader. "Look at what one of the Patriarch Cyril's rabid monks did to me," he said, pointing to a large gash in his forehead, still fresh. The unrest among Christians had begun to reach a fever pitch as Cyril fought for supremacy over his rivals, aiming for control of the church and its networks of monks and followers.

Hypatia turned away from Orestes's wound, shaken by this physical evidence of human hatred and the body's frailty. She, like others who followed Neoplatonic ideals, sought to rise above the limitations (as well as the desires) of the human body—and to seek out the higher plane of the spiritual world instead.

In fact, her rejection of male attraction to her own body had become legendary. A famous story circulated about a student who had become enamored of her physical beauty and pursued her. She rejected his advances, but he kept at it. Hypatia then used her lyre to try to soothe him with music in the Pythagorean style, but to no avail. Ultimately, she dramatically showed him a menstrual rag, symbolizing the physical impurities of the body, and told him, "It is this that you love, not something beautiful."[7] The man promptly reconsidered.

Hypatia preferred to live in celibacy, and she and her students, including Synesius—who later became a Christian bishop—felt attached to each other through a nonsexual love.[8] That love among the members of her inner circle could only take her so far. Unfortunately for Hypatia, Governor Orestes was right. Hypatia was publicly accused of driving a wedge between Orestes and Cyril to prolong the dispute and, even more seriously, of practicing magic and "bewitching" Orestes.

In March 415 CE, Hypatia (who lacked the armed guards that protected Orestes) was violently pulled from her carriage and dragged into a Christian church. She was killed there by a riotous mob of Christian followers of Cyril, at the instigation of a lector named Peter. The crowd tore her body apart with broken roof tiles and eventually burned her remains.[9] Her brutal death was mourned by many in the ancient world. Hypatia's memory is honored today in historical accounts, novels, films, and the title of a modern journal of feminist philosophy.[10]

The last form of Platonism

Hypatia was a Neoplatonist. But what, exactly, is Neoplatonism? It was the last of the major Hellenistic philosophies to develop, beginning with Plotinus of Lycopolis (modern Egypt) in the third century of the common era, that is, almost seven centuries after Plato. Of course, at the time Neoplatonists would not have called themselves that. As far as they were concerned, they were just Platonists.[11]

The story of Neoplatonism begins with Plotinus (204–270), continues with his student Porphyry of Tyre (modern Lebanon, 234–305), and then with Porphyry's own student, Iamblichus of Chalcis (modern Syria, 245–325). It ends with the late flourishing of the Academies in Athens and Alexandria during the fifth and sixth centuries and the figure of Proclus of Constantinople (412–485). A few decades after Proclus's death, the Byzantine Christian emperor Justinian closed the Academy, and all the other schools in 529, thus inaugurating the Dark Age.* Interestingly, it was a revival of interest in Neoplatonism that

---

* "Dark Age" is a term no longer used by modern historians. But we are echoing the opinion of the Tuscan scholar Petrarch, who coined the term in the 1330s, and who was instrumental in the Renaissance that brought the Middle Ages to an end.

contributed to the Renaissance of the fifteenth century. But that, obviously, is another story.

Neoplatonist metaphysics has a strong mystical flavor, and much of it is counterintuitive by modern standards. Nevertheless, let's see if we can make some sense of it. Plotinus[12] recognizes three fundamental metaphysical principles: the One (also called the Good), the Intellect, and the Soul. Notice the capital letters, indicating universal principles, as distinct from individual instantiations of such principles in specific beings or aspects of the cosmos.

The One is self-caused and is itself the cause of everything else in the cosmos. The Intellect, in turn, derives from the One. It engages in contemplation, and such contemplation generates a number of distinct thoughts, which are the famous Forms that Plato talks about in three of his dialogues: *Phaedo*, *Republic*, and *Phaedrus*.

The Soul is the principle that originates desires, so everything that has a soul—including plants, animals, and of course, human beings—acts out of desire and seeks external things, like food, water, sleep, and so on. In a sense, the Soul is the source of our troubles, because it often makes the error of valuing externals over contemplation, which is how Plotinus explained the origin of evil. It is the activity of the Soul that produces individual souls, such as our own. These individual souls, metaphysically speaking, are the actualizations of the potential inherent in the Forms generated by the Intellect.

According to Plotinus, a rational soul always chooses the Good, but when the soul forgets what it is, or otherwise becomes ignorant of its own nature, it engages in evil. Salvation, then, comes not from faith or prayer but from dialectic engagement, that is, from philosophical investigation.

One way to look at Plotinus's philosophy is that it achieved a synthesis of the original Platonism and Aristotelianism, meaning that he took Plato's mythical stories (such as those in *Timaeus*) and filtered them through Aristotelian logic to arrive at a coherent, if complex, system of metaphysics and ethics. Accordingly, scholars sometimes consider Plotinus the last true representative of the Greek philosophical spirit, before the final advent of Christianity.

One of Plotinus's goals was to defend Platonism from the encroachment of both Orthodox Christianity and Gnosticism,[13] an early form of Christian theology that was making inroads at the time. According to the Gnostics (a word that means "having knowledge"), salvation comes from personal spiritual knowledge, not from orthodox teachings. You can see why they were declared heretics by other Christians, were accordingly persecuted, and their books largely destroyed.

For the Gnostics, the world is characterized by two principles (instead of three as in Plotinus): God and a malevolent lesser divinity known as the Demiurge, who is responsible for creating matter. (Demiurge is also the word used by Plato to indicate the entity that created the world out of the available materials, and it means "craftsman" or "artisan.") For the Gnostics, God and spirit are good, of course, while the Demiurge and matter are evil. They didn't talk about sin and repentance, as did what later became mainstream Christianity, but of illusion and enlightenment. Misguided people lack knowledge, so they live in the thralls of illusions about the world. If and when they acquire knowledge, they achieve enlightenment.

Neoplatonism after Plotinus

The next big figure in Neoplatonism is Plotinus's student, Porphyry.[14] He had a stint as a Christian, so much so that Saint Augustine talks of him as if he were an apostate. Porphyry had a broad range of interests, including music and astronomy, and he wrote a biography of Pythagoras. He thought that the soul could ascend to higher levels of existence through the practice of virtue in the form of good works. This is interesting because it means that salvation is a gradual process, as opposed to Plotinus's idea that it could be the result of an instantaneous enlightenment achieved by philosophical reflection. Porphyry believed in astrology, which was popular throughout the Hellenistic period. He thought that astrology was a way to help the soul orient itself toward its place in the cosmos, which would somehow speed up salvation.

Iamblichus,[15] the third major Neoplatonic figure, was, in turn, a student of Porphyry, and therefore a "grand-student" of Plotinus. He made a bit of a mess out of Plotinus's metaphysics, likely because he did not understand it. Iamblichus thought that there is a Supreme One even higher than Plotinus's One, which seems like metaphysical overkill. He also, again unnecessarily, divided Soul into three components: cosmic, rational, and irrational.

Not content with these complications to the Neoplatonist system, Iamblichus posited a series of intermediate beings, including demons, angels, and the souls of heroes. The idea was that we can invoke such beings to help us toward salvation. He also established the practice of theurgy, or divine magic, whereby the soul is helped by ritualistic acts that somehow transcend the alleged limits of reason, again all in the service of speeding up salvation. Oh, and Iamblichus also wrote a biography of Pythagoras, a figure that Neoplatonists regarded highly on account of his penchant for mysticism.

The last great Neoplatonist was Proclus.[16] He was a religious universalist, meaning that he saw something valuable in all religions. And he put his money where his mouth was, managing to get initiated into all the mystery religions that were current at the time. While for Plotinus the Intellect stems from the One, for Proclus the Intellect is the culmination of the activity of the One, though it isn't clear exactly what that means. For Proclus, unlike for Plotinus, matter is not evil.

The very last name that the historical record associates with Neoplatonism is that of Pseudo-Dionysius,[17] who was active in the late fifth century. He attempted to reconcile Platonism and Christianity, but Justinian was about to close the Academy, thus ringing down the curtain on the entirety of antiquity.

Can we live like Neoplatonists today?

Neoplatonism was certainly a coherent (if mystical) life philosophy, and its adherents practiced the philosophy as a way of life. For example, the life of Plotinus was a simple, contemplative one in which he ate plant-based foods[18] and practiced moderate asceticism in order to curb his desire for the mere material and clear the way for higher "purificatory" virtues. This, in turn, was meant to achieve a "likeness to God."[19] And therein lies the rub. Just like the Pythagoreans, the Neoplatonic way of life leans heavily on a mystical metaphysics that would be hard for many of us to adopt wholesale.

But in a loose sense, many people today live in accordance with some aspects of Neoplatonism, since the philosophy had a massive impact on many domains of modern thought. If you're a Christian, some of what you believe could be traced to Neoplatonism, either because Christianity adopted aspects of it, or because it changed in reaction to it. For instance, the apophatic nature of God (being able to speak only about what God is *not*—God is without limits) can be traced in part to Origen, who shared a teacher with Plotinus. And Augustine's concept of an immutable God can arguably be linked to Neoplatonic thought as well.[20]

Neoplatonism also had a major influence on Sufism.[21] And some of the early Jewish Kabbalists were explicitly Neoplatonist,[22] with the *sefirot** being strongly influenced by the Neoplatonic theory of emanation.[23] Some scholars have even argued that it was the Hellenistic-Jewish philosophy of Philo of Alexandria that laid the groundwork for Plotinus's invention of Neoplatonism![24]

Thus, all the Abrahamic religions have been touched by Neoplatonism. Not only that, but modern occultism, which can trace its roots to the nineteenth century, again has a strong Neoplatonic influence. For example, Helena Blavatsky's activities at the Theosophical Society leaned heavily on Neoplatonism.[25] And the Hermetic Order of The Golden Dawn explicitly practiced theurgy. Contemporary occultists are still strongly influenced by Neoplatonism, and some of them are attempting to elaborate on ancient techniques.[26]

Modern occultists' expansion of Neoplatonic techniques is necessary for those who wish to actually put Neoplatonism into practice, since there's so little information in the ancient literature detailing exercises. Scholars have sketched out aspects of such a practice, such as "paying attention to the objects of mind" to help concentrate the soul, but the details of how to actually achieve this are opaque.[27] Some have even speculated that Eastern-style meditation may have played a role in Neoplatonic practice.[28] However, the paucity of evidence concerning Neoplatonic contemplative techniques is one more reason that we've mapped this philosophy in the dark, uncharted seas.

That said, if the occult or the mystical piques your fancy, perhaps exploring Neoplatonism for yourself would be worthwhile. Plotinus's *Enneads* are beautifully written, if somewhat baffling at times. Attempting to digest the *Enneads* could be viewed in a certain light as a spiritual exercise in itself.

---

* *Sefirot* (plural; singular is *sefirah*) are a set of ten emanations that (to oversimplify) describe how God is revealed in the world and how the physical and metaphysical are generated. It's a major idea in Kabbalah.

REFLECTION

Here is your final set of prompts to help you reflect on aspects of Neoplatonism.

- If you hold a mystical or religious worldview, in what ways is Neoplatonism similar to your views, and in what ways is it different? If you are more atheistically or scientifically minded, describe at least one aspect of Neoplatonism that accords with your worldview.

- Recall that Porphyry's take on Neoplatonism implied that ethical and spiritual progress occurs more gradually, whereas Plotinus believed in something more akin to instant enlightenment. Which viewpoint do you agree with more: that moral/spiritual progress occurs quickly, or gradually? Why? What do you think causes this kind of progress in you? Do some experiences (challenging life circumstances, specific spiritual experiences) allow for rapid spiritual or moral progress? If so, what are they? Have you experienced any?

- Proclus believed that all religions have value. If you are religious, do you agree? Why or why not? If you are not religious, feel free to reflect instead on whether all philosophies have some value. If you're not sure what you think about practicing religion, what parts of religion interest you or have value?

_____

_____

_____

_____

_____

_____

_____

_____

Finally, catalog any interesting or practicable ideas from the Neoplatonists in the space that follows.

_____

_____

_____

_____

_____

_____

_____

_____

_____

_____

_____

_____

_____

_____

_____

_____

_____

EPILOGUE

Over the course of your journey, you've visited three ports and explored unknown waters. Now it's time to choose your own destination. This choice may be daunting; after all, we've covered several hundreds of years' worth of Greco-Roman thought and practices over the course of this book. But don't fret. In the following, we'll help you make sense of what you've learned and think through where you can take your own practice in a few steps.

Step 1: Review your logs

We left space at the end of each chapter to allow you to write out your thoughts concerning each philosophy of life we've covered. Now's the time to put those thoughts to use.

Go back over your notes and take some time to consider your impression of each philosophy. Then consolidate your thoughts in the chart that follows.

1. Rate each philosophy of life by circling the appropriate emoji. Did you find the philosophy useful (😃), so-so (😐), or not useful (🙁)?

   Perhaps you skipped over some chapters. That's not a problem. If you skipped a chapter because you knew it wouldn't be helpful for you, mark the philosophy with a 🙁 . If you skipped it because of lack of time or because you were more interested in other philosophies, consider going back and working through the philosophy you skipped before you proceed.

2. Briefly summarize the ideas you found particularly useful or inspiring for each philosophy.

If you skipped the chapter or found the philosophy a complete mismatch for you, leave this blank.

3. Briefly summarize the practices for each philosophy that were particularly impactful for you. If none were, leave this blank.

PORT OF PLEASURE	
Cyrenaicism (Ch. 1) 😀 😐 ☹️	Epicureanism (Ch. 2) 😀 😐 ☹️
Favorite ideas:	Favorite ideas:
Favorite exercises:	Favorite exercises:

PORT OF CHARACTER			
Aristotelianism (Ch. 3) 😀 😐 ☹️	Stoicism (Ch. 4) 😀 😐 ☹️	Cynicism (Ch. 5) 😀 😐 ☹️	Political Platonism (Ch. 6) 😀 😐 ☹️
Favorite ideas:	Favorite ideas:	Favorite ideas:	Favorite ideas:
Favorite exercises:	Favorite exercises:	Favorite exercises:	Favorite exercises:

PORT OF DOUBT			
Socraticism (Ch. 7) ☺ ☹ ☹	Sophism (Ch. 8) ☺ ☹ ☹	Academic Skepticism (Ch. 9) ☺ ☹ ☹	Pyrrhonism (Ch. 10) ☺ ☹ ☹
Favorite ideas:	Favorite ideas:	Favorite ideas:	Favorite ideas:
Favorite exercises:	Favorite exercises:	Favorite exercises:	Favorite exercises:

HERE BE DRAGONS		
Pythagoreanism (Ch. 11) ☺ ☹ ☹	Megarianism (Ch. 12) ☺ ☹ ☹	Neoplatonism (Ch. 13) ☺ ☹ ☹
Favorite ideas or practical takeaways:	Favorite ideas or practical takeaways:	Favorite ideas or practical takeaways:

Step 2: Put your astrolabe to use

An astrolabe (the same kind of instrument Hypatia used; see chapter 13) was invented around the second century and used for over a thousand years to determine your ship's latitude by means of the positions of the stars. The chart you filled out in the previous step can serve a similar purpose: to help you see where you are in terms of which philosophy (or philosophies) of life you found most suitable.

If you take a close look at your chart, one of four patterns probably emerges.

1. **Cloudy Sky**: Overall, you found none of the practices or philosophies in this book interesting or compelling.

2. **North Star**: You found one of these philosophies in this book much more compelling than the rest.

3. **Constellation**: You found one of the ports (pleasure, character, doubt, or—for the more adventurous among you—uncharted waters) much more compelling than the others, but you jibed with multiple philosophies within that group.

4. **Milky Way**: Many of the philosophies across all the sections of this book gelled with you, and there's no clear winner.

Take some time to look for one of the four patterns listed previously. When it becomes apparent to you, write in the space that follows which pattern (Cloudy Sky, North Star, Constellation, or Milky Way) you fit into.

_____

_____

_____

_____

_____

_____

If you fit best into the Cloudy Sky pattern, your job is done. After thoroughly exploring the major practical Greco-Roman philosophies of life, you found none to be suitable. If that's the case, we hope you don't feel disappointed! Greco-Roman philosophies are only one of several possible ways to live a happy life. Perhaps other traditions would suit you better, or perhaps you found that you don't quite buy this life philosophy stuff at all. If so, you've still learned something about yourself and a subset of ancient life philosophies! Having ruled this group out, you can now be more efficient in your life's journey.

If you fit into one of the other three patterns, use the space that follows to summarize your current thoughts, depending on which pattern categorizes you the best.

- **North Star:** Write down the philosophy you found most compelling, and rewrite it to show why you found it to be the best fit for you.

- **Constellation:** Write down the port (pleasure, character, doubt, or uncharted waters) that you found most appealing, along with why you think this goal is the best fit for you.

- **Milky Way:** A major assumption of many of the ancient philosophies of life we've covered here is that there's *one single* thing to pursue in life that will lead to flourishing. You probably disagree! In the space that follows, list out the benefits that each philosophy provided to you personally. If it's possible (it may not be!), try to rank the benefits from most important to least important. For example, if you appreciated the mysticism of Neoplatonism and the mental tranquility of Epicureanism, which is more important to you: mysticism or tranquility?

_____

_____

_____

_____

_____

_____

Step 3: Rig your sails

Now that you've found where you are, it's time to embark on a more intentional, philosophical life by making a plan to practice philosophy. But we'll be frank: A philosophical life requires long, consistent, dedicated practice. The purpose of this book has been to lay the groundwork for such a life, but there is a lot more to learn and explore through pondering, trial and error, and experience. So don't think of this goal as committing to a single practice or philosophy for the rest of your life. Instead, think of it as just enough to help you get started on your journey.

Your plan will look a little different depending on whether you fit most into the North Star, Constellation, or Milky Way categories. So we'll lay out three different approaches depending on your results from the previous step. Proceed by skipping to the section that applies to you.

North Star

Since you found one specific philosophical approach to be the best fit for you, our advice is to make a plan to practice it daily while learning more about it through the resources for your specific philosophy in step 4. We also encourage you to search the internet and bookstores for more information. Since you've chosen a single life philosophy, you'll be able to dedicate a lot of attention to it if you so choose.

Since you fell into the North Star category, you probably value the goal that your philosophy of choice strives to achieve (maximal physical pleasure) and believe that that particular philosophy of life seems like a good way to achieve it. We suggest that you put this belief to the test as you dip your toes into your favorite philosophy's waters. After a few weeks of consistent practice, do you see any fruits? If not, you may want to reassess your practice, or perhaps your philosophy.

In order to start your practice, look at your favorite exercises from the philosophy that you wrote in Step 1. In the space that follows, write an action plan for how you would like to practice for a set amount of time. For example, if your North Star was Aristippus and his philosophy of Cyrenaicism, you could plan to spend a week on each of the exercises from Days 2 to 5. We suggest creating a SMART plan: one that's Specific (so you know exactly what you'll be doing), Measurable (so you know that you actually did your practice), Achievable (so that you have a high chance of succeeding), Relevant to the goal (in the case of Cyrenaicism, physical pleasure), and Timed (so you know when or for how long you'll do the practice).

_____

_____

_____

_____

_____

_____

You can also revisit the chapter on your philosophy of choice for further inspiration. Look through the life of the philosopher who was profiled and the theory behind the philosophy to see if any other ideas for consistent practice pop up. You're also welcome to invent your own exercises: Anything that is consistent with the philosophical theory that leads to the philosophy's goal is fair game! If any more ideas for practice come to you, add them to the previous space. Once you've laid out your plan for practice, move on to Step 4 for ways to learn more about your philosophy.

Constellation

If you fall into this category, you found one specific *goal* more worthwhile than the others. However, multiple approaches to achieve this goal resonated with you; there was no single philosophy or approach that stood out. Since that's the case, it's worth taking a bit more time to explore *why* this goal was appealing to you, since that may help shape which practices you choose to start pursuing.

In the space that follows, take some time to put down your thoughts about why the goal is a good fit for you. For example, if you found character building to be your Constellation, write the reasons why you think this will lead to a worthwhile life for you.

_____

_____

_____

_____

_____

_____

Now that you've clarified your reasons for finding this goal desirable, go back to the exercises you found most compelling from the philosophies under this goal and find the ones you think are most likely to move you closer to the goal. For instance, let's say you found the idea of character building appealing because it puts you in a better position to try to make the world a better place, as Plato attempted to do (chapter 6). However, political activism requires a bit of courage, and based on your score for courage in chapter 4, Day 2, you may have found yourself to be less courageous than you'd like. In that case, your plan for practicing could be to become more politically active while applying Epictetus's fundamental rule (chapter 4) to keep a level head and proceed slowly and steadily. Using this approach, you're able to borrow from several philosophies while achieving a single, clear goal.

In the space that follows, write out an action plan for how you would like to practice for a set amount of time. We suggest creating a SMART plan: one that's Specific (so you know exactly what you'll be doing), Measurable (so you know that you actually did your practice), Achievable (so that you have a high chance of succeeding), Relevant to the goal (in our example, improving your character), and Timed (so you know when or for how long you'll do the practice).

_____

_____

_____

_____

_____

_____

_____

After you've written an action plan to test the waters, move on to Step 4 to discover resources that can help you learn more about your favorite set of philosophies as you begin your practice.

Milky Way

If you fall in this category, you're an eclectic: You found utility in a lot of the philosophies you've explored in this book. We have good news and bad news for you. The good news is that you've gotten your money's worth from this book! You've found many of the philosophies that we've explored to be fascinating and potentially useful in helping you craft a worthwhile life. The bad news is that you have your work cut out for you. Having found so much to be useful, it can be hard to know what to turn your attention to, both in theory and in day-to-day practice.

That's why we asked you to attempt to rank the benefits you received from each philosophy in Step 2: Knowing what was *most* beneficial to you can help you choose which philosophies you can spend the majority of your time pursuing.

If you were able to rank the benefits in Step 2, use the space that follows to create a plan for how to continue practicing your most impactful philosophies, focusing on the top one or two to start with. Try to create a SMART plan: one that's Specific (so you know exactly what you'll be doing), Measurable (so you know that you actually did your practice), Achievable (so that you have a high chance of succeeding), Relevant to the benefits you outlined in Step 2, and Timed (so you know when or for how long you'll do the practice).

_____

_____

_____

_____

_____

_____

_____

_____

_____

_____

_____

_____

_____

If you weren't able to rank the benefits, a different approach is required. Perhaps you'd be better served by having a "tool kit" of your favorite philosophies to use at appropriate times. For instance, if you find yourself in a rut due to a stifling social convention, perhaps chapter 5's Cynic exercise could be of use (page 108). However, if you found that Pyrrho's methods of doubt laid out in Day 4 of chapter 10 brought you peace of mind, you can turn to those methods when you're stressed (page 219–20). Different situations require different actions, and as an eclectic, you have a wealth of resources to choose from!

In the space that follows, build your own philosophical tool kit from your favorite philosophies that you laid out in Step 1. It may be useful to put them in an if/then format; for example, "If I feel confused about a decision, I'll take a Carneadean approach to the evidence that I learned in chapter 9," or "When I feel like I'm overindulging in a kinetic pleasure, I'll try to exchange it for a katastematic one, such as in Days 4 and 5 of chapter 2."

If/when _____	I will _____	Reference (chapter, philosophy, or specific exercise)
Example: People have told me I'm too confident in a belief I hold.	Apply Socratic self-examination.	Chapter 7, Days 1 & 2

We suggest reviewing your tool kit at least once a day so that if an opportunity arises, you will remember how to put your game plan into practice. Once you've laid out your plan, move on to Step 4 for opportunities to learn more about some of your favorite philosophies.

Step 4: Refine your map

This book has provided a basic map for your philosophical journey. In the previous step, you laid out the basics of how to embark on practicing a philosophical life. However, there is much more to explore.

One place to start would be to look at one of our major sources for this book: Diogenes Laërtius, who lived around the third century CE. He was an ancient historian of philosophy and covered most of the philosophers we include in this book. We recommend the following edition of his work: *Lives of the Eminent Philosophers* (Oxford University Press, 2018), translated by Pamela Mensch and edited by James Miller. The following is a handful of additional recommended resources to help deepen your understanding of the specific philosophies that interest you the most.

- **Cyrenaicism**
  - » Kurt Lampe, *The Birth of Hedonism: The Cyrenaic Philosophers and Pleasure as a Way of Life*, Princeton University Press, 2014.
    The best source wfor those who want to dive deeply into the philosophy of Cyrenaicism.
  - » Tim O'Keefe, "Cyrenaics," *Internet Encyclopedia of Philosophy*, iep. utm.edu/cyrenaics.
    A free, easily accessible overview of Cyrenaicism.

- **Epicureanism**
  - » John Sellars, *The Fourfold Remedy: Epicurus and the Art of Happiness*, Allen Lane, 2021.
    A brief overview of Epicurean philosophy from a top scholar of Greco-Roman philosophy.
  - » Society of the Friends of Epicurus, societyofepicurus.com
    The website for the modern-day Epicurean movement that provides a range of resources.

- **Aristotelianism**
  - » John Sellars, *Aristotle: Understanding the World's Greatest Philosopher*, Pelican, 2023.
    An excellent overview of Aristotle's rich, complex philosophy.
  - » Joe Sachs, "Aristotle: Ethics," *Internet Encyclopedia of Philosophy*, iep.utm.edu/aristotle-ethics.
    A solid, free overview of Aristotelian ethics.

- **Stoicism**
  - » Massimo Pigliucci, "Stoicism," *Internet Encyclopedia of Philosophy*, iep.utm.edu/stoicism.
    A free, broad overview of the Stoic philosophical system from one of the authors of this book.
  - » Gregory Lopez and Massimo Pigliucci, *A Handbook for New Stoics: How to Thrive in a World Out of Your Control—52 Week-by-Week Lessons*, The Experiment, 2019.
    A practical handbook that can help you put Stoicism into practice, by two of the authors of this book.

- **Cynicism**
  - » Laura Grams, "Hipparchia," *Internet Encyclopedia of Philosophy*, iep. utm.edu/hipparch.

    An overview of the life of one of the few women philosophers in ancient Greece, which also links to an overview of Cynicism as a philosophy.
  - » Ansgar Allen, *Cynicism*, MIT Press, 2020.

    A unique journey of a book that captures the spirit of ancient Cynicism, and explores how the word arrived at its modern usage.

- **(Political) Platonism**
  - » Robin Waterfield, *Plato of Athens: A Life in Philosophy*, Oxford University Press, 2023.

    An excellent modern biography of one of the world's most influential philosophers.
  - » Heather L. Reid and Mark Ralkowski, eds., *Plato at Syracuse*, Parnassos Press, 2019.

    A volume of scholarly articles (which are open access and available at: jstor.org/stable/j.ctvcmxptk) focusing on Plato's life and political exploits in Syracuse.

- **The Socratic Method**
  - » Debra Nails and S. Sara Monoson, "Socrates," *Stanford Encyclopedia of Philosophy*, plato.stanford.edu/entries/socrates.

    A sweeping, free, accessible overview of Socrates's life and philosophy.
  - » Ward Farnsworth, *The Socratic Method: A Practitioner's Handbook*, Godine, 2021.

    A unique overview of what the Socratic Method is, where it came from, and how to wield it in practice.

- **Sophism**
  - » Mauro Bonazzi, "Protagoras," *Stanford Encyclopedia of Philosophy*, plato.stanford.edu/archives/fall2020/entries/protagoras.

    An overview of the ideas and life of the main Sophist we covered in chapter 8.
  - » Robin Waterfield, *The First Philosophers: The Presocratics and the Sophists*, Oxford University Press, 2000.

    While only part of this book covers the Sophists, it provides a solid overview.

- **Academic Skepticism**

  » James Allen, "Carneades," *Stanford Encyclopedia of Philosophy*, plato. stanford.edu/entries/carneades.
    An overview of this influential Academic Skeptic's philosophy and life, who was the focus of chapter 9.

  » *Skepticism: From Antiquity to the Present*, eds. Diego E. Machuca and Baron Reed, Bloomsbury Academic, 2018.
    Chapters 3 to 7 cover the major philosophers from the skeptical phase of the Academy.

- **Pyrrhonism**

  » Douglas C. Bates, *Pyrrho's Way: The Ancient Greek Version of Buddhism*, Sumeru Press, 2020.
    An introduction to Pyrrhonism from a modern Pyrrhonian practitioner.

  » *Skepticism: From Antiquity to the Present*, eds. Diego E. Machuca and Baron Reed, Bloomsbury Academic, 2018.
    Chapters 2 and 10 cover the lives and ideas of Phyrro, Timon, and Sextus Empiricus.

- **Pythagoreanism**

  » Carl Huffman, "Pythagoreanism," *Stanford Encyclopedia of Philosophy*, plato.stanford.edu/entries/pythagoreanism.
    A broad but deep overview of the major Pythagoreans throughout history.

  » Carl A. Huffman, *A History of Pythagoreanism*, Cambridge University Press, 2014.
    A deep, sweeping overview of the Pythagoreans, their way of life, and their influence throughout history.

- **Megarianism**

  » James Allen, "Megara and Dialectic," in T. Bénatouïl & K. Ierodiakonou, eds., *Dialectic after Plato and Aristotle*, Cambridge University Press, 2018, pp. 17–46.
    A modern overview of the Megarian and Dialectical schools.

» Eduard Zeller, *Socrates and the Socratic Schools*, Longmans, Green, and Co., 1877, pp. 249–81.

   While quite an old book that doesn't cover the more recent scholarship concerning the possible multiplicity of Megarian schools, this still provides an excellent overview of this little-known school (or schools, as the case may be). It's also in the public domain, and can be found for free on Google Books.

• **Neoplatonism**

» Christian Wildberg, "Neoplatonism," *Stanford Encyclopedia of Philosophy*, plato.stanford.edu/entries/neoplatonism.

   An excellent overview of this complex, mystical philosophy.

» Pauliina Remes, *Neoplatonism*, Routledge, 2008.

   A comprehensive book covering the Neoplatonists from Plotinus through the closure of the Academy, along with an overview of Neoplatonic theories of psychology, ethics, and politics.

With these four steps, you've been able to narrow your focus, make a plan for starting your practice, and discover resources to learn more.

At this point, we hope you have enough provisions for your journey. Fair winds and following seas!

NOTES

Part 1: The Port of Pleasure

1. A. Delle Fave et al., "Hedonism and Eudaimonism in Positive Psychology," in *Psychological Selection and Optimal Experience Across Cultures. Cross-Cultural Advancements in Positive Psychology*, vol. 2 (Springer, 2010), 3–18.

2. S. Frederick and G. Loewenstein, "Hedonic Adaptation," in *Well-Being: The Foundations of Hedonic Psychology*, eds. D. Kahneman et al. (Russell Sage Foundation, 1999), 302–29. See also John Mathews, "The Hedonic Treadmill: From Consumerism to Minimalism," *Virginia Counseling*, December 21, 2015, vacounseling.com/hedonic-treadmill.

1 Seek pleasure with Aristippus

1. This scene, along with most of this biographical sketch, was informed and inspired by biographical details in Diogenes Laërtius, *Lives of the Eminent Philosophers*, trans. Pamela Mensch, ed. James Miller (Oxford University Press, 2018), Book 2:65, 95–111. The chapter on Aristippus says that he "consorted with Laïs the courtesan," and the exchange included here comparing a courtesan with a house and a ship is detailed on page 98.

2. Joshua J. Mark, "Aristippus of Cyrene," World History Encyclopedia, worldhistory.org/Aristippus_of_Cyrene, and Tim O'Keefe, "Aristippus," Internet Encyclopedia of Philosophy, iep.utm.edu/aristippus.

3. Mark, "Aristippus of Cyrene," op. cit. See also "Dionysius I," *Encyclopedia Britannica*, britannica.com/biography/Dionysius-I.

4. Laërtius, *Eminent Philosophers*, 2.78, 100.

5. Laërtius, *Eminent Philosophers*, 2.66, 95 (citing Cynic philosopher Diogenes). The footnote of the Mensch translation (edited by Miller) explains: "Cynics were often termed 'dogs.' A 'royal dog' however, being both spoiled and subservient, would be the opposite of the Cynic ideal."

6. The obol was a unit of ancient Greek currency worth one-sixth of a drachma. An unskilled worker earned about two obols a day. For more info, see "Ancient Greek Coins," Ashmolean, ashmolean.org/sites/default/files/ashmolean/documents/media/learn_pdf_resources_greece_ancient_greek_coins_notes_for_teachers.pdf.

7. Laërtius, *Eminent Philosophers*, 2.75, 99.

8. Ibid., 100.

9. Plutarch, *Moralia*, 524a–b, cited in *The Birth of Hedonism: The Cyrenaic Philosophers and Pleasure as a Way of Life*, Kurt Lampe (Princeton University Press, 2014), 59.

10. Vitruvius, "Introduction," *The Ten Books on Architecture*, trans. Morris Hicky Morgan, lexundria.com/vitr/6.0/mg.

11. Ibid.

12. Mark, "Aristippus," op. cit.

13. For an in-depth treatment of Cyrenaic philosophy see Tim O'Keefe, "Cyrenaics," Internet Encyclopedia of Philosophy, iep.utm.edu/cyrenaics.

14. Laërtius, *Eminent Philosophers*, 2.66, 105.

15. Mark J. Amiradakis, "Is social networking fostering the fungibility of the Other?," *Communicatio* 42, no. 2 (2016): 238–52.

16. Peter Markie, and M. Folescu, "Rationalism vs. Empiricism," *The Stanford Encyclopedia of Philosophy*," September 2, 2021, plato.stanford.edu/entries/rationalism-empiricism.

17. Cicero, *Tusculan Disputations* 3.28, in *The Complete Works of Cicero*, trans. D. Yonge (Delphi Classics, 2014).

18. Lampe, *The Birth of Hedonism*, op. cit.

19. Ibid.

2 Avoid pain and stress with Epicurus

1. For more on the Garden, see William Morison, "The Garden of Epicurus," Internet Encyclopedia of Philosophy, iep.utm.edu/garden. See also Carlo Diano, "Epicurus," *Encyclopedia Britannica*, britannica. com/biography/Epicurus. Seneca, in his letters, also referenced the Epicureans' love of barley-meal and water, the simplest of foods and drinks. See Seneca's citations here: "Seneca: References to Epicurus," New Epicurean, newepicurean.com/suggested-reading/ senecas-references-to-epicurus.

2. David Stuttard, *A History of Ancient Greece in 50 Lives* (Thames & Hudson, 2021) 214.

3. Diogenes Laërtius, *Lives of the Eminent Philosophers*, trans. Pamela Mensch, ed. James Miller (Oxford University Press, 2018), 10.3, 493.

4. Stuttard, *50 Lives*, 212–13.

5. Laërtius, *Eminent Philosophers*, 10.3, 492.

6. From Epicurus's "Fragment 551," sometimes translated as "Live unknown," in *Selected Fragments*, trans. Peter Saint-Andre, 2011, monadnock.net/epicurus/fragments.html.

7. See Tim O'Keefe, "Epicurus," Internet Encyclopedia of Philosophy; see especially his description of Epicurus's views on friendship: iep.utm.edu/epicur/#SH5f.

8. Seneca, Letter 21, "On the Renown Which My Writings Will Bring You," trans. Richard M. Gummere, in *Letters from a Stoic* (Lexicos Publishing, 2011), 69.

9. Laërtius, *Eminent Philosophers*, 10. In 10.7, he cites some who complained about Epicurus (494), but Laërtius quickly changes course to say "those people are out of their minds" and to proclaim Epicurus's "matchless courtesy" and "incomparable goodness" in 10.9, 496.

10. Laërtius, *Eminent Philosophers*, 10.16.

11. Stuttard, *50 Lives*, 215.

12. Laërtius, *Eminent Philosophers*, 10.9, 496.

13. Marcus Aurelius, *Meditations*, 7.64.

14. For more on the loose but plausible connecting strands from the Reformation through to the Shakers, as well as how Epicureanism compares, see Alex C. Parrish's master's thesis, "Quietism: Perceptions of Withdrawal in Epicureanism and Other Philosophical and Religious Movements" (York University, 2008), collectionscanada .gc.ca/obj/thesescanada/vol2/002/MR51576.PDF?oclc_ number=714264050.

15. For more on the Oneida Community, see Beth Quinn Barnard, "The Utopia of Sharing in Oneida, N.Y.," *The New York Times*, August 3, 2007.

16. Foundation for Intentional Community, 2024, ic.org.

17. Society of Friends of Epicurus, societyofepicurus.com.

18. Hiram Crespo, *Tending the Epicurean Garden* (Humanist Press, 2014). See also Catherine Wilson, *How to Be an Epicurean: The Ancient Art of Living Well* (Basic Books, 2019).

Part 2: The Port of Character

1. C. B. Miller, *The Character Gap: How Good Are We?* (Oxford University Press, 2017). See also Massimo Pigliucci, *The Quest for Character: What the Story of Socrates and Alcibiades Teaches Us About Our Search for Good Leaders* (Basic Books, 2022).

2. Rosalind Hursthouse, *On Virtue Ethics* (Oxford University Press, 1999), 172.

3. John M. Doris, *Lack of Character: Personality and Moral Behavior* (Cambridge University Press, 2002).

4. Miller, *The Character Gap*, op. cit.

3 Strike the right balance with Aristotle

1. David Stuttard, *A History of Ancient Greece in 50 Lives* (Thames & Hudson, 2021), 185. Also discussed in Diogenes Laërtius, trans. Pamela Mensch, ed. James Miller, *Lives of the Eminent Philosophers* (Oxford University Press, 2018), Book 5, chapter 1. Much of this chapter's background comes from these sources, along with James Miller, *Examined Lives: from Socrates to Nietzsche* (Farrar, Straus & Giroux, 2011).

2. Stuttard, *50 Lives*, 183.

3. James Miller, *Examined Lives*, 93.

4. Sources name various reasons that could explain why Aristotle wasn't chosen to lead the Academy: because of anti-Macedonian sentiment, because he was not an Athenian citizen, because Aristotle may have thought the Academy was placing too much emphasis on mathematics and theory rather than on "practical sciences," or because there may have been disharmony between Plato and Aristotle. See Miller, *Examined Lives*, 94; Stuttard, *50 Lives*, 184; Rupert Woodfin and Judy Groves,*Introducing Aristotle* (Totem Books, 2001), 9; and Robin Waterfield, *Plato of Athens: A Life in Philosophy* (Oxford University Press, 2023), 225–26.

5. Woodfin and Groves, *Introducing Aristotle*, 13.

6. Stuttard, *50 Lives*, 185.

7. Ibid., 188.

8. Miller, *Examined Lives*, 97. Miller quotes Plutarch's *Parallel Lives* on Aristotle's experience teaching Alexander.

9. Stuttard, *50 Lives*, 190.

10. Miller, *Examined Lives*, 100.

11. Ibid., 104.

12. Jonathan Barnes, *Aristotle: A Very Short Introduction* (Oxford University Press, 2000), 11.

13. Miller, *Examined Lives*, 90.

14. Ibid., 89.

15. Woodfin and Groves, *Introducing Aristotle*, 3.

16. Aristotle, *Nicomachean Ethics*, 1107a, 7–8.

17. Ibid., 1103b, 23–25.

18. Aristotle, *Physics*, 7, 247b.

19. Joe Sachs, "Aristotle: Ethics," Internet Encyclopedia of Philosophy, iep.utm.edu/aristotle-ethics.

20. Aristotle, *Nicomachean Ethics*, 1103a, 24–25.

21. Ibid., 1153b, 17–20.

22. Ibid., 1179a, 13.

23. The scholar Pierre Hadot counted Aristotle's philosophy as a way of life, but given the picture we painted of his theory-heavy ethics that's short on practicality, this is certainly up for debate. To get a nuanced view of this debate, see J. Sellars, "Aristotle and Philosophy as a Way of Life," in *Hadot and Foucault on Ancient Philosophy*, eds. M. Faustino and H. Telo (Brill, 2024). To make a long story short, Sellars's thesis is that while Aristotle may not present strong practical guidance on how to live a good life, his view of philosophy is that it consists of an active practice. In that sense, Aristotle did espouse a practical way of life, and followed through with his theory in the way he lived his own life.

24. These virtues, excesses, and deficiencies can be found in Aristotle, *Nicomachean Ethics*, 1107b–1108a, with the exception of justice (at least the sense of justice which is a "part of virtue" and not "the whole of virtue"), which is spelled out in 1130b–1131a. We've intentionally taken minor liberties with interpreting some of the virtues. For example, we've focused more on the nonmaterial aspects of justice to make the separation from generosity a bit cleaner conceptually, even though Aristotle does mention distribution of both material and nonmaterial things as falling under justice. Also, some virtues are combined and simplified (*megaloprepeia* and *eleutheriotēs*— "magnificence" and "generosity"), while others that may be hard to understand outside of an aristocratic ancient Greek context (*megalopsuchia* or "greatness of soul") are skipped.

25. Aristotle, *Nicomachean Ethics*, 1104b, 30.

26. For more on this, see the section on intellectual virtues at: Joe Sachs, "Aristotle: Ethics," Internet Encyclopedia of Philosophy, iep.utm.edu/aristotle-ethics/#InteVirt.

27. Aristotle, *Nicomachean Ethics*, 1103b, 4.

28. Ibid., 1105a, 30.

4 Focus on what's up to you with Epictetus

1. "Archaeological site of Nikopolis," UNESCO World Heritage Convention, January 16, 2014, whc.unesco.org/en/tentativelists/5861. See also Ancient Nicopolis, 2020, actianicopolisarchaeopark.gr/en/nikopolis/romaiki-nikopoli.

2. Christopher Gill, "Introduction," in Epictetus, *Discourses, Fragments, Handbook*, trans. Robin Hard (Oxford University Press, 2014), viii.

3. Ibid., vii.

4. Philip Matyszak and Joanne Berry, *A History of Ancient Rome in 100 Lives* (Thames & Hudson, 2023), 162.

5. Keith H. Seddon, "Epictetus," Internet Encyclopedia of Philosophy, iep.utm.edu/epictetu. Seddon cites "a story told by the author Celsus (probably a younger contemporary of Epictetus)—quoted by the early Christian Origen (c. 185–254 CE) at *Contra Celsum* 7.53" that relates this incident.

6. For an exploration of Nero's court and times that seeks to rehabilitate his reputation, see Joshua Levine, "The New, Nicer Nero," *Smithsonian*, October 2020, smithsonianmag.com/history/new-nicer-nero-history-roman-emperor-180975776.

7. Gill, "Introduction," viii.

8. Robert Dobbin, "Introduction," in Epictetus, *Discourses and Selected Writings* (Penguin Classics, 2018), 18. Dobbin cites Origen, a Christian writer of the third century, who said "Plato is only found in the hands of those reputed to be philologists. By contrast, Epictetus is admired by ordinary people who have the desire to be benefited and who perceive improvement from his writings," *Contra Celsum*, 6, 2.

9. Epictetus, *Discourses*, 1.18.15 and 1.29.21. See Robin Hard translation cited in note 2 of this chapter.

10. Gill, "Introduction," viii–ix.

11. Ibid., viii.

12. Lucian of Samosata, *The Works of Lucian of Samosata—Volume 03*, trans. H. W. Fowler and F. G. Fowler, gutenberg.org/cache/epub/6829/pg6829.txt. Lucian writes: "I believe the man is still alive who paid 120 pounds for the earthenware lamp of Epictetus the Stoic. I suppose he thought he had only to read by the light of that lamp, and the wisdom of Epictetus would be communicated to him in his dreams, and he himself assume the likeness of that venerable sage."

13. See Philippa Foot, *Natural Goodness* (Clarendon Press, 2001), as well as Frans de Waal et al., *Primates and Philosophers: How Morality Evolved* (Princeton University Press, 2006).

14. Epictetus, *Discourses*, 1.9.1.

15. Epictetus, *Enchiridion*, 1.1.

16. Cicero, *De Finibus Bonorum et Malorum*, 3.22.

17. Epictetus, *Discourses*, 3.3.

18. For more on this, see Chris Fisher, "What is Traditional Stoicism?," *Traditional Stoicism*, November 28, 2015, traditionalstoicism.com/what-is-traditional-stoicism.

19. Epictetus, *Discourses*, 3.2.

20. Ibid., 3.3.

5 Be a rebel like Hipparchia

1. This scene is drawn from a description in Diogenes Laërtius, *Lives of the Eminent Philosophers*, trans. Pamela Mensch, ed. James Miller (Oxford University Press, 2018), 6.96–98, 306–6. For more background on Hipparchia, see also Laura Grams, "Hipparchia," Internet Encyclopedia of Philosophy, iep.utm.edu/hipparch.

2. Laërtius, *Eminent Philosophers*, 6.94, 304.

3. Ibid., 6.96, 305.

4. Ibid., 6.92, 302.

5. Joshua J. Mark, "Hipparchia of Maroneia," World History Encyclopedia, May 27, 2021, worldhistory.org/Hipparchia_of_Maroneia.

6. Ansgar Allen, *Cynicism* (MIT Press, 2020).

6 Work toward a just society with Plato

1. The background for the biographical scenes in this chapter comes from two sources, one ancient, one modern: Plato, Letter 7, and Robin Waterfield, *Plato of Athens: A Life in Philosophy* (Oxford University Press, 2023). For Plato's Letter 7, see "Plato's Seventh Letter," trans. Jonah Radding, in *Plato at Syracuse*, eds. Heather L. Reid and Mark Ralkowski (Parnassos Press, 2019).

2. Waterfield, *Plato of Athens*, 117–18.

3. Plutarch, *Life of Dion*, 13.3.

4. Plato, Letter 7, 348a.

5. Carolina Araújo, "What was Plato up to in Syracuse?," in *Plato at Syracuse*, eds. Heather L. Reid and Mark Ralkowski (Parnassos Press, 2019), 89.

6. Archestratus, a fourth-century BCE poet from Gela, wrote that Syracusans "ruined" good fish by cooking it with cheese and vinegar. For more on the food culture of ancient Syracuse, see Sergio G. Grasso, "The Food Culture of Siracusa," *Siracusa Culture*, February 2021, siracusaculture.com/en/2022/02/18/the-food-culture-of-siracusa.

7. For more on Plato at the court of Dionysius in Syracuse, see Waterfield, *Plato of Athens*, chapter 7.

8. Constance C. Meinwald, "Late dialogues of Plato," *Encyclopedia Britannica*, britannica.com/biography/Plato/Late-dialogues. A side note on Plato's influence on Rome: In his introduction to his translation of Marcus Aurelius's *Meditations*, Gregory Hays also points out that Marcus "is said to have been fond of quoting Plato's statement in *The Republic*: 'States will never be happy until rulers become philosophers or philosophers become rulers.'" Hays mentions that many people have pointed to the Roman emperor himself as a sort of philosopher-king, though he thinks that Marcus would have rejected the term. See Marcus Aurelius, *Meditations: A New Translation*, trans. Gregory Hays (Modern Library, 2002).

9. There is debate among scholars about just how many of Plato's dialogues were actually written by Plato. Robin Waterfield counts only twenty-eight as authentic. See *Plato of Athens: A Life in Philosophy* (Oxford University Press, 2023).

10. For more on Plato's political philosophy, see W. J. Korab-Karpowicz, "Plato: Political Philosophy," Internet Encyclopedia of Philosophy, iep.utm.edu/platopol.

11. Plato, *The Republic*, trans. Desmond Lee (Penguin Classics, 2003).

12. Ibid., 331d.

13. Ibid., 332d.

14. Ibid., 335a.

15. Ibid., 331e.

16. John Rawls, *A Theory of Justice* (Belknap Press, 1971).

17. Plato, *The Republic*, 338c.

18. Ibid., 351d.

19. Ibid., 347c–d.

20. Massimo Pigliucci, *The Quest for Character: What the Story of Socrates and Alcibiades Teaches Us about Our Search for Good Leaders* (Basic Books, 2022).

21. David Stuttard, *Nemesis: Alcibiades and the Fall of Athens* (Harvard University Press, 2018).

22. Plato, *Alcibiades Major*, 26.

23. See "Aristocracy," Online Etymology Dictionary, etymonline.com/word/aristocracy.

24. Plato, Letter 7, 326a.

25. Ibid., 324c.

26. Ibid., 324d–e.

27. Yacov Tsur, "Political Tenure, Term Limits and Corruption," *SSRN*, June 16, 2021.

28. Daniel E. Bergan, "Constituent contacts can influence how legislators vote," United States Policies and Politics Blog, London School of Economics, April 29, 2015, blogs.lse.ac.uk/usappblog/2015/04/29/constituent-contacts-can-influence-how-legislators-vote.

Part 3: The Port of Doubt

1. Diego E. Machuca and Baron Reed, eds., *Skepticism: From Antiquity to the Present* (Bloomsbury Academic, 2018).

7 Question everything with Socrates

1. "Delphic oracle," *Encyclopedia Britannica*, britannica.com/topic/Delphic-oracle.

2. Plato, "Apology," trans. Henry Cary, in *Delphi Complete Works of Plato* (Delphi Classics, 2015), 61. Socrates recounts his friend's visit to Delphi, the question he asked and answer he received, and how it prompted him to seek wisdom among the Athenians, inspiring this scene.

3. For biographical and contextual details on Socrates, see Debra Nails and S. Sara Monoson, "Socrates," *Stanford Encyclopedia of Philosophy*, May 26, 2022, plato.stanford.edu/entries/socrates.

4. Plato, "Apology," op. cit.

5. Xenophon, "Memorabilia," trans. E. C. Marchant, *Delphi Complete Works of Xenophon* (Delphi Classics, 2013), 6.5, 739.

6. Ibid.

7. Nails and Monoson, "Socrates," op. cit.

8. Xenophon, "Memorabilia," op. cit.

9. Plato, *The Apology*, op. cit.

10. Ibid., 74.

11. Plato, "Plato's Seventh Letter," trans. Jonah Radding, in *Plato at Syracuse*, eds. Heather L. Reid and Mark Ralkowski (Parnassos Press, 2019).

12. For an excellent overview of Socratic philosophy see James M. Ambury, "Socrates," Internet Encyclopedia of Philosophy, iep.utm.edu/socrates.

13. Plato, *Euthyphro*, 5d.

14. Ibid., 6e–7a.

15. Ibid., 9e.

16. Plato, *Euthyphro*, 12d.

17. Ibid., 12e.

18. Ibid., 14e.

19. Ibid., 15b.

20. Ibid., 15e.

21. This definition was challenged only in 1963 by Edmund Gettier, who articulated a series of special cases that appear to be exceptions to the Socratic/Platonic conception of knowledge. So-called Gettier cases have stimulated a bit of a cottage industry of responses and counter-responses that we certainly do not need to get into here. However, the interested reader can check out Stephen Hetherington, "Gettier Problems," Internet Encyclopedia of Philosophy, iep.utm.edu/gettier.

22. This particular way of thinking about what counts as true is known as the correspondence theory of truth, and it is usually deployed in both common and scientific discourse. There are, however, other conceptions of truth, perhaps the most useful alternative being the coherence theory of truth, used in mathematics and logic. If I say, for instance, that the Pythagorean theorem is "true," I cannot mean the word in the same sense as in the case of the claim that Saturn has rings. For a geometrical theorem like Pythagoras's to be true means that it is internally logically coherent and has been properly derived from certain starting axioms, such as those of Euclidean geometry. For a good discussion of theories of truth, including both the correspondence and coherence ones (as well as others), see Bradley Dowden and Norman Swartz, "Truth," Internet Encyclopedia of Philosophy, iep.utm.edu/truth.

23. Plato, *Euthyphro*, 5a.

24. Diogenes Laërtius, *Lives of the Eminent Philosophers*, trans. Pamela Mensch, ed. James Miller (Oxford University Press, 2018), 2.29.

8 Practice relativism with Protagoras

1. Protagoras's words and the scene in this chapter were inspired by Plato's dialogue *Protagoras*, written in c. 380 BCE. See Plato, *Protagoras*, trans. Benjamin Jowett, classics.mit.edu/Plato/protagoras.html. The setting of this dialogue in 434 BCE was suggested by "The Dramatic Order of Plato's Dialogues," Monadnock Valley Press, September 19, 2024, monadnock.net/plato/order.html, based on work by Christopher Planeaux.

2. Robin Waterfield, *Plato of Athens: A Life in Philosophy* (Oxford University Press, 2023), 41.

3. Ibid., 42–43. In a footnote, Waterfield explains that Sophists went to teach in Athens due to its wealth (much of which was generated by its empire), which gave its citizens leisure time for "non-practical pursuits such as education. The Greek word for 'leisure' is *skholê*, from which we get the word 'school.'"

4. Plato, "Protagoras," trans. David Horan, *The Dialogues of Plato*, note 6, platonicfoundation.org/protagoras.

5. Waterfield, *Plato of Athens*, 43.

6. Mauro Bonazzi, "Protagoras," Stanford Encyclopedia of Philosophy, September 8, 2020, plato.stanford.edu/archives/fall2020/entries/protagoras.

7. Ibid.

8. Ibid.

9. Robin Waterfield, *The First Philosophers: The Presocratics and the Sophists* (Oxford University Press, 2000), 207.

10. Adapted from Plato, *Protagoras*, 316d.

11. Waterfield, *The First Philosophers*, 205.

12. Cited in Diogenes Laërtius, *Lives of the Eminent Philosophers*, trans. Pamela Mensch, ed. James Miller (Oxford University Press, 2018), 9.50–56, 460–63; and Cicero, *De Natura Deorum*, 1.23.63, penelope.uchicago.edu/Thayer/E/Roman/Texts/Cicero/de_Natura_Deorum/1B*.html.

13. Laertius, *Eminent Philosophers*, 9.50–56, 460–63.

14. Bonazzi, "Protagoras," op. cit.

15. Waterfield, *Plato of Athens*, chapter 2.

16. Ibid.

17. Plato, *Protagoras*, 319a.

18. In the so-called great speech of Plato's *Protagoras*, 320c–328d.

19. Laërtius, *Eminent Philosophers*, 9.51–52.

20. Socrates explaining Protagoras's position in Plato's *Theaetetus*, 167c.

21. Laërtius, *Eminent Philosophers*, 9.51.

22. Plato, *Theaetetus*, 167b–c.

23. Laërtius, *Eminent Philosophers*, 9.50.

24. H. Diels and W. Kranz, eds., *Die Fragmente der Vorsokratiker* (Weidmann, 1974), fragment DK80b4.

25. Ibid., fragment 21B15–16.

26. Laërtius, *Eminent Philosophers*, 2.8.

27. Sextus Empiricus, *Against the Mathematicians*, 9.24.

28. Quoted in *Against the Mathematicians*, 9.24.

29. Plato, *Meno*, 91e.

30. Plato, *Cratylus*, 384b.

31. Plato, *Greater Hippias*, 282e.

32. André Laks and Glenn W. Most, eds. and trans., *Early Greek Philosophy: Sophists, Part I* (Harvard University Press, 2016), D28.

33. For more on this possibility, see Bonazzi, "Protagoras," op. cit.

34. For example, see Marcus Aurelius, *Meditations*, 9.38, and Marcus's fifth reminder to himself in *Meditations*, 11.18.

35. Plutarch, "Parallel Lives," in *Early Greek Philosophy*, 8.36.3, D30.

36. For more on this charitable take, see Bonazzi, "Protagoras," op. cit.

9 Embrace uncertainty with Carneades

1. Plutarch, "Carneades Visit to Rome from Life of Cato the Elder," Ancient History Sourcebook, Fordham University, ed. Paul Halsall, October 4, 2024, sourcebooks.fordham.edu/ancient/plut_carneades.asp.

2. Mentioned in Craige Champion, "Carneades at Rome: Philosophos Pragmatikos," in *Mediterranean Antiquity* (2016), 72. Champion cites Cicero (via a passage from Lactantius) and Quintilian.

3. Melvyn Bragg, Angie Hobbs, Jonathan Ree, and David Sedley, "Stoicism," *In Our Time*, BBC Radio podcast, March 4, 2005. One thing the Roman Cato objected to was that "philosophy was a Greek thing, and it was taking place in the Greek language, and he thought this was distracting people from their national duty" (in the words of Jonathan Ree).

4. The source for the reconstruction of Carneades's Roman speech is Marcus Tullius Cicero, *The Republic*, Book 3, in which he included Philus's speech summarizing Carneades's case against justice delivered in his Roman oration, and also Laelius's speech, incorporating pro-justice arguments that may echo what Carneades said the day before. See translation by C. W. Keyes (1928) at attalus.org/cicero/republic3.html.

5. James Allen, "Carneades," Stanford Encyclopedia of Philosophy, 2020, plato.stanford.edu/entries/carneades/#LifeWork.

6. See Cicero's text on Philus's speech. The Voconian law (Lex Voconia) was passed in Rome in 169 BCE (with the support of Cato the Elder) to limit women's ability to inherit. See "Voconian Law," LSD Law, lsd.law/define/voconian-law, and "lex Voconia," Oxford Classical Dictionary, February 26, 2018, oxfordre.com/classics/display/10.1093/acrefore/9780199381135.001.0001/acrefore-9780199381135-e-8201?rskey=grAlwH&result=11.

7. Plutarch, *Life of Cato the Elder*.

8. Champion, "Carneades at Rome," 73.

9. Allen, "Carneades," op. cit.

10. Diogenes Laërtius, *Lives of the Eminent Philosophers*, trans. Pamela Mensch, ed. James Miller (Oxford University Press, 2018), 4.62, 207.

11. Allen, "Carneades," op. cit.

12. Champion, "Carneades at Rome," 66.

13. Plutarch, *Life of Cato the Elder*.

14. Diogenes Laërtius, *Lives of the Eminent Philosophers*, Vol. I, Books 1–5, trans. R. D. Hicks, Loeb Classical Library 184 (Harvard University Press, 1925).

15. Laërtius, *Eminent Philosophers*, 4.65.

16. Allen, "Carneades," op. cit.

17. Robin Waterfield, *Plato of Athens: A Life in Philosophy* (Oxford University Press, 2023).

18. Diego E. Machuca and Baron Reed, eds., *Skepticism: From Antiquity to the Present* (Bloomsbury Academic, 2018), chapters 3, 4, 6, and 7.

19. Cicero, *Academica*, 2.47.

20. Allen, "Carneades," op. cit.

21. Sharon Bertsch McGrayne, *The Theory That Would Not Die: How Bayes' Rule Cracked the Enigma Code, Hunted Down Russian Submarines, and Emerged Triumphant from Two Centuries of Controversy* (Yale University Press, 2012).

22. Edward Clayton, "Cicero," Internet Encyclopedia of Philosophy, iep.utm.edu/cicero-roman-philosopher.

23. Damian Fernandez-Beanato, "Cicero's demarcation of science: A report of shared criteria," *Studies in History and Philosophy of Science* 83 (2020): 97–102.

24. Cicero, *On Duties*, 2.7, 3.20.

25. Bruce Arroll, "Common cold," *BMJ Clinical Evidence* (2011): 1510.

10 Suspend judgment with Pyrrho

1. Diogenes Laërtius, *Lives of the Eminent Philosophers*, trans. Pamela Mensch, ed. James Miller (Oxford University Press, 2018), 9.62–108. This source provides much of the biographical information that we have on Pyrrho. Discussed in Christopher I. Beckwith, *Greek Buddha: Pyrrho's Encounter with Early Buddhism in Central Asia* (Princeton University Press, 2015), 190–92, with reference to Plutarch's retelling of the ship story. For background, see also Richard Bett, "Pyrrho," Stanford Encyclopedia of Philosophy, September 15, 2022, plato.stanford.edu/entries/pyrrho.

2. Laërtius, *Eminent Philosophers*, 9.61.

3. Ibid., 9.58–60

4. Tim O'Keefe, "Anaxarchus," Internet Encyclopedia of Philosophy, iep.utm.edu/anaxarchus.

5. Laërtius, *Eminent Philosophers*, 9.61, and Beckwith, *Greek Buddha*, op. cit. Beckwith discusses in detail the early practitioners of Buddhism whom Pyrrho may have encountered in India.

6. Beckwith, *Greek Buddha*, 28, and Laërtius, *Eminent Philosophers*, 9.63. According to Beckwith, the men's motionless endurance of pain may have been an early form of yoga. He and Laërtius cite the story about Anaxarchus.

7. Laërtius, *Eminent Philosophers*, 9.62–108, and Beckwith, *Greek Buddha*, op. cit.

8. Laërtius, *Eminent Philosophers*, 9.66.

9. Ibid.

10. Ibid.

11. Ibid., 9.67.

12. Ibid., 9.62

13. Ibid., 9.69.

14. Ibid., 4.3. Laërtius quotes Ariston, who parodied a passage of the *Iliad* on the chimera, turning it into this description of Arcesilaus: "He's Plato in front, Pyrrho behind, Diodorus in the middle." (Diodorus was a master dialectician.)

15. He lived in the second or third century CE, and his *Outlines of Pyrrhonism* is the fullest ancient account of Pyrrhonian skepticism. See Benjamin Morison, "Sextus Empiricus," Stanford Encyclopedia of Philosophy, July 12, 2019, plato.stanford.edu/entries/sextus-empiricus.

16. See Beckwith, *Greek Buddha*, and Bett, "Pyrrho," op. cit.

17. Laërtius, *Eminent Philosophers*, 9.62.

18. Ibid.

19. Ibid., 9.64.

20. Ibid., 9.61.

21. On Pyrrhonism's connection with Buddhism, see the fascinating but quite speculative Beckwith, *Greek Buddha*, op. cit.

22. The questions are reported by Pyrrho's student, Timon, though we know about them because they were recorded by Aristocles, a second-century peripatetic, and later reported by the Christian commentator Eusebius, *Praeparatio Evangelica*, 14.18.1–5.

23. Laërtius, *Eminent Philosophers*, 4.28, and Cicero, *Academica*, 45.

24. Sextus Empiricus, *Outlines of Pyrrhonism*, 1.232, and Plutarch, *Adversus Colotes*, 1120c.

25. Harald Thorsrud, "Ancient Greek Skepticism," Internet Encyclopedia of Philosophy, iep.utm.edu/ancient-greek-skepticism.

26. For instance, in the second century, by Aulus Gellius in his *Attic Nights*, 1.5.6.

27. The main resource for modern Epicurean practice we're aware of is the Society of Friends of Epicurus, societyofepicurus.com.

28. For more information on modern Pyrrhonism, see the Modern Pyrrhonism Movement, pyrrhonism.org.

29. E. M. Cioran, *The Trouble with Being Born* (Seaver Books, 1976).

30. W. B. Britton et al., "Defining and Measuring Meditation-Related Adverse Effects in Mindfulness-Based Programs," *Clinical Psychological Science* 9, no. 6 (2021): 1185–1204.

31. Douglas C. Bates, *Pyrrho's Way: The Ancient Greek Version of Buddhism* (Sumeru Press, 2020), 260.

32. Bates, *Pyrrho's Way*, 74 and 262.

33. Ibid., 94.

34. Ibid., 98.

Part 4: Here Be Dragons

1. "Here be dragons" probably wasn't on many ancient maps or globes, but we like the spirit of this popular myth, so we'll use it! For more info, see "Here be dragons," Wikipedia, last modified July 6, 2024, en.wikipedia.org/wiki/Here_be_dragons.

2. Lloyd P. Gerson ed., "On the Life of Plotinus and the Order of His Books by Porphyry of Tyre," in *Plotinus: The Enneads*, trans. George Boys-Stones et al. (Cambridge University Press, 2017), 10.1–12.

3. Porphyry, "On the Life of Plotinus," 10.14–31.

4. See Peter S. Adamson, *Classical Philosophy* (Oxford University Press, 2014), and *Philosophy in the Hellenistic and Roman Worlds* (Oxford University Press, 2015).

11 Pythagoras the mystic

1. Diogenes Laërtius, *Lives of the Eminent Philosophers*, trans. Pamela Mensch, ed. James Miller (Oxford University Press, 2018), 8.36, 410. The story is cited by Laërtius in a passage from a poem by Xenophanes (c. 570–c. 478 BCE), a Greek philosopher-poet who was a contemporary of Pythagoras. (The poem may have been a humorous effort to poke fun at Pythagoras, but it represents one of his key ideas nonetheless.)

2. Laërtius, *Eminent Philosophers*, 8.4–5, 396.

3. Ibid., 8.3, 396.

4. Ibid., 8.10, 399.

5. Ibid., 8.34, 408.

6. Ibid., 8.9, 398.

7. Ibid., 8.10, 399.

8. Josceyln Godwin, "Foreword," and David R. Fideler, "Introduction," in *The Pythagorean Sourcebook and Library*, ed. Kenneth Sylvan Guthrie (Phanes Press, 1987), 12–13 and 20.

9. Iamblichus, "The Life of Pythagoras," in *The Pythagorean Sourcebook and Library*, 59.

10. Godwin and Fideler, *The Pythagorean Sourcebook*, 12–13, and 20.

11. Iamblichus, "The Life of Pythagoras," 58.

12. Laërtius, *Eminent Philosophers*, 8.11, 399.

13. Godwin and Fideler, *The Pythagorean Sourcebook*, 20.

14. Iamblichus, "The Life of Pythagoras," 64.

15. Carl Huffman, "Pythagoras," Stanford Encyclopedia of Philosophy, February 5, 2024, plato.stanford.edu/entries/pythagoras.

16. Ibid.

17. Ibid., and "Pythagoreanism," Stanford Encyclopedia of Philosophy, March 5, 2024, plato.stanford.edu/entries/pythagoreanism.

18. Jeremy Bentham, *An Introduction to the Principles of Morals and Legislation* (1789).

19. "Glucose-6-phosphate dehydrogenase deficiency," MedlinePlus, March 31, 2024, medlineplus.gov/ency/article/000528.htm.

20. Porphyry, *Life of Pythagoras*, 19.

21. Iamblichus, *On the Pythagorean Way of Life*, 31.

22. Aristotle, "Fragment 91," in *The Complete Works of Aristotle*, Vol. 2, ed. Jonathan Barnes, trans. Jonathan Barnes and Gavin Lawrence (Princeton University Press, 1984).

23. Laërtius, *Eminent Philosophers*, 8.69.

24. Aristotle, "Fragment 91," op. cit.

25. Ibid., 129.

26. Porphyry, *Life of Pythagoras*, 7.

27. Iamblichus, *On the Pythagorean Way of Life*, 82.

28. Ibid., 233.

29. Stobaeus, *Anthology*, 1.10.13.

30. Iamblichus, *On the Pythagorean Way of Life*, 189–94.

31. Polybius, *The Histories*, 2.39.

32. Robin Waterfield, *Plato of Athens: A Life in Philosophy* (Oxford University Press, 2023). See chapter 5, especially the sections "A Diverse Academy" and "The Curriculum."

33. Flora R. Levin, ed., *The Manual of Harmonics of Nicomachus the Pythagorean* (Phanes Press, 1994), 86–87.

34. Gregory would like to thank Crockett Marr, who pointed out this particular story and helped in pondering its practical implications.

35. Levin, *Manual of Harmonics*, chapter 6.

36. Aristides Quintilianus, *De Musica*, 3.2.

37. Levin, *Manual of Harmonics*, 93–94.

38. Ironically, testing the implications of the story as told by Nicomachus leads to the conclusion that it's quite flawed. The tones that hammers produce when striking anvils don't depend on the hammers' weights alone. And hanging weights off strings using the ratios Nicomachus describes would not recreate the fourth, fifth, and octave. For details, see Levin, 92–93.

12 Stilpo the Megarian

1. Cicero, *De Fato*, 5.

2. Diogenes Laërtius, *Lives of the Eminent Philosophers*, trans. Pamela Mensch, ed. James Miller (Oxford University Press, 2018), 2.113–20, 115–18. Also Catherine Hundleby, "Nicarete of Megara," *Women in World History: A Biographical Encyclopedia*, Encyclopedia.com, October 14, 2024, encyclopedia.com/women/encyclopedias-almanacs-transcripts-and-maps/nicarete-megara-fl-300-bce.

3. Laërtius, Eminent Philosophers, *2.113–14, 115.*

4. Ibid.

5. Suggested by Laërtius in some translations of *Lives of the Eminent Philosophers*. See note to chapter on Pyrrho, page 466.

6. Ibid., 7.24, 322.

7. Ibid., 2.119, 117–18.

8. Ibid., 2.116, 115.

9. Ibid., 2.120, 118.

10. See J. Allen, "Megara and Dialectic," in *Dialectic after Plato and Aristotle*, eds. T. Bénatouïl and K. Ierodiakonou (Cambridge University Press, 2018), 17–46. See also Eduard Zeller, "The Megarian and the Elean-Eretrian Schools," in *Socrates and the Socratic Schools* (Longmans, Green, and Co., 1877).

11. Laërtius, *Eminent Philosophers*, 2.115, 116.

12. James Ladyman and Don Ross, *Every Thing Must Go: Metaphysics Naturalized* (Clarendon Press, 2007).

13. Again, we don't wish to push too far the notion that the Greek thinkers anticipated modern science, but it is interesting to note that Einstein's General Theory of Relativity does imply that time is fundamentally different from how we perceive it, and that it doesn't, in fact, "pass." This idea is referred to as the block universe, and Parmenides would have been pleased. For a broader discussion of modern philosophy of time, see Nina Emery et al., "Time," Stanford Encyclopedia of Philosophy, plato.stanford.edu/entries/time. See also Bradley Dowden, "Time," Internet Encyclopedia of Philosophy, iep.utm.edu/time.

14. Susanne Bobzien, "Ancient Logic," Stanford Encyclopedia of Philosophy, April 15, 2024, plato.stanford.edu/entries/logic-ancient.

15. Epictetus, *Discourses*, 2.19.

16. Daniel Dennett, Elbow Room: *The Varieties of Free Will Worth Wanting* (MIT Press, 1984).

17. Laërtius, *Eminent Philosophers*, 2.106.

13 Hypatia the Neoplatonist

1. The background for this chapter was informed by Edward J. Watts, *Hypatia: The Life and Legend of an Ancient Philosopher* (Oxford University Press, 2017). See also interview with Watts: Josh Landy and Ray Briggs, "Hypatia of Alexandria," *Philosophy Talk*, July 23, 2023, philosophytalk.org/shows/hypatia-alexandria, and Philip Matyszak and Joanne Berry, *A History of Ancient Rome in 100 Lives* (Thames & Hudson, 2023), 240–42.

2. Watts, *Hypatia*, 159.

3. For more on Hypatia's teaching and her leadership, see Watts, *Hypatia*, chapters 3 and 6.

4. Watts, *Hypatia*, chapter 2.

5. Ibid., chapter 1, especially page 14.

6. Ibid., chapter 6.

7. Ibid., chapter 5. Watts cites the Neoplatonic philosopher Damascius, page 75. Damascius wrote *The Life of Isidore* and served as the last scholarch of the Athenian Neoplatonic school, 515–529 CE.

8. Watts, *Hypatia*, chapter 5, especially page 74.

9. Ibid., chapter 8. Some accounts say she was attacked with shards of pottery or with shells; all agree about her brutal death.

10. Ibid., chapters 9 and 10. Recent depictions of Hypatia include a cameo in the TV comedy series *The Good Place*, where she was played by Lisa Kudrow, and the main character of the film *Agora*, where she was portrayed by Rachel Weisz.

11. See Edward Moore, "Neo-Platonism," Internet Encyclopedia of Philosophy, iep.utm.edu/neoplato. Also see Christian Wildberg, "Neoplatonism," Stanford Encyclopedia of Philosophy, January 11, 2016, plato.stanford.edu/entries/neoplatonism.

12. Lloyd P. Gerson, ed., *The Plotinus Reader* (Hackett, 2020). Also Pierre Hadot, *Plotinus or the Simplicity of Vision*, trans. Michael Chase (University of Chicago Press, 2022).

13. Edward Moore, "Gnosticism," Internet Encyclopedia of Philosophy, iep.utm.edu/gnostic.

14. Jonathan Barnes, ed. and trans., *Porphyry's Introduction* (Oxford University Press, 2006). See also Gillian Clark, trans., *Porphyry: On Abstinence from Killing Animals* (Bloomsbury Academic, 2014).

15. *Complete Works of Iamblichus*, trans. Thomas Taylor et al. (Delphi Classics, 2021).

16. Radek Chlup, *Proclus: An Introduction* (Cambridge University Press, 2016).

17. *Pseudo-Dionysius: The Complete Works*, trans. Paul Rorem (Paulist Press, 1987).

18. Lloyd P. Gerson ed., "Life of Plotinus 2," in *Plotinus: The Enneads*, trans. George Boys-Stones et al. (Cambridge University Press, 2017), 10.1–12.

19. Paul Kalligas, "Plotinus," *Stanford Encyclopedia of Philosophy*, September 25, 2024, plato.stanford.edu/entries/plotinus.

20. W. R. Inge, "The Permanent Influence of Neoplatonism upon Christianity," *American Journal of Theology* 4, no. 2 (1900): 328–44

21. K. Godelek, "The Neoplatonist roots of Sufi philosophy," *The Paideia Archive: Twentieth World Congress of Philosophy* 5 (1998): 57–60.

22. Raphael Jospe, "Chapter 3: Jewish Neoplatonism: Isaac Israeli and Solomon ibn Gabirol," in *Jewish Philosophy in the Middle Ages* (Academic Studies Press, 2009).

23. Moshe Idel, *Absorbing Perfections: Kabbalah and Interpretation* (Yale University Press, 2002), 245–46. See also Moshe Idel, "Jewish Kabbalah and Platonism in the Middle Ages and Renaissance" in *Neoplatonism and Jewish Thought*, ed. Lenn Goodman (State University of New York Press, 1992), 319–52.

24. Adam Afterman, "Chapter 2: From Philo to Plotinus: The Emergence of Mystical Union" in *And They Shall Be One Flesh: On the Language of Mystical Union in Judaism* (Brill, 2016).

25. Nicholas Goodrick-Clarke, "Chapter 11: Helena Blavatsky and the Theosophical Society," in *The Western Esoteric Traditions: A Historical Introduction* (Oxford University Press, 2008).

26. For example, Bruce MacLennan, "Twenty-first Century Theurgy," web.eecs.utk.edu/~bmaclenn/papers/MacLennan%20ISNS%20 2014%20rev.pdf. Also see two YouTube videos on the topic: "Neoplatonism in Magic Esotericism Witchcraft Occult," October 25, 2020, youtube.com/watch?v=Jyplc67lcA0, and "Metamodern Spirituality | Updating Neoplatonic Spirituality (w/ John Vervaeke)," March 26, 2023, youtube.com/watch?v=Seg3Q5ndkmw.

27. Sara Ahbel-Rappe, "Neoplatonic Contemplative Ethics: Mind Training," in *The Reception of Greek Ethics in Late Antiquity and Byzantium*, eds. S. Xenophontos and A. Marmodoro (Cambridge University Press, 2021), 52–68.

28. J. M. Chase, "Did Socrates Meditate? On Some Traces of Contemplative Practices in Early Greco-Latin Philosophy," *Religions* 13, no. 6, 479.

ACKNOWLEDGMENTS

Massimo would like to thank all the people who taught him about practical Greco-Roman philosophy, and especially Larry Becker, Rob Colter, Bill Irvine, Anthony Long, Donald Robertson, and John Sellars.

Gregory is grateful to the longtime attendees and supporters of the New York City Stoics who allowed him to level up his understanding of Greco-Roman philosophies over the past couple of years, as well as modern practitioners of non-Stoic philosophies, including Hiram Crespo and Douglas C. Bates for their conversations and for their work in bringing ancient philosophies back to life.

Meredith would like to thank her husband, Bob Kunz, and her daughters, Elizabeth and Shannon, for their love and encouragement as she worked on this book. Raising her daughters sparked her interest in practical philosophy and especially Stoicism, and she has relied on her family's invaluable support, insight, and humor as she journeyed into the ancient past to get to know the thinkers who still inspire us to live more fully today. Meredith would also like to thank her parents, Susan Alexander and the late Herb Alexander, for their love and guidance. Their brilliance and intellectual curiosity motivated her to "dare to know" and to live a life of the mind.

The authors would also like to thank our editor, Batya Rosenblum, for her unwavering support and careful edits to the first draft of this book.

ABOUT THE AUTHORS

MASSIMO PIGLIUCCI is an author, blogger, and podcaster, as well as the K. D. Irani Professor of Philosophy at the City College of New York. His academic work is in evolutionary biology, philosophy of science, the nature of pseudoscience, and practical philosophy. Massimo publishes a regular column in *Philosophy Now* titled "The Art of Living." His books include *How to Be a Stoic: Using Ancient Philosophy to Live a Modern Life* (Basic Books) and *Nonsense on Stilts: How to Tell Science from Bunk* (University of Chicago Press). Massimo's latest book is *The Quest for Character: What the Story of Socrates and Alcibiades Teaches Us about Our Search for Good Leaders* (Basic Books). More by Massimo at newstoicism.org and thephilosophygarden. substack.com.

GREGORY LOPEZ is the founder of the New York City Stoics, cofounder and board member of The Stoic Fellowship, cohost of Stoic Camp New York, and on the team at the Modern Stoicism organization. He received a master's degree in molecular biophysics from Johns Hopkins University and a PharmD from the University of Maryland, Baltimore. He has published essays on Stoicism in the *Stoicism Today* blog and in *The Philosophers' Magazine* and has given several invited talks on Stoicism to groups ranging from small Unitarian congregations to over a thousand people at Stoicon 2020. He is the co-author with Massimo Pigliucci of *A Handbook for New Stoics: How to Thrive in a World Out of Your Control* (The Experiment, 2019). You can find out more and contact him at his personal website: greglopez.me.

MEREDITH ALEXANDER KUNZ, a writer and editor, created The Stoic Mom blog in 2016 to explore the many ways that parents and kids can benefit from practicing Stoic philosophy. She is a communications leader in Silicon Valley and a Stoic-inspired leadership coach. Meredith earned a bachelor's degree in history and literature from Harvard College and a master's degree in history from Stanford University. Her writing has appeared in *Newsweek*, *The Daily Journal*, *The Industry Standard*, *The STOIC* magazine, and the *Stoicism Today* blog. She has given talks on Stoicism to a range of international audiences and has been interviewed on podcasts and NPR-affiliate KCRW radio. Learn more and follow her work at thestoicmom .substack.com, thestoicmom.com, and meredithkunz.com.

Also Available by Massimo Pigliucci and Gregory Lopez

A HANDBOOK FOR NEW STOICS
How to Thrive in a World Out of Your Control

Here are 52 week-by-week lessons to help you overcome adversity and find tranquility in the modern world.

"In 52 pithy and practicable lessons, Pigliucci and Lopez explain how lessons plucked from an ancient Greco-Roman philosophy can reshape one's sense of self. . . .This successful blend of knowledge and action items will entice readers looking for thoughtful prompts for self-reflection."
—*Publishers Weekly*

"In an age that equates virtue with frenzies of outrage and denunciations of others' failings, *A Handbook for New Stoics* serves as an inspired self-help cure that, with insight and sympathy, will nudge you in the direction of the happiness and equanimity born of strength of character and wisdom."
—**Rebecca Newberger Goldstein,** author of *Plato at the Googleplex* and National Humanities Medal recipient

"A wonderfully simple approach to the core concepts and techniques of Stoicism, *A Handbook for New Stoics* gives readers an easy way to train themselves in Stoic practices, broken down into weekly exercises spanning a whole year. Through this book, Pigliucci and Lopez have managed to make Stoicism accessible to anyone."—**Donald Robertson,** cognitive-behavioral psychotherapist and author of *How to Think Like a Roman Emperor*

Flexibind paperback | $22.95 | 336 pages | ISBN 978-1-61519-533-6